▮•test driving
linux

▐•test driving
linux

from windows to linux
in 60 seconds

David Brickner

Beijing • Cambridge • Farnham • Köln • Paris • Sebastopol • Taipei • Tokyo

Test Driving Linux
by David Brickner

Published by O'Reilly Media, Inc., 1005 Gravenstein Highway North,
Sebastopol, CA 95472.

O'Reilly books may be purchased for educational, business, or sales promotional use.
Online editions are also available for most titles (*safari.oreilly.com*). For more information, contact our corporate/institutional sales department: (800) 998-9938 or
corporate@oreilly.com.

Editor:	Andy Oram
Production Editor:	Emily Quill
Cover Designer:	Mike Kohnke
Interior Designer:	Marcia Friedman
Printing History:	April 2005: First Edition.

 This book uses RepKover™, a durable and flexible lay-flat binding.

ISBN: 0-596-00754-X
[M]

Table of Contents

PREFACE

Before you buy a car, you take it for a test drive. You do this regardless of whether the car is new or used, if you're buying it from a dealer or from your best friend. The purpose of the test drive is to make sure you feel comfortable with the car—that you can see out of it, that it doesn't have any glaring blind spots, that it handles well and performs to your expectations. It's simply a wise thing to do before you commit a lot of money.

Likewise, it's a good idea to test-drive an operating system before you switch to it full-time. The OS is at the heart of everything you do on a computer, and if you aren't comfortable with the OS, you won't be happy with your computer. Changing to a new operating system, even just an upgrade from one version of Windows to another, is never as simple as all the marketing ads would have you believe.

This book is about taking the Linux operating system for a test drive on your Windows computer. I wrote it because I believe you need to know what you're getting into before making a commitment to a new operating system. Linux is the only viable alternative desktop operating system you can run on your current Windows computer. In this book, you'll learn what Linux is, how it works, what it can do for you, and what it can't. You'll see how to use Linux for everyday tasks like surfing the Web, reading email, sending instant messages to friends, writing reports, and playing music.

Most other Linux books on the market right now contain CDs that allow you to install Linux on your hard drive. The problem is that this can sometimes be a difficult task, requiring you to make choices you may not be prepared for, such as how to partition your hard drive or configure the boot loader. And until you install Linux on your hard drive, the rest of those books are useless. You are forced to make a commitment to Linux before you even know if you like it.

But the CD included with this book takes a completely different approach. With the *Move* Live CD, you can run Linux *without* having to install it to your hard drive. There are no difficult choices to make and no risk to your Windows system. Simply pop the CD into your CD drive and boot up. After a few minutes and a few simple questions, your computer will be running Linux—right from the CD.

And that is why this book is called *Test Driving Linux*. You can truly just take Linux for a spin, and when you're done, just put the CD away and go back to using Windows again.

Don't count on wanting to, though. My guess is that once you take Linux for a test drive, you'll want to drive it off the lot for good.

Desktop Linux Only

This book will not teach you how set up or administer Linux on a server. It is strictly for people who want to use Linux on their desktop.

Audience

The way I see it, there are two types of computer users in the world: those who use Linux as their desktop OS, and those who are going to.

This book is mainly written for the second group—for Windows users who have heard of Linux and want to find out what all the fuss is about without committing a lot of time or hard-drive space in that endeavor. If you are frustrated by buggy software, weekly security patches, and spyware on your computer, read this book. I don't assume you have any prior knowledge of Linux at all—just a willingness to learn and the ability to click a mouse and type on a keyboard.

But this book also doesn't ignore people who already use Linux on their desktop. Though you won't learn any dirty details about compiling your kernel or setting up WEP encryption with your wireless card, you'll find out a lot more about the KDE desktop environment and programs like KMail, Konqueror, OpenOffice.org, and GnuCash. This book can turn existing Linux users into more effective Linux users.

System Requirements and USB Memory Key

The *Move* CD is designed to run on Pentium-class PCs (including AMD processors) with at least 128 MB of RAM, although 256 MB is highly recommended. And since *Move* runs from CD, you need a dependable (and fast) CD-ROM or DVD drive. The faster your processor is (faster than 1 Ghz is good) and the more memory you have, the better your overall experience. (And of course, you should also be sure to keep the CD clean and free of smudges or scratches.)

These guidelines also serve as good minimum requirements for a computer on which to install Linux. Like Windows, Linux will run even better the more resources you give it. To really enjoy Linux and not feel that your hardware is holding you back, I recommend a 1.5 Ghz or faster processor and 512 MB of memory.

Since *Move* runs from CD and does not write anything to your computer's hard disk, it is perfectly safe to use and will not affect your Windows system in any way. The disadvantage of this, however, is that you will lose all of your changes and settings each time you shut down *Move* because there is no storage space to write changes to. This problem can be solved with the addition of a USB memory key. The key will allow you to store system configuration files and personal data, which means *Move* will keep your customizations between reboots. The combination of the USB memory key and the *Move* CD also means you can take your new Linux desktop everywhere you go and use it on any PC you have access to. Using the memory key is as simple as making sure it is plugged in at all times—*Move* will take care of the rest. You'll have the best experience if you use a USB 2.0 memory key, which is faster than the older 1.1 standard.

USB key problems?

Unfortunately, not all USB keys work equally well with *Move*. If you are experiencing problems with your memory key, consult the appendix for troubleshooting tips.

And if you don't have a USB key, don't worry—even without it, this book and CD will still give you an excellent introduction to using the Linux operating system.

Organization of This Book

This book is divided into 13 chapters and an appendix. I did my best to present the material in an interesting, logical order that would get you performing useful tasks right at the beginning. I recommend reading this book from cover to cover, but if you already know some of the material, feel free to skip around. Though there are plenty of screenshots to help you understand the text, for the best experience you should run *Move* and try out the recommended steps as I describe them.

Chapter 1, *Getting Started*

This chapter introduces you to Linux, the *Move* CD, and the KDE desktop environment.

Chapter 2, *Surf the Web*

Perhaps the biggest reason people buy computers is to get on the Internet. This chapter shows you how to use the Konqueror web browser, a capable alternative to Internet Explorer, and popular add-on software such as Adobe Acrobat Reader, Flash, and RealPlayer.

Chapter 3, *File Management*

This chapter covers the Konqueror file manager, and shows you how to manage your files on your Linux desktop as well as over a network on remote Windows and Linux machines. The very end of the chapter shows you how to access the files on your Windows hard drive, which is useful if you want to play music or view images from your Windows setup.

Chapter 4, *Music and Videos*

Sometimes it really is all about the music. This chapter proves to you that Linux takes multimedia seriously. Here, you will learn about MP3 and video players, CD burning, and music encoding.

Chapter 5, *Play Games*

This chapter introduces you to the games on the *Move* CD, shows you where you can find more games on the Web, and covers the state of gaming in Linux. You've got to try out Tux Racer!

Chapter 6, *Email, Organizers, and Instant Messaging*

Linux is an excellent platform for email and instant messaging. This chapter covers the email client KMail, the calendar program KOrganizer, the contact manager KAddressbook, and the multi-network instant messenger client Kopete.

Chapter 7, *Edit Digital Images*

The GIMP is the open source image-editing program of choice. This chapter teaches you how to use the GIMP and its supporting programs to manage and edit your digital image collection.

Chapter 8, *Customize Your Desktop*

Fully configuring your desktop environment can be very satisfying and a lot of fun to boot. This chapter covers the KDE Control Center, which lets you configure styles, themes, colors, fonts, and window decorations.

Chapter 9, *A Free Office Suite*

OpenOffice.org is the only real contender to the dominance of Microsoft Office. This chapter provides a basic introduction to the word processor and spreadsheet components.

Chapter 10, *Manage Your Finances*

GnuCash is Linux's alternative to Quicken and Money. This chapter quickly gets you up to speed on this personal finance program.

Chapter 11, *The Command Line*

True Linux users aren't afraid of the command line. This chapter is an easy introduction to the text-based underside of the Linux operating system. Learn how to manipulate files, directories, and program processes quickly and easily without using the mouse.

Chapter 12, *Great Programs That Aren't on the CD*

The *Move* CD doesn't have enough room for every great open source program. This chapter introduces several popular programs that didn't fit on the CD.

Chapter 13, *Pre-Switching Information*

If you enjoyed your test drive of Linux, you may be wondering what you should do next. This chapter introduces you to the other versions of Linux you can try out, and gives information on additional resources you can turn to on your open source journey.

Appendix, *Solutions to Common Problems*

Nothing is perfect—not even Linux. There are several quirks to using the *Move* CD, and this appendix attempts to help you solve them. The appendix also shows you how to set up your printer and configure your modem so you can get on the Internet.

Conventions Used in This Book

The following typographical conventions are used in this book:

Plain text

Indicates menu titles, menu options, menu buttons, and keyboard accelerators (such as Alt and Ctrl).

Italic

Indicates new terms, URLs, email addresses, filenames, file extensions, pathnames, directories, and Unix utilities.

Constant width

Indicates commands, options, the contents of files, or the output from commands.

Constant width bold

Shows commands or other text that you should type literally.

Constant width italic

Shows text that should be replaced with values supplied by you.

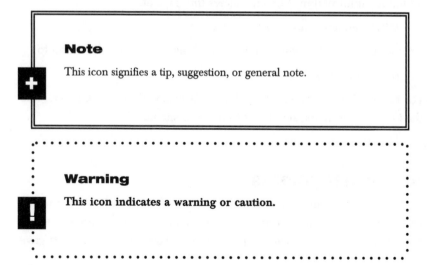

Note

This icon signifies a tip, suggestion, or general note.

Warning

This icon indicates a warning or caution.

Safari Enabled

 When you see a Safari® Enabled icon on the cover of your favorite technology book, that means the book is available online through the O'Reilly Network Safari Bookshelf.

Safari offers a solution that's better than e-books. It's a virtual library that lets you easily search thousands of top tech books, cut and paste code samples, download chapters, and find quick answers when you need the most accurate, current information. Try it for free at *http://safari.oreilly.com*.

We'd Like to Hear from You

Please address any comments and questions concerning this book to the publisher:

> O'Reilly Media, Inc.
> 1005 Gravenstein Highway North
> Sebastopol, CA 95472
> (800) 998-9938 (in the United States or Canada)
> (707) 829-0515 (international or local)
> (707) 829-0104 (fax)

There is a web page for this book, which lists errata, examples, and any additional information. You can access this page at:

> *http://www.oreilly.com/catalog/tdlinux*

To comment or ask technical questions about this book, send email to:

> *bookquestions@oreilly.com*

For more information about books, conferences, Resource Centers, and the O'Reilly Network, see the O'Reilly web site at:

> *http://www.oreilly.com*

Acknowledgments

I would like to thank my wife, Claire, for making it possible for me to write this book. By this I don't just mean allowing me the time to work, but for supporting me every step of the way. Her love and support gave me the confidence to take on this project. And the edits she made to my writing helped to make this a much better book than it could have been without her.

Many thanks go to Andy Oram, my editor and co-worker. He graciously took on this project on short notice, provided me with quality feedback, and put up with the crazy schedule as the deadline approached.

Large portions of Chapters 1 and 2 are based upon earlier material by Phil Lavigna; Chapter 9 is a condensed version of Sam Hiser's material that originally appeared in *Exploring the JDS Linux Desktop* (O'Reilly); and Chapter 10 was written by Breckin Loggins. My thanks to all three for their contributions. The excellent and timely feedback from my reviewers, Charles Stafford and Kevin Shockey, made this book more relevant and correct than it would have been otherwise. Any errors that remain are entirely my own.

Emily Quill was the production editor for this book and performed the copyedit. Without her work, this book would be an embarrassment to my high school English teacher. Thank you, Emily.

And, of course, my thanks to Richard Stallman, Linus Torvalds, and everyone else who works on, supports, documents, and advocates free and open source software.

GETTING
STARTED

The first time I ever drove a car was on a one-mile stretch of straight country road at 5 A.M. After a ten-second driving lesson from my cousin, I found myself driving in the middle of the road with the headlights off. Another car approached and we started to panic. My cousin yelled at me to get in my own lane and turn on the head-lights, and I responded by almost veering off the road as I frantically searched the dashboard for the control to turn on the lights. Driving bumper cars at the carnival had not prepared me for this.

Many people wanting to try Linux for the first time find themselves simi-larly unprepared. They are often worried that they'll lose data, crash the machine, spend endless hours learning how to perform common tasks, or even make their Windows machine unbootable. But these potential Linux users needn't be afraid. Using Linux is far less accident-prone than learning to drive.

This book, along with its accompanying CD, is an excellent way to explore the exciting world of Linux and open source software. The *Move* CD is a customized version of the popular Mandrake Linux distribu-tion. It runs "on the fly" directly from the CD. There's nothing to install, and all of your computer's data remains perfectly safe. It's like driving a car that you can crash as hard as you want without ever damaging the car or yourself.

Move includes hundreds of applications for just about every type of daily computer task. The CD contains a complete Microsoft Office–compati-ble office suite called OpenOffice.org. Other programs allow you to surf the Web, create and modify graphics, listen to music, and watch videos. Whatever it is you want to do, you'll probably find an an open source program for it on this CD.

This is not a demonstration CD, nor is it an interactive video, such as those frequently used in software training. *Move* is a real operating ver-sion of Linux that runs from CD instead of from a hard drive. This is truly the easiest way to test-drive Linux.

What Is Linux?

Linux is a free and open source operating system that you can run on your current PC in place of Microsoft Windows. It was first created by college student Linus Torvalds in 1991. Because Linus made all of his programming code (usually referred to as *source code*) available to others,

Linux has since been further developed by thousands of programmers from around the world. As many people point out, Linux itself is not a complete operating system. In fact, it is only the core of an operating system, known as a *kernel*. A kernel is combined with many programs, libraries, and utilities to make up an operating system. The GNU project, an organization of programmers and others devoted to creating source code that can be distributed freely, has supplied many of the programs and libraries that combine with the Linux kernel to make a complete operating system. Taking the GNU project into account, many people refer to the operating system based on the Linux kernel as GNU/Linux (pronounced guh-noo'/Lynn'-nucks). Throughout this book, the term Linux refers to the entire open source operating system, unless otherwise stated.

A comparison to a car may help you understand this arrangement better. The kernel can be thought of as the car's engine, transmission, and wheels, while the belts, hoses, frame, pumps, and fuel injectors are supplied by the GNU project. At this point you have a usable car, but it isn't very pretty. KDE (described in a later section) and other graphical environments are the sheetmetal that defines the actual *look* of the car, as well as the interior and the details that make it comfortable and fun to drive.

What's in a name?

KDE stands for Kool Desktop Environment. While using it, you can't help but notice that the developers like to name their KDE programs so they begin with a K: Kontact, KMail, Konqueror, KWrite, and so on.

Linux is everywhere. More web sites run Linux than Windows, and the National Security Agency (NSA) in the U.S. loves Linux so much that it created its own highly secure version called SELinux (and then shared it with everyone). The U.S. Department of Defense uses clusters of Linux servers to run battlefield simulations, and everyone's favorite personal video recorder, TiVo, runs Linux inside (but not on Intel processors). Amazon runs on Linux, and so does Google. And, as this book will teach you, Linux is a free alternative to Microsoft Windows on many desktop computers.

What Do Open Source and Free Software Mean?

Though you can often get Linux at no cost or for just a few dollars, its "free"-ness does not actually refer to its price. Instead, it means that you should feel free to modify the code that makes up Linux in whatever way you see fit. The only restriction is that in most situations you must share your changes with everyone else, so that they too can benefit from your improvements. Despite what Bill Gates says, this isn't communism. Personally, it makes me think of communities coming together to build a barn, or friends who help you move. They ask nothing in return except for your willingness to return the favor when the time comes.

You will also hear Linux described as an *open source* program. This recently coined term is meant to make the notion of free software more acceptable to businesses and governments. For some strange reason, businesses think something that costs nothing is worth nothing. What qualifies as open source software is more broadly defined than free software, which means some open source software may not be free software.

Though open source software is the more commonly used term, free software is the traditional one. Many people seeking to encompass both terms use the acronym FOSS, which logically enough stands for Free Open Source Software. For more information about free software, visit *http://www.gnu.org*; for more information about open source software, visit *http://www.opensource.org*.

Many Distributions of Linux

It's important to be aware that *Move* is just one of several hundred "flavors" of Linux. Each flavor is known as a *distribution*. You might have already heard of the most popular ones: Red Hat, Mandrake, Novell Suse, and Debian. Different distributions are akin to different car models. When buying a car, you get to choose the model with the look, performance, safety features, and price point that suit you best. Linux distributions give you the same freedom of choice. What a boring world it would be if the only car available was a Ford Focus!

Starting Up the Move CD

So let's get started with using Linux by booting the enclosed CD. Before booting into *Move*, be sure to plug in and turn on any peripheral devices that are attached to your PC, such as zip drives, printers, scanners, etc., so that *Move* will have the greatest chance of configuring things automatically. If you have a USB memory key, insert it before the system boots up so that *Move* can use it to store your configuration.

System requirements

The preface of this book provides all the dirty details about system requirements and the usefulness of having a USB memory key. The short of it is: if your computer can run Windows, it can run Linux. And if you have a USB memory key, you can save data and settings from your *Move* session.

To use the CD, simply insert it into your CD-ROM drive and boot your computer. If your computer is set to boot from the CD drive (and most of them are), you will shortly see a screen that looks like Figure 1-1. If your computer is not set to boot from CD, you'll probably need to make a change in your computer's BIOS. The Appendix provides instructions for doing this. When you see the screen shown in Figure 1-1, simply press Enter to launch *Move*.

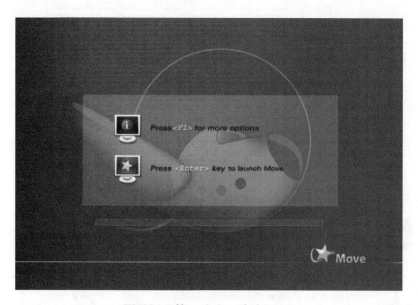

FIGURE 1-1. Move startup splash screen

F1 options

The menu options accessible by pressing F1 are for advanced features of the CD. You don't need to use this menu unless referred to it by the troubleshooting steps in the appendix.

You'll see a few automated screens go by. You'll then be prompted to choose a preferred language, agree to the licensing terms, detect a USB key, choose a login name and password, and so on (Figure 1-2).

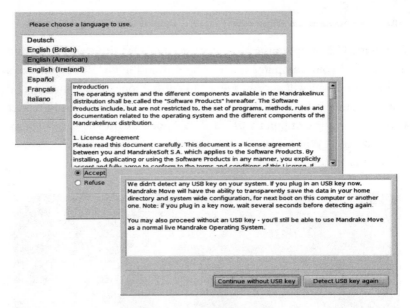

FIGURE 1-2. Initial configuration screens

Move is completely safe

At no point during this startup is anything being done to your hard drive. Using this CD does not hurt your current computer setup. Also, the length of time it takes to boot *Move* is not an indicator of the performance of Linux itself. When the entire operating system runs from a CD there are some tradeoffs, one of which is speed.

In the first screen you need to choose a language. Although this CD has support for only a few languages, Linux itself supports more than 70 languages, which is one of the reasons why Linux is so popular outside the United States. Microsoft must have financial reasons to include support for a particular language; Linux needs only the time and interest of someone who can speak the language—one of the many benefits of open source.

In the second screen you need to agree to the licensing terms for *Move*. If you agree with the terms, check the Accept box and click OK. If not, click Quit to cancel the setup procedure and reboot your computer.

Check out the Linux license

Most people don't read the "click-thru" licenses that appear when they install software. But, just for kicks, you should read *Move*'s license terms and compare them to the terms on a typical Windows program. If you can stomach the legalese, you will come away with a better understanding of the differences between free and proprietary software.

In the third screen you have to set up a user account for *Move*. Because Linux is designed to be a multiuser operating system, it requires that each user have an account. Each account has its own set of files, preferences, and permissions that is independent of and secured from other users. *Move* only requires you to set up a single user account. You can press Tab or use your mouse to move between fields on the account creation screen.

First, type your full name into the Real Name field. In the User Name field type in a nickname or a short version of your full name. It is traditional, and best, to make your username all lowercase without any spaces. For example, if your name is Joshua Harris, you would put Joshua Harris in the Real Name field, and maybe just jharris in the User Name field. From here on, the computer will "think" of you as jharris. You are asked to enter your password twice, to make sure you didn't make a mistake the first time you typed it. Click Next after you fill out all the requested information (Figure 1-3).

```
Enter a user
Enter your user information, password will be used for
screensaver

Real name        | Joshua Harris
User name        | jharris
Password         | *******
Password (again) | *******|

[ Advanced ]                                    [ Next ]
```

FIGURE 1-3. Setting up a user account in Move

Advanced choices

The Advanced button lets you select a particular command-line shell to use. Don't worry about this until after you have read Chapter 11. Nearly all Linux users use the recommended default shell *bash*, which stands for Bourne Again SHell.

If you didn't put in a USB memory key before you booted, the next screen displays a dialog box prompting you to insert a key. If you have one but have not inserted it yet, plug it into any free USB port, wait a few seconds, and click the "Detect USB key again" button. If you don't have a USB key, simply click "Continue without USB key."

USB key problems?

Unfortunately, not all USB memory keys are created equal. Some keys are not recognized by *Move*. This is a failing of the live CD. An actual installation of Linux on your machine should not have a problem with any USB memory key you can use under Windows.

Depending upon the hardware attached to your computer, some additional screens may appear, perhaps to set up a printer or to configure certain types of mice or keyboards. Responding to these screens should be fairly straightforward. If you're in doubt, the default is probably just fine.

After the initial question-and-answer session is complete, *Move* attempts to boot into the desktop environment. One minor problem I have noticed on a few computers is that the screen will go blank and won't come back up. If this happens, just press any key on the keyboard and the screen should come back up. After the hardware setup is complete, you are transported to the KDE desktop.

If you encounter any problems getting the CD to boot, the Appendix provides suggestions to solve the most common problems *Move* users encounter.

The KDE Desktop

KDE is a powerful and full-featured graphical desktop environment for Linux computers. Unlike Microsoft Windows or the Macintosh, Linux is not limited to just one graphical user interface (GUI). Instead, Linux provides a *platform*, called the X window system, on which many different GUIs can run. KDE is one of the most popular Linux GUIs and is very easy for Windows users to learn. Chapter 12 introduces another GUI, but since it isn't included on the *Move* CD it's not described in great detail.

Much of this book focuses on using the KDE environment. Don't let this confuse you—*you are still using Linux when you use KDE.* You are just interacting with Linux through a particular set of graphical programs that belong to the KDE environment. This is no different from using Windows, where your interaction with the core of the operating system, the kernel, is controlled by the graphical environment known as the Explorer shell. Didn't know that, did you?

In Figure 1-4 you can see the default KDE desktop provided by *Move*, which consists of:

- The desktop, on which frequently used files, folders, and wallpaper may be placed.

- A panel, called the *kicker*, across the bottom of the screen, which is used to launch applications and switch between desktops. This is similar to the Windows start button and taskbar, but much more versatile.

- A welcome screen with some helpful tips to get you started with *Move*. Click Close to remove this window from your desktop.

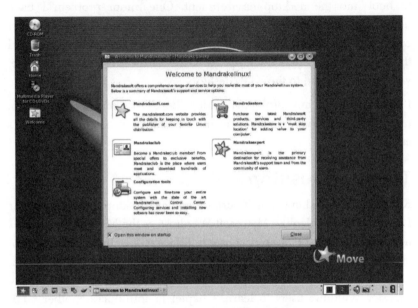

FIGURE 1-4. The default KDE desktop

You may be surprised to see that the KDE desktop looks pretty much like the Windows desktop you have been using for years. As you will find out, KDE behaves a lot like Windows too. In fact, KDE is designed so that users of other operating systems will feel right at home.

The desktop shown in Figure 1-4 contains shortcuts to important directories and devices that *Move* detected during startup. There is an icon leading to your Home directory (similar to My Documents in Windows), an icon for the *Move* CD-ROM, and a Trash can for storing items before deletion. Feel free to rearrange the icons to your liking by dragging them to different areas of the desktop. For a tidier arrangement, right-click an empty area of the desktop to expose a context menu, then select Icons → Line Up Vertically to align the icons up and down across the left edge of the screen. The desktop icons can also be lined up horizontally, across the top of the desktop. Pretty standard stuff for Windows users. The important thing is to not be afraid to experiment with your new Linux desktop. After all, it all runs from CD, which means that if you mess things up, you can just reboot and start over.

The *kicker* (Figure 1-5) is the long panel across the bottom of the KDE desktop. It already contains icons to run several popular applications. The kicker also includes a desktop *pager* for switching between virtual desktops (numbered 1 and 2), a *taskbar* that shows any applications that are currently running, a *system tray* that holds icons for programs that run in the background, and a clock.

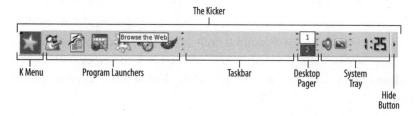

FIGURE 1-5. The kicker panel at the bottom of the KDE desktop

The button with the star in the leftmost corner of the kicker is the *K Menu* or Application Starter (it works just like the Start button in Windows). The K Menu offers easy access to the installed applications, as well as a few special options such as logging off the computer or launching a Run window, which lets you launch a program by typing its name.

A Quick Tour of the Kicker

The *kicker* is similar to what is commonly called the Start Bar or taskbar in Windows and consists of several small programs known as *applets*. The kicker is basically just a holding place where applets can be placed.

The K Menu is located on the leftmost side of the kicker. When you click the K Menu icon, a pop-up menu displays the applications available on the *Move* CD. Pressing the Windows key, present on most keyboards, is a quick way to bring up the K Menu.

The kicker also contains shortcuts to several popular KDE applications, represented by icons. These shortcuts include the Show/Hide desktop (which toggles between minimizing and maximizing all application windows), your Home directory (like the My Documents folder in Windows), a web browser, an email application, and others. As you can see in Figure 1-5, holding the cursor over an icon displays a descriptive tooltip (here, "Browse the Web").

The taskbar is the blank area to the right of the shortcut icons. Whenever an application is running, or when a window is open in KDE, an icon representing that window appears in the taskbar. When a window or application is minimized, click its icon to restore the window; click once more to minimize it.

The desktop pager, shown as a grouping of two small numbered boxes, allows you to switch between virtual desktops. Virtual desktops are fully covered later in this chapter. Believe me, you're going to like them.

The system tray (on the right side of the kicker) contains small applications that run in the background, such as a clock, a screen resizing program, a laptop battery monitor, and others. Click the clock with the left mouse button to display a small calendar. Click it again to close the calendar.

Finally, on the extreme right side of the kicker is an arrow. Click it once to hide the kicker, and again to restore it.

Chapter 8 covers the various settings adjustments that can be made to control the behavior of the kicker, but here are a couple of easy changes you can make.

Changing the kicker size

For some reason the Mandrakesoft programmers who created *Move* set the default kicker size too small, which can be difficult to read. To change the kicker size, right-click the K Menu button, choose Panel Menu → Size, and select a size. Try them all and pick a size that's right for you. I like the normal size.

Adding items to the kicker

If you often use a particular application or tool, you'll probably want faster access to it than the K Menu can provide. In KDE, you can add a single program or an entire menu as a quick-launch button on the kicker.

To add an application to your kicker open the K Menu and drag a menu item (such as the Play games → Frozen-Bubble item) to an empty area of the kicker. The taskbar section is fine, if the icon area is already full. This should give you a brand-new icon on your panel, similar to the one in Figure 1-6.

FIGURE 1-6. Drag and drop a menu item to the kicker

If you don't like where the icon is placed, right-click it and select Move. The icon will now follow your mouse movements and move to another place on the kicker. When you're done, click the left mouse button to "set" the icon.

And if you're tired of a certain icon on the kicker, right-click the icon and select Remove from the context menu.

Making Selections

Much of your interaction with a computer involves selecting items so you can perform an action upon them. You click and double-click icons, highlight text to edit, select items to delete, and so on. Most of the selection techniques you use in Windows also work in KDE and in other KDE programs, such as the file manager Konqueror and the email application Kontact. Try the following with the desktop icons:

- Right-click on the desktop, choose Icons, and select a method to organize your icons.
- Select more than one item by holding down the Ctrl key and clicking different icons.
- Select several icons with the lasso method (or rubber band). Just click an empty area near the desired items and hold down the mouse button while moving the cursor across any icons you want to select.
- To add icons to a group you've already selected with the rubber band method, press the Ctrl key while lassoing or clicking more icons.

- To remove items from a selection, hold down the Ctrl key and click an item to deselect it.
- To select all files or folders, drag a large bounding box around all the icons or press Ctrl-A to select all.
- To deselect all items, simply click an empty area of the desktop or window.

Getting comfortable with the mouse

Rumor has it that the game Solitaire was first included with Windows to teach users mouse techniques like click, drag, and double click. Regretfully, *Move* doesn't include a solitaire game, but practicing with the icons gives the same benefits (and is much less addictive).

The Home Directory

The Home icon in the kicker and on the desktop is a shortcut to your own personal directory. This is where you can store all your stuff—work files, downloads from the Internet, digital camera images, music files, etc. If you're using a USB memory key, your Home directory is on the key. Just double-click the Home icon to see the contents of your Home directory. File management is covered in Chapter 3.

There's no place like Home

In Linux, each user has a Home directory that contains all of that user's files and data. Inside this directory are many hidden files and directories that control preferences for KDE and other programs. These files are normally hidden by the file manager, so you don't have to worry about deleting them accidentally.

Using a Typical KDE Application

Most Linux applications look and behave very much like the applications you use every day in Windows. Even how you launch programs is similar. For example, to launch the text editor KWrite, you would click K Menu → All Applications → More applications → Editors → KWrite. This is similar to launching Notepad in Windows: Start Menu → Programs → Accessories → Notepad. Launch KWrite now so you can perform the tasks in this section. Most KDE applications behave similarly to KWrite, so it is a good "starter" program.

KDE application windows contain a title bar, drop-down menus, a toolbar with buttons for commonly used commands, and a work area. In the case of KWrite, the work area is a place to do some typing. In other applications, the work area might be your email or a web page.

Go ahead and explore the menus and toolbar buttons offered by KWrite. Pause the cursor over any of the buttons to display tooltips that describe the functions of the various buttons (Figure 1-7). Also worth noting is the Help menu that appears in most KDE applications. Choose Help → KWrite Handbook from the menu to see the help files for KWrite.

FIGURE 1-7. The tooltip for the Print icon on the KWrite toolbar

When you're done exploring the menus and toolbar, go ahead and type a few lines of text in the work area. For some strange reason, I've always had the compulsion to type the opening lines of J.R.R. Tolkien's *The Hobbit.*

Most KDE programs can be customized by using various options under the Settings menu. In KWrite, go to Settings → Configure Editor to load its configuration window. You'll notice that for a text editor, KWrite has an awful lot of options to configure. This is because KWrite is a very capable text editor, much more powerful than Notepad, and includes many features to meet the needs of advanced users who want to write programs, web pages, and complex documentation.

Just for practice, change the font for KWrite. From the main configuration window, click the Font tab (Figure 1-8); select a new font and font size and click OK to accept the changes. As you can see, the changes are accepted immediately and affect the current text, even though you didn't have it highlighted.

FIGURE 1-8. Configuring KWrite

When you use other programs on this CD, you should always check out the Settings menu. Try out a bunch of options and see how the choices affect the application's behavior. And as always, if you end up scrambling the application so much that it doesn't work as expected, you can simply reboot—just one great feature of learning Linux from a live CD.

The Open and Save File Windows

In many programs, the most common tasks you perform are opening and saving files. KDE provides a standardized way to perform these tasks that incorporates a lot of the features found in recent versions of

Windows. Figure 1-9 shows a typical KDE Save dialog. To see it for yourself, type some text in KWrite and choose File → Save from the drop-down menu, or click the Save button in the toolbar.

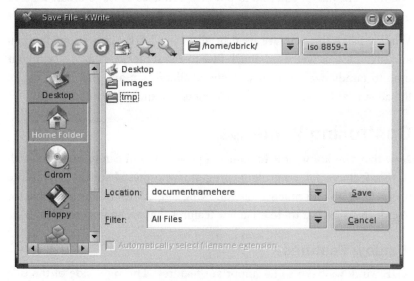

FIGURE 1-9. A typical KDE dialog window

The Save dialog window is divided into several parts. The space in the center displays the folders and files in your current directory. You can descend into folders by double-clicking them. The Location field is where you type your new file's name before clicking Save to save it. The Filter drop-down list doesn't say much in KWrite, but in some programs it presents numerous entries that can help you quickly filter out all of the files that don't meet your filter criteria.

Along the top of the Save window are several icons to help you navigate the filesystem. The first four look like those in a web browser, and perform the same functions. The folder icon lets you create a new folder; the star icon lets you set a bookmark (a quick way to go to preferred folders); and the wrench icon presents a menu to help you control the display of items in the center. The drop-down list on the top shows you the location of the current file and of those you most recently visited. The final option on the top of the bar is particular to the KWrite application and controls the type of file encoding for your text document. This option is not something you will use all that often.

Along the left-hand side of the Save window are some quick links to specific locations on the computer. If you right-click in this space you get a context menu that lets you delete or add new entries. If you have several different places you like to put files, it makes sense to create a quick link to those folders.

Windows like this one are used in all of the KDE applications to open and save files, as well as to attach files to email messages. It is worth your time to familiarize yourself with the available options and make use of the advanced features such as bookmarks and quick link icons.

Controlling Windows

Now that you know how to launch a program, you can experiment with KDE's features for controlling program windows. Launch the KWrite program again and practice the following steps. Most of this is old hat for Windows users, but there are a few features that are unique to KDE.

Window Features

KDE windows have some important features. The right side of the title bar contains three buttons, just like those in Windows. From left to right these are:

Minimize
> This hides the window, leaving only an icon in the taskbar.

Maximize
> This expands the window to the largest possible size. If the window is already maximized, it will be restored to its previous size.

Close
> This closes the window. The keyboard shortcut for this is Alt-F4.

KDE windows also contain a window menu to provide quick access to the most common operations. Right-click the title bar (or press Alt-F3) to see the window operations menu. Under the Advanced option, you can specify whether this window should always be on top of other windows or always below them. I find this option handy for multimedia programs such as an MP3 player, or instant messenger windows, where I always want the program to float on top of my other windows so I can control my music or keep track of an instant message conversation.

Another interesting feature is the "windowshade." Double-click the title bar to roll up a window, then double-click it again to roll it back down. This is a handy way to hide a game of Frozen-Bubble when your boss walks by.

Resizing and Moving Windows

You probably resize windows all the time. Programs often open windows that are too small, or you have to drag and shrink windows to get them out of the way so you can get to a program or icon beneath them. KDE provides numerous ways to resize windows:

- Resize a window horizontally by dragging the left or right edge to make the window wider or narrower.
- Resize a window vertically by dragging the top or bottom edge to make the window taller or shorter.
- Resize a window in both directions at the same time by dragging any corner of a window.
- Or, while pressing the Alt key, hold down the right mouse button inside the window, and drag the cursor to resize the window. If you click near a corner, you will be able to resize in both directions.

Retrain your mouse finger

This option is a particularly handy one, but one that I had to train myself to use. Once I got used to it, I found it to be the most convenient way to resize a window, because it doesn't require precise mouse pointing to grab the window's edge to get the resizing cursor.

- Move a window by simply clicking and holding the title bar while dragging it to a new location.
- Or, press and hold the Alt key while dragging anywhere in the open window to move a window.

Virtual Desktops

Two things have long pained me when watching other people use their
computers. One is that the user often has dozens of icons on his desktop. So many, in fact, that he sometimes spends a minute just looking for
the proper icon to click. The other is the poor window management
options that Windows provides. A user may have several programs open
at a time, and when he wants to launch a new program, usually from an
icon on his desktop, he often has to drag windows out of the way, minimize them, or both. Not only is this a time-consuming process just to
find an icon to launch a program, but it also means the user has to locate
and move the previous program windows back into place when it comes
time to use them again.

Fortunately, KDE has some nifty features that can help you organize
your icons and open windows. Chapter 8 contains information on customizations you can make to the kicker to create quick-launch icons for
programs and assign keyboard shortcuts to launch your favorite applications. But you can start using a feature right now that can help you manage open windows. It's called a virtual desktop, and once you start using
it, you won't be able to get by without it.

In KDE, you can have several different desktops—each with its own windows and settings. *Move*'s default configuration provides only two desktops, though you can configure KDE to use up to sixteen. The concept of
virtual desktops is a little difficult to understand for people who haven't
used them before, so it may be best to explain them with an analogy
everyone should be familiar with: changing television channels.

Two of my favorite shows, *Smallville* and *Lost*, air at the same time on Wednesday nights. By using my remote I can switch channels between the two shows. My TV picture adjusts to display what is being broadcast on the other channel, and I can switch back to the first channel at any time. Back and forth, back and forth. The same TV, but different channels, each one showing a different show. It's so simple that it almost seems absurd to explain it.

Well, virtual desktops work the same way. Each desktop is displayed on the same monitor, but shows you a different "channel." What this means is you can have a program like Frozen-Bubble running on your first virtual desktop, and another program like KWrite running on the second one. And with a simple keyboard command or click of a mouse, you can switch between these different desktops and see the other program.

Virtual desktops allow you to better organize your open applications. Linux users often put different applications on different desktops and change between applications by switching desktops instead of minimizing and maximizing applications. Some Windows users who try out Linux never grasp the flexibility that virtual desktops allow them and continue to work in their normal manner on only one desktop. But the virtual-desktop converted enjoy the uncluttered feeling of virtual desktops and sincerely feel their loss when they are forced to use an OS that doesn't support them.

Task-oriented virtual desktops

I like to use four desktops. I run email applications on Desktop 2, word processing applications on Desktop 3, and web browsers on Desktop 4. Desktop 1 I reserve for those occasional odd programs that I run, like a remote connection to another system, so most of the time it is empty. If I kept icons on my desktop, an empty Desktop 1 would allow me easy access to them.

Switching between virtual desktops is easy—all you have to do is click on a mini version of the virtual desktop, which is shown in the desktop pager in the kicker panel. As you recall, the desktop pager is the small group of two numbered boxes on the righthand side of the kicker. If you're not running any programs, Desktop 1 looks exactly like Desktop 2, so you won't feel like you've changed "channels" at all when you switch between them. (Which makes it a lot like watching a Presidential address on different networks, but without the odd changes in color or volume.)

So let's perform the following little test just to confirm that virtual desktops do work. From Desktop 1, launch the KWrite application, type "This application is on Desktop 2" in the window, and then right-click the title bar and select To Desktop → 2 Desktop 2, as shown in Figure 1-10. The KWrite window disappears from your current screen. Now launch the Frozen-Bubble game in Desktop 1 by clicking K Menu → Play games → Frozen-Bubble. (This is a fun game—you should play it sometime. But not now!) Now go to Desktop 2 by clicking on the number 2 in the desktop pager or by pressing Ctrl-Tab. You can now type away in the KWrite application. Feel like playing some Frozen-Bubble? Switch back to Desktop 1 by clicking on the number 1 in the pager or by pressing Ctrl-Tab again. See? Using virtual desktops is just like changing TV channels!

Sometimes you want the same window to appear on every desktop. For example, maybe you need a small chat window or an alarm clock to always be visible. You can make this happen by right-clicking on the title bar and choosing To Desktop → All Desktops.

Quick desktop switches

Pressing Ctrl-F1 or Ctrl-F2 sends you immediately to the corresponding desktop. Pressing Ctrl-Tab cycles through the desktops in ascending order; Ctrl-Shift-Tab cycles through in descending order. Moving past the last desktop brings you back to the first one.

You can change the number of virtual desktops by right-clicking the desktop and choosing Configure Desktop. In the window that appears, click the Multiple Desktops icon, then in the configuration pane to the

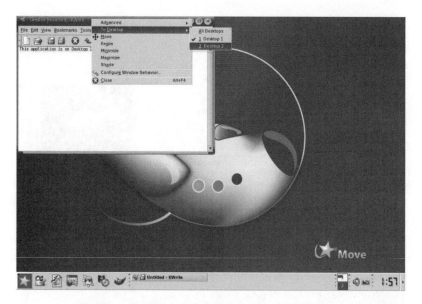

FIGURE 1-10. Send a window to the second virtual desktop

right of the icon, move the slider to the desired number. More desktops can make it easier to manage your active applications, but too many can make it difficult to remember which application is on which desktop. The taskbar, by default, is configured to show all running applications, so clicking on a program in the taskbar switches to the appropriate desktop and brings the application to the front.

Setting Your Desktop Background

From pictures of their family and pets to pictures of Russell Crowe and fast cars, people love to personalize their computer desktops with background images. KDE, of course, provides the ability to do this. In fact, the program that displays wallpaper allows for even more types of images and more image effects than you can get in Windows.

To get started, right-click an empty area of the desktop and choose Configure Desktop. Figure 1-11 shows the configuration screen for changing the background. There are a lot of options.

First off, you can choose whether this wallpaper change affects all virtual desktops or just a specific one. Then you can choose either a color background, a picture you select from a drop-down list or with the file

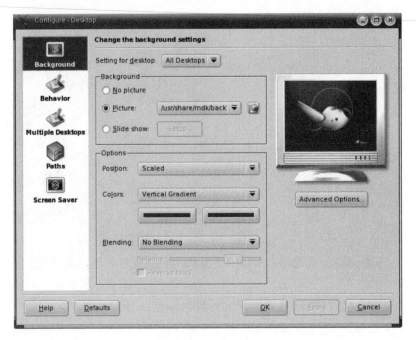

FIGURE 1-11. Changing the desktop wallpaper with Configure Desktop.

selector, or a slide show that lets you choose which pictures to display and for how long. The Options section further affects the color or picture choices. The most useful option is the Position drop-down list, which lets you choose how a picture should be scaled to fit the screen. Small images look best when they are *tiled*, and large images look better *scaled*. Tiling is when an image is repeated until it fills the screen; scaling is when an image is stretched equally in all directions until it fills the screen. A small preview screen shows you how your selection will look.

You can use practically any image file as wallpaper, including any Windows wallpapers you may already have on your hard drive. Chapter 3 tells you how to do this. In the meantime, you can download a lot of great Linux-related wallpapers from *http://www.kde-look.org*. When you're happy with the desktop wallpaper in the preview screen, press OK to accept your change and close the window.

Virtual desktop-specific wallpapers

+

Setting different wallpapers for different virtual desktops makes it easier to remember which desktop you are on and lets you enjoy multiple wallpapers. Use the "Setting for desktop" drop-down list to choose which desktop wallpaper to change. After applying the change, press Ctrl-Tab to switch to the desktop and check the results.

Linux Equivalents to Your Windows Programs

There are so many open source applications available that it can be difficult to know which one you need. Table 1-1 lists a few Linux programs that can be used to perform common tasks. (The program listed first is the one that is available on the *Move* CD or that is fully described in this book.)

TABLE 1-1. Linux programs for common tasks

Task	Linux application name	How to launch
Web browsing	Konqueror Firefox Opera	K Menu → Surf the Internet → Browse the Web
Email	Kontact Evolution Thunderbird	K Menu → Surf the Internet → Read and send e-mail
File management	Konqueror	K Menu → All Applications → Home
Office productivity (Word processors, spreadsheets, and presentations)	OpenOffice.org (Writer, Calc, and Impress)	K Menu → Use office tools → Create a (text document, spreadsheet, presentation, drawing)
Calendar	Kontact Evolution	K Menu → Organize → Organize your time

TABLE 1-1. Linux programs for common tasks (continued)

Task	Linux application name	How to launch
Instant messaging	Kopete Gaim	K Menu → Surf the Internet → Chat
Personal finances	GnuCash	K Menu → Organize → Manage your finances
Image editing	The GIMP	K Menu → View, modify and create graphics → Edit images and photos
Watching videos	Totem xine Mplayer	K Menu → Enjoy music and video → Watch videos
Creating web pages	Mozilla Composer Quanta	K Menu → All Applications → Internet → Web editors → Mozilla Composer
Viewing PDF files	Acrobat Reader KPDF	K Menu → All Applications → Office → Publishing → Acrobat Reader
Listening to music	Totem XMMS amaroK	K Menu → Enjoy music and video → Listen to music files

If you can't find what you need in the list above, visit *http://www. freshmeat.net.* This web site is a searchable database of thousands of open source programs, so there's a good chance you can find what you're looking for. Though you can't install these programs while using *Move,* you will be able to use them once you install Linux. Keep in mind that just because an open source program has an unfamiliar name or looks a little different from what you're used to, it doesn't mean that it won't do what you need. An example of this is the chat program Kopete. This oddly named program lets you chat on the AOL, Yahoo, MSN, Jabber, and IRC networks, which makes it much more flexible than the instant message clients that AOL or Microsoft provides.

Logging Out of KDE

When you're done for the day, log out of Linux by clicking K Menu → Logout or by right-clicking an empty area of the desktop and selecting Logout. Figure 1-12 shows you the logout screen.

FIGURE 1-12. The options for logging out of KDE

The restart and turn off options are self-explanatory; selecting End Session logs you out of KDE and then logs you back in. This odd behavior occurs because *Move* has only the single user you created when you started it up. On a regular Linux system with more than one user account, this option presents you with a login box after KDE closes so you can select which user to log in as.

2 + ! SURF THE WEB

Depending on how much time you spend on the Internet, your web browser may be one of the most important programs on your computer. Just a few years ago, Linux users had only one graphical web browser available: the venerable Netscape Communicator. But today, Linux users are treated to a wide selection of world-class web browsers, including two browsers based upon Netscape—Mozilla and the wildly popular Firefox—and a commercial offering called Opera.

The default web browser on the *Move* CD is *Konqueror*, a full-featured browser that is part of the KDE desktop environment. In fact, the technology behind Konqueror is compelling enough that Apple chose to base its own Mac OS X web browser, called Safari, on Konqueror's code. And because the Konqueror project is open source, Apple returned their improvements back to the community—their changes were added to Konqueror to make it even better.

Jack of all trades

The Konqueror file manager you'll learn about in Chapter 3 and the web browser covered in this chapter are one and the same. Konqueror is not just a program; it also provides a framework for running whatever programs its creators choose to embed into it. That includes programs such as FTP clients, terminal windows, PDF and image viewers, and even a tool for CD ripping and MP3 encoding.

These days, it's worth trying an open source web browser for security reasons alone. Microsoft's Internet Explorer web browser has proven to be riddled with security holes that can be severe enough to make your system unusable or even destroy your important files. Microsoft attempts to fix these security problems as they pop up, but the patches are a) not always successful, b) sometimes not provided until months after a security hole is found, and c) often available only to Windows XP users. Even when patches are available that *do* work, you may not feel comfortable using them. This is the reason millions of Windows machines have become so compromised that they can now be remotely controlled by an unsavory group of Internet citizens known as *crackers*. Crackers hijack many ordinary home Windows computers by exploiting security holes in Internet Explorer. Then, adding insult to injury, the crackers use these computers to send a huge portion of the world's spam email!

In 1965, Ralph Nader published a book called *Unsafe at Any Speed*, which detailed the reluctance of the big car companies to improve the safety of their cars through better testing or inclusion of sensible safety devices like seat belts. Similarly, Microsoft's Internet Explorer web browser is also "unsafe on any computer." In fact, the U.S. Department of Homeland Security has even recommended that Americans stop using Internet Explorer!

The good news is you can switch at any time to a web browser that is safe. Do yourself and your computer a favor: install a safe web browser, such as Firefox or Mozilla. Both of these excellent web browsers can be found at *http://www.mozilla.org*, run on Windows, and are a breeze to download, install, and use.

Using Konqueror as a Web Browser

The Konqueror web browser supports all the usual features required by a browser, including HTML 4.0, JavaScript, the ability to run Java applets, Cascading Style Sheets, SSL, and lots more. But that's really just a lot of technical jargon; what it basically means is that Konqueror should have no problem correctly displaying the web sites you visit most. You can launch the web browser directly from the Konqueror icon in the kicker panel (it looks like a small blue world with some spikes coming out of it). Or you can start it up by selecting K Menu → Surf the Internet → Browse the Web. The default startup page for the version of Konqueror on *Move* is a welcome page that offers helpful links for Mandrake users (Figure 2-1).

Browsing the Web

Using Konqueror is no different from using any other browser, such as Internet Explorer. To navigate to a new page, double-click the text in the Location field to highlight it (the keyboard shortcut for this action is Alt-O). Then enter the new address (including the suffix, such as *.com* or *.org*) and press Enter to load the page. (The Location field serves the same purpose, and is in the same place below the menus, as the Address field in Internet Explorer.)

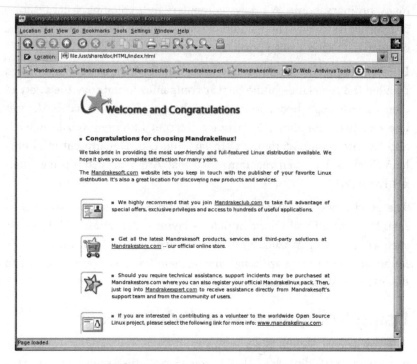

FIGURE 2-1. The main Konqueror page in Move

Using the Run window

A useful way to launch the web browser directly from the desktop is by pressing Alt-F2 to display the Run dialog. Then type a URL (such as *google.com*) and click Run. This launches Konqueror and automatically loads the requested web page.

Besides using your mouse to move around on a page, you can also use several different keyboard commands, as shown in Table 2-1. Some of these commands will be familiar to IE users who navigate with the keyboard.

TABLE 2-1. Common web browsing shortcuts

Keyboard shortcut	Used to...
Ctrl-Shift-N	Create a new tab
Ctrl-N	Open a new browser window
Ctrl-W	Close the active tab
Ctrl-Q	Close the browser window
Alt-left arrow	Go back a page
Alt-right arrow	Go forward a page
Ctrl-R or F5	Reload a page
Ctrl-left click	Open the link in a new tab
Page Down	Scroll down one screen
Page Up	Scroll up one screen
Alt-O	Put the cursor in the Location field and highlight the text
Ctrl-+	Increase font size
Ctrl-—	Decrease font size
Ctrl-[	Move to the browser tab to the left of your current one
Ctrl-]	Move to the browser tab to the right of your current one

Just as in other browsers, Konqueror's Forward and Back buttons keep a history of the most recently viewed pages (Figure 2-2). If you click and hold your mouse over one of these buttons, a small menu appears from which you can select the page you want to move back to. Jumping back five pages this way is much faster than clicking the Back button five times and waiting for each page to load.

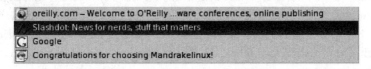

FIGURE 2-2. Using the Back button submenu to jump back several pages

As you can see, for basic use, Konqueror is not really any different from Internet Explorer. But don't let Konqueror's ease of use fool you. It has several advanced features that make it a compelling replacement for IE.

Searching from the Location Bar

One of the most useful things on the Internet is the Google search engine. Many users visit Google dozens of times a day as the starting point for their Internet fun. Though Google usually loads very quickly, it is still annoying to have to go to it each time you want to perform a search. Many IE users install the Google toolbar so they can have a search field on their browser at all times. With Konqueror, there is no need to install this extra software because the location bar itself can be used to automatically Google things. To use this feature, just double-click the text in the Location field to highlight it, then type a search word or phrase directly into the Location field and press Enter. Konqueror automatically uses the Google search engine to look up what you typed. You can even use all the features you would normally use with the Google search field, like quotes around exact phrases and minus (-) signs to force the search to ignore certain words.

Googling from the Run window

Bring up the Run dialog by pressing Alt-F2, then type **gg: mandrake** to perform a Google search of the word mandrake. (Or try an even more exciting word, like Linux.)

If Google is not your search engine of choice, you can easily change the default search engine from within Konqueror by clicking Settings → Configure Konqueror → Web Shortcuts. In the configuration panel, click on the drop-down list for "Default search engine" and select the search engine you wish to use. Click OK to apply your choice and close the settings screen.

General search engines like Google are not the only, or even the best, way to find information on the Internet. There are many specialized web sites that can help you find specific types of information with a high rate of success. One of the most well known is the Internet Movie Database (IMDB) at *http://www.imdb.com*. This site has a huge amount of information about actors and actresses, movies, and TV shows. It is an indispensable resource for those who like to keep track of such things.

But, just as you can search Google without actually visiting the Google web site, you can search IMDB from the Location field in Konqueror as well. For example, to search for Ted Danson, simply type the following query into the Location field (Figure 2-3) and press Enter:

```
imdb:Ted Danson
```

FIGURE 2-3. Entering an IMDB query in Konqueror

What you will get back is the IMDB web page on Ted Danson, just as if you had visited IMDB and typed your search directly into its search field (Figure 2-4). Typing **imdb:** in the Location field in Konqueror is an example of using a *web shortcut.*

FIGURE 2-4. The IMDB results for Ted Danson

Konqueror has dozens of web shortcuts already conveniently set up for you. Simply open Settings → Configure Konqueror → Web Shortcuts to see a list of them. The Shortcut column tells you what you need to enter in the Location field to start your search. For instance, to search the online Merriam-Webster dictionary, you can enter `dict:` or `webster:` followed by the word you want to search for. Press Enter to start your search.

➕ Deciphering computer acronyms

A very useful web shortcut to use in conjunction with technical books like this one is the Acronym database. This web site (known as ad for short) tells you what many acronyms in this book mean. For example, to search for the acronym HTML, type `ad: HTML` in the Location field and press Enter.

You can modify these web shortcuts by highlighting the ones you want to edit and clicking Change. Then you can edit the words in the "URI shortcuts" field or add new words by placing a comma after the last word and entering a new shortcut word. Note that there is no space after the comma in these entries. If you put in a space after a shortcut, that shortcut will stop working, and when you attempt to use it Konqueror will instead perform a general search using Google.

Customizing Konqueror

Because Konqueror can wear so many hats (acting as a file manager, web browser, and FTP client, among other things), it needs to remember all your preferences for these very different functions. Konqueror keeps track of your preferences through *profiles*. These profiles remember what size window you prefer, your default startup web page (homepage), and your favorite toolbar configuration. There are five default profiles: File Management, Web Browsing, File Preview, Midnight Commander, and Trash, and you can create more profiles to suit your purposes. The most frequent changes made to the default Web Browsing profile are to the default startup page and to the size of the browser window.

Making Konqueror Remember Its Size

As you use Konqueror, you may become annoyed by the fact that it doesn't remember your preferred window size each time you restart it. I don't know the reason it was programmed this way; after all, KDE remembers the window sizes of other programs. Thankfully, there is an easy solution to this annoyance. To configure the web browser so that it automatically appears in your preferred window size, all you need to do is update the Web Browsing profile.

First, set the Konqueror window to the size you want. Then, inside Konqueror, select Settings → Save View Profile "Web Browsing" to load the profile manager shown in Figure 2-5.

FIGURE 2-5. The Web Browsing profile configuration dialog

Near the bottom of the window, uncheck the box next to "Save URLs in profile" and check the box next to "Save window size in profile." Then click Save. The next time you launch the Konqueror web browser, it will open to your preferred size. Problem solved!

Setting a Homepage

When the web browser starts up in the *Move* CD, it displays a default page that was set by Mandrakesoft. But you can change the startup page to anything you want—say, the homepage of your favorite news site or sports team.

To specify a different homepage, first load the desired page into Konqueror. Then click Settings → Save View Profile "Web Browsing" to load the profile preferences. Make sure the "Save URLs in profile" option is checked, then click Save. The next time you start up the web browser, it will display your newly selected homepage.

Like any web browser, Konqueror loads faster if no default page is set. To set Konqueror to a blank page, simply perform the step above with the "Save URLs in profile" option unchecked.

Changing the Font Sizes

One annoying thing that Linux and Mac users have to deal with are web designers who create pages with only Microsoft Windows in mind. This problem manifests itself in several ways. For example, sometimes a web page won't load because it irritatingly insists that you use Internet Explorer. Or the text on a page may show up in a teensy-tiny little font. Take a look at Figure 2-6, which shows Microsoft's homepage displayed in Konqueror. If you can read that extremely tiny text, then congratulations—you probably don't need glasses. But if you feel the beginnings of a headache coming on, then relief is available. Konqueror provides a way to specify font sizes that should cut down on these problems.

FIGURE 2-6. Extremely small text on a web page designed for Windows

To set your font size preferences, just open the Preferences window by selecting Settings → Configure Konqueror and clicking on the Fonts icon. You'll see that the Font panel includes an option for setting minimum and medium font sizes. The first setting tells Konqueror to enlarge any text to at least the minimum requested size; the second controls the size of typical body text.

Select a font size that's comfortable for you (try 10 points minimum and 12 points medium). After making the desired changes, click the OK button to accept the changes and close the window. Your currently viewed page should be automatically updated, but if you're in doubt that any change occurred, click the Refresh button. Figure 2-7 shows the Microsoft homepage after these settings were adjusted.

FIGURE 2-7. The same web page after setting a minimum and medium font size

You can also change the font size "on the fly" using a keyboard shortcut. Pressing Ctrl combined with + or – respectively increases or decreases the font sizes on a page in real time. This is useful for when you encounter a web site that has particularly odd font sizes and you only need a temporary fix.

As you might guess, you can also use this Font configuration panel to control the fonts you want to display. Experiment and discover which fonts make for the most comfortable reading. You won't see many familiar font names in the Konqueror font listing because most fonts have to be licensed from their creators in order to be used. No free distribution of Linux can legally include such licensed fonts. Some Linux companies do buy fonts and distribute them with their versions of Linux, but these versions of Linux must be purchased.

Simplifying the Toolbar

Konqueror, like most KDE applications, has a rather messy default toolbar (as shown in Figure 2-8). This may come from the KDE development philosophy of making as many features as possible available to you. This is great because it gives you a lot of control over all the applications, but it can be distracting if you prefer a simple look. Thankfully, KDE allows you to modify the toolbars.

FIGURE 2-8. The default Konqueror toolbar

The procedure to change Konqueror's default toolbar is fairly simple. To start customizing, just right-click in any blank space on the toolbar containing the Back and Forward buttons and choose Configure Toolbars. In the Configure Toolbars window, first select the toolbar you want to modify from the Toolbar drop-down list.

Change the right toolbars

Note that the default toolbar you see in Konqueror is actually made up of two toolbars: the Main Toolbar <Konqueror> and the rather confusingly named Main Toolbar <khtmlpart>. You need to make adjustments to *both* of these toolbars in order to remove unnecessary icons.

The Configure Toolbars window has two lists. The list on the left, labeled "Available actions," contains icons and actions you can add to your toolbar. The list on the right, labeled "Current actions," contains icons and actions you can remove from your toolbar. The left and right arrow icons between the lists control whether a selected item is moved from the left-hand list to the right-hand list or vice versa, and the up and down arrow icons move selected items up and down the list. The order of icons in the list is the order in which the icons appear on the actual toolbar. Click OK or Apply to accept any changes. If you make a mistake, just click Cancel to close the window without making any changes permanent.

So to remove an item from your toolbar, for example, select it in the "Current actions" list, click the left arrow icon to send the selected item to the "Available actions" list, and click OK or Apply to make your changes permanent. That's it! Figure 2-9 shows you what the Configure Toolbars window looks like with the Cut action highlighted and ready to be removed.

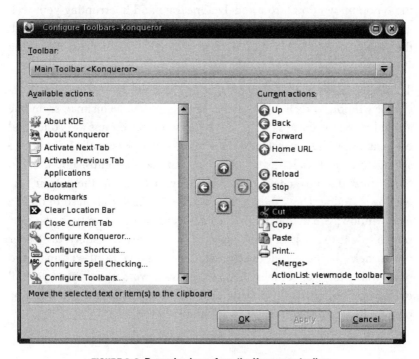

FIGURE 2-9. Removing icons from the Konqueror toolbar

My personal preference is to remove all the default icons except for Back, Forward, Home, Reload, Stop, and Printer. In order to do this, I have to remove items from both the Main Toolbar <Konqueror> and the Main Toolbar <khtmlpart>. I also like to set the icons to be a little larger, which you can do by right-clicking on the toolbar, selecting Icon Size, and choosing a new size. Figure 2-10 shows my customized version of the Konqueror toolbar.

FIGURE 2-10. A simplified Konqueror toolbar

Disabling Pop-Up Ads

Those stupid ads that seem to pop up everywhere are definitely one of the most annoying things about surfing the Web. A great feature of Konqueror, and most other Linux web browsers, is the ability to prevent these pop-up windows from rudely appearing and interrupting your web surfing. Microsoft recently incorporated this functionality into IE with the release of Service Pack 2 for Windows XP. This is great if you use Windows XP, but not very useful for the 80 million people who don't.

To disable pop-ups in Konqueror, open the Settings → Configure Konqueror window and click the Java & JavaScript icon. This may seem like an odd place for these settings, but because most pop-ups are controlled by JavaScript code, it actually does make sense. Figure 2-11 shows the settings on the JavaScript tab that you can use to control pop-ups. To block most pop-ups, check off either Deny or Smart in the "Open new windows" dialog. Deny means that JavaScript is never allowed to open a new window; Smart means that a new window opens only if you purposefully clicked a JavaScript-enabled link. Smart is usually the better option here, because it doesn't break the functionality of web mail and bank web sites that sometimes open separate windows to have you fill out a form. So just click on Deny or Smart, press OK, and you won't be bothered with annoying pop-ups anymore.

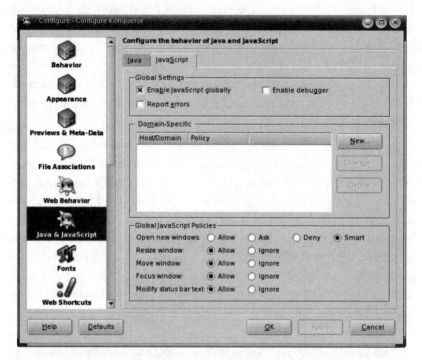

FIGURE 2-11. Disabling pop-up ads in the JavaScript panel

If even the Smart option prevents a web site from working properly, you need to create an exception for that site and allow it to create pop-up windows. To do this, click on the New button in the Domain-Specific section of the JavaScript tab. In the window that appears, type in the domain name (like *oreilly.com* or *nyt.com*) in the "Host or domain name" field, set the JavaScript policy drop-down list to Accept, and check off the Allow box for the "Open new windows" option. Click OK to apply your changes. From now on, the web site you specified should always allow pop-up windows.

Exploring Tabbed Web Browsing

Tabbed browsing is a great feature for power web surfers. In normal web browsing, clicking on a link changes the current page to display the contents of the link you clicked on, or sometimes a clicked link opens up a new browser window. The eventual result is that after 20 minutes of surfing you end up with several open browser windows cluttering up your desktop.

The solution to this browsing mess is *tabs*. Tabbed browsing allows you to have several pages open at the same time within one window. Tabbed browsing, which originated in the web browser Opera, has become so popular that all modern web browsers except Internet Explorer (who would have guessed?) include the feature. Don't ask me why Microsoft hasn't added it yet; until recently, they were way behind with pop-up ad blocking, too.

One of the best ways to show off the power of tabs is to visit a site that has a lot of links to articles you want to read. A news site is a good choice. A favorite site among Linux users is *http://www.slashdot.org*, which proclaims itself to be "News for Nerds. Stuff that Matters." To see how tabbed browsing works, open the Slashdot site, hold down the Ctrl key, and left-click on several article links. Each link opens in a new tab located just below the Location field. Figure 2-12 shows three tabs; Google and Slashdot are in the background, and the tab in the foreground is displaying oreilly.com. You can also click your middle mouse button on a link for the same effect.

FIGURE 2-12. Each tab represents a different web page

What's the deal with the middle mouse button?

A middle mouse button click entails different things, depending upon the type of mouse you have. If you have a mouse with a scroll wheel, it means clicking the scroll wheel as if it were a button. If you have a three-button mouse, it means clicking the middle mouse button. If you have a two-button mouse, it means clicking both the left and right mouse buttons simultaneously, a process known as *chording*.

Using tabs in this manner is useful because it allows sites you are interested in to be loaded in the background. While you continue to read your main news page, other articles can load in the tabs and will be ready for reading when you get done with the main page. It also means you don't lose your starting place while chasing down a series of links that caught your interest, but that were only tangential to the reason you opened your browser in the first place.

To bring a tabbed page to the front, click its tab with the mouse or press Ctrl-[or Ctrl-] to cycle through the tabs. Close the active tab by right-clicking it and selecting Close, by clicking the Close icon to the far right of the tab bar, or by pressing Ctrl-W on the keyboard.

You can open a new blank tab in several convenient ways. You can select Location → New Tab from the Konqueror menu, or press Ctrl-Shift-N (a particularly difficult combination to remember). Or, if a tab is already visible, you can right-click it and select New Tab. Regardless of your method, the tab will open, ready for you to enter an address or a search phrase in the Location field.

Though tabs are enabled by default, two settings that make tabs more useful are turned off. It's definitely worth taking the time to fix this. The configuration settings for tabs can be found by clicking on Settings → Configure Konqueror → Web behavior. From here, check the box next to "Open links in new tab instead of in new window." Then, click the Advanced Options button and check off "Open as tab in existing Konqueror when URL is called externally" (see Figure 2-13). Click OK, then press Save to close the Settings window. From now on, when you click

Load your favorite web sites automatically

One particularly great use for tabs is to have your web browser open with all your favorite sites loading automatically. To do this, create a bunch of tabs and load a different preferred site in each one. Then go to Settings → Save View Profile "Web Browsing" and save your web browsing profile with the "Save URLs in profile" option checked. Close and reopen Konqueror, and watch the magic happen.

on a link that would normally open in a new window, it will open in a new tab instead, and clicking on a link in another application, such as email, will open the URL in a new tab of an already running instance of Konqueror, instead of launching a new Konqueror window. These settings help keep things neat and tidy.

FIGURE 2-13. Konqueror's tab configuration panel

Teaching Konqueror to Lie

It is a sad fact that Microsoft's Internet Explorer web browser has over 90 percent of the web browser market. What's even sadder is that many web sites insist that you use Internet Explorer if you want to visit the site at all. They do this because they want to make sure you have the best browsing experience possible and mistakenly believe that only IE can provide it. Some web sites advise you to use an updated browser and then suggest something like Internet Explorer Version 4.0 or higher. Konqueror is a far more advanced web browser than IE 4 ever was, and arguably more advanced than IE 6 is now, but that doesn't stop these web sites from mistakenly thinking you have an outdated browser.

In the end, if you want to visit these sites, you have no choice but to lie to them. (Extreme, but necessary!) Use the following steps to configure Konqueror to pretend to be a web browser that is acceptable to troublesome web sites.

Click Settings → Configure Konqueror → Browser Identification. In this panel, click the New button under Site Specific Identification. In the dialog that appears, type in the URL for the web site you intend to lie to. For example, if your problem is with the Weight Watchers web site, enter `weightwatchers.com` in the field "When browsing the following site." In the next field, "Use the following identification," select the web browser you will pretend to be. The best selection in the list is probably Safari 1.0 on Mac OS X, because as mentioned at the beginning of the chapter, Safari is based upon Konqueror code. If choosing Safari doesn't get you in, try using one of the Mozilla options, or IE on Mac PPC.

Send a message to web site owners

Web servers track the types of browsers that visit their sites. Therefore, by choosing something other than IE on Windows, you are reminding those running the web site that they should program for a broader set of users. Who knows—if enough people visit using a non–Internet Explorer browser, the web site owners just might change their policy

Figure 2-14 shows a completely filled out "pretend" browser identification dialog. The Update List button simply downloads a fresh list of available browser identifications.

FIGURE 2-14. Configuring Konqueror to identify itself as IE on PPC

The best way to let a web site know that you want them to support your browser is to send them an email and tell them. If you can't find an address on the web site to send complaints to, you can always try *webmaster@websitename*. Let them know which browser you use, and whether the web site functioned correctly after you pretended to be IE. Web sites are more likely to add support for something that already works well.

Using Bookmarks

Like all good web browsers, Konqueror supports saved web site links known as *bookmarks*. Bookmarks, also known as Favorites to those who use Internet Explorer, make it easy to revisit your favorite web sites with the single click. In Konqueror, bookmarks can be used for web sites, FTP sites, or even a directory on your hard drive.

Adding a Bookmark

To bookmark a page you're currently viewing, simply select Bookmarks → Add Bookmark from the drop-down menu. The keyboard shortcut is Ctrl-B, and there is also a right-click context menu option called Bookmark This Location. Once you create a new bookmark, open the Bookmark menu once again, and you will see the new bookmark at the bottom of the list. By default, new bookmarks are also displayed on the

Bookmark toolbar. In Konqueror, this is the toolbar directly below the Location field, and it is probably already populated with several links to Mandrakesoft.

Managing Bookmarks

You've probably bookmarked dozens of web sites you visit regularly, and even more sites that you find of occasional interest and don't want to forget how to get there. But your bookmarks, some of which have very obscure names, can quickly become difficult to navigate if you don't apply some sort of organization scheme to them. Konqueror has a very useful bookmark manager feature to help with this task. To organize your list of bookmarks, select Bookmarks → Edit Bookmarks to open the bookmark manager.

Since Konqueror just appends new bookmark entries to the bottom of the list, you may find that your bookmarks get messy quite quickly. You can easily rearrange bookmarks inside the bookmark manager by dragging them to desired positions on the list or into folders. You can create new folders by clicking the Create New Folder icon on the toolbar (it's the one that looks like a folder), by pressing Ctrl-N, or by right-clicking inside the manager and choosing Create New Folder (as shown in Figure 2-15). New folders are added to the top of the bookmark list.

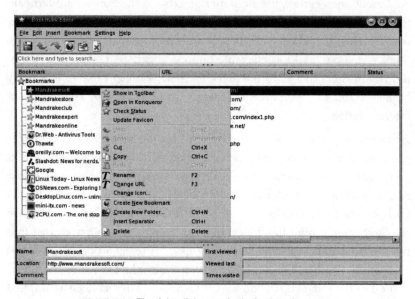

FIGURE 2-15. The right-click menu in the bookmark manager

Bookmarking for neat freaks

If you frequently bookmark pages, cleaning up bookmarks later on can be time consuming. A nice feature of Konqueror is the ability to place a bookmark in a specific folder at the time you create it. The easiest way to do this is through the Bookmarks menu. While viewing a page you want to bookmark, just click the Bookmarks menu, navigate to the folder you want to put the link in, and select Add Bookmark.

To remove any unwanted entries, select the items so that they become highlighted (use Shift-click or Ctrl-click to select more than one item). Then delete your selections by choosing Edit → Delete, by right-clicking an entry and selecting Delete, or simply by pressing the Delete key. Repeat the process until all unwanted entries have been removed.

After tidying things up, choose File → Quit to close the manager and save your changes. The new and improved bookmark list is now ready to use.

Using the Bookmark Toolbar

As I mentioned earlier, the Bookmark toolbar is the thin bar underneath the Location field. This is a convenient place to store bookmarks to your most frequently visited web sites. Since the Bookmark toolbar displays all of your bookmarks as clickable buttons, it can get cluttered very easily. If you don't like the Bookmark toolbar, you can remove it entirely by deselecting the Settings → Toolbars → Show Bookmark Toolbar (Konqueror) option.

However, if you like the convenience of having your favorite web sites just a single click away, you'd probably rather just specify the exact links you want on the toolbar. To do this, go to Bookmarks → Edit Bookmarks, and in the Bookmark Editor, click Settings and select "Display Only Marked Bookmarks in Konqueror Bookmark Toolbar." Then click the Save icon. Doing this hides all your Bookmark toolbar entries (but not the bookmarks in your Bookmark list). To select a bookmark to put back on the toolbar, simply right-click on the bookmark inside the Bookmark Editor and choose "Show in Toolbar." Your change is applied once you click the Save icon or close and save the Bookmark Editor.

Playing with the Bookmark and History Sidebar

Like IE, Konqueror provides a sidebar on the left side of the browser window to display bookmarks and your browsing history. You can toggle the appearance of the sidebar by pressing the F9 key. When the sidebar is visible, there is a collection of icons along the left side that control the contents of the sidebar. Some of these items are relevant only when Konqueror is being used as a file manager, but the bookmark and history icons are useful when browsing the Web.

Click once on the bookmark icon (a star) to show your entire bookmarks collection inside the sidebar. This is the same list displayed by clicking the Bookmarks menu item, but this way it's off to the side and out of your way, but at the same time always visible so you can quickly click on a link.

The history icon looks like a small clock. Clicking it lists all of the web sites you have visited in a specified time period (see Figure 2-16). You can change the time period (as well as other things) in the History preference panel, which you can reach by clicking Settings → Configure Konqueror → History Sidebar. The history gives you an easy way to get back to web sites that you've visited recently. If you're concerned about your privacy and don't want others to see your history, just use the Clear History button to erase your tracks. Unfortunately, there is no way to prevent the history from being created, but you can set the "Maximum number of URLs" to 1, which means that only your most recently visited web site gets saved.

Dealing with Helper Applications

Helper applications are programs that work with a web browser to handle certain types of files, such as PDFs, Flash animations, and videos. Helper applications often require you to make some changes in your computer setup (also known as your *configuration*) so that your web browser knows which application to launch when it encounters certain types of files.

The *Move* CD includes the following helper applications:

Acrobat Reader
> You can use this program to view Portable Document Files (PDFs). These files often show up on the Internet as links on various web sites. PDFs are used when their creators want to be certain you see the document exactly the way they want it displayed. The Acrobat

FIGURE 2-16. The History view in the sidebar

Reader program is provided by Adobe and includes a small browser plug-in that makes it possible to view PDF images inside your web browser.

Macromedia's Flash Player

Many web sites contain multimedia sections that are viewable only with the Flash Player. These so-called Flash animations are very common on the Internet; many web sites use Flash to create interactive games or experiences for visitors. This program is the most commonly downloaded plug-in in the world.

Real's RealPlayer

You can use this program to view streaming sound and video over the Internet. Many news and music web sites provide multimedia streams that require this program.

Some other popular helper applications, such as Macromedia's Shockwave, do not run on Linux, so Konqueror doesn't support them. And although the *Move* CD does not contain support for Microsoft's WMA or Apple's QuickTime programs, it is possible to use these programs in Linux once you install a Linux distribution on your hard drive.

Changing a Helper Application

One of the great but confusing things about Linux is that there is often more than one program to accomplish any given task. There are multiple desktop environments (KDE, GNOME, WindowMaker, Xfce, and more), multiple web browsers (Konqueror, Firefox, Mozilla, Opera, Galeon, and others), and even more than one program for viewing PDF files.

On the *Move* CD, PDF files are by default displayed in a program called KGhostview. KGhostview, shown in Figure 2-17, is a great PDF viewer that loads quickly and has an interface that integrates nicely with the rest of the KDE desktop. However, you may come across some files that do not display properly in KGhostview. If that happens to you, there's an easy fix—just set Adobe's Acrobat Reader to be your default PDF viewer.

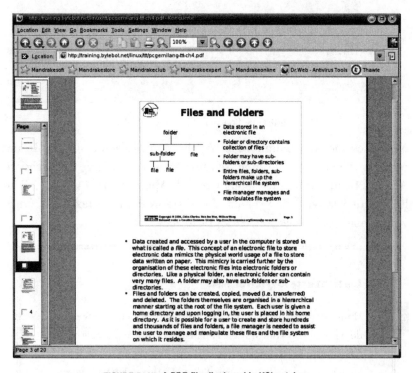

FIGURE 2-17. A PDF file displayed in KGhostview

To change your default PDF viewer, go to Settings → Configure Konqueror → File Associations. In the "Configure file associations" panel, shown in Figure 2-18, expand the application group by clicking the plus sign next to it, then click once on the pdf entry. Alternatively, you also just type **pdf** into the "Find filename pattern field" and then click pdf.

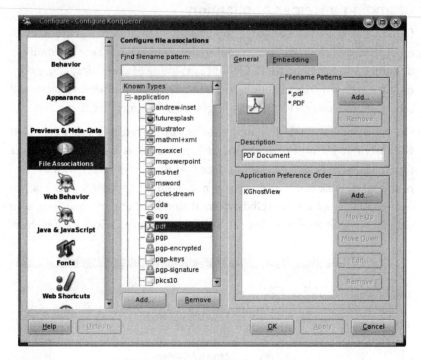

FIGURE 2-18. Creating a PDF file association

Now click the Add button under Application Preference Order. In the resulting Choose Application selector shown in Figure 2-19, choose Acrobat Reader from the menu under All Applications → Office → Publishing, or just type the program name **acroread** in the text field. Once you've made your selection, click OK to accept it.

Learning on the job

Until you really become familiar with Linux (which usually means doing a lot of work on the command line, a topic covered in Chapter 11), you probably won't know the actual commands to launch even your most frequently used programs. Don't worry— you probably don't know the commands in Windows, either.

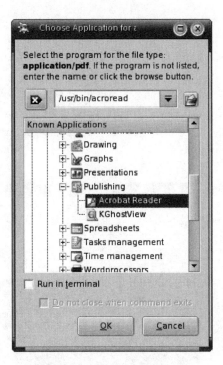

FIGURE 2-19. Choosing Acrobat Reader

A minor annoyance

The first time Acrobat Reader runs, you have to accept a license. This window may get hidden behind other applications, so if the PDF doesn't open within a few seconds, look at your taskbar to find the license window so you can accept Adobe's terms.

Acrobat Reader should now appear in the Application Preference Order list. If it's not already at the top of the list, select it so that it becomes highlighted and click the Move Up button until it's at the top. Finally, press OK to accept the change. KDE then tells you that it is updating the system configuration. The next time you click a link to a PDF file, you'll be offered the option of either downloading the file or opening it in Acrobat Reader.

Flash Player

Flash Player is a plug-in program for viewing Macromedia Flash animations. *Move* is preconfigured to use this plug-in, so you don't need to change anything to enjoy Flash-enabled web sites, such as the one shown in Figure 2-20. If you have kids or are a kid at heart yourself, you might want to check out some of the great Flash games on the Web. Do a Google search for Flash games or just go straight to the aptly named *http://www.addictinggames.com*.

FIGURE 2-20. Konqueror playing a Flash game

RealPlayer

RealPlayer is a popular program for listening to and viewing online streaming audio and video files. RealPlayer is not an application that gets embedded into your web browser like Flash; instead, a separate application, RealPlayer G2, is launched when you click a link for a RealPlayer audio or video file.

You can find RealPlayer audio and video streams all over the Internet. For a quick test to make sure everything is working (and to hear a great Boston band whose lead singer and guitarist happen to work at O'Reilly), head on over to *http://www.thecharms.net/charms2/discography2. htm* and click one of the Streaming links. This loads a page where you can select streams for one of three songs.

When you click on one of the streaming links, you are presented with a dialog asking you if you want to save or open the link; choose Open. The next dialog presents a similar choice, but this time select Open with RealPlayer G2. If you check off the option "Do not ask again," you won't get this dialog in the future. Instead, RealPlayer will immediately launch each time you click on a link to a RealPlayer file.

+

Just say no to spam

The first time you use RealPlayer, you need to go through a little setup routine (in which you enter your email address, zip code, connection speed, etc.). One little checkbox that you might want to pay attention to is "Inform me of updates and events." This checkbox is preselected for you. If you don't unclick it, you will get spam-like email from Real.com at the email address you provide.

SHOUTcast

SHOUTcast (and Icecast) are streaming audio formats often used by independent radio stations. You don't need a special plug-in to enjoy these types of files because Totem, KDE's built-in media player, can handle them quite nicely.

To test out these formats, locate a web site that offers these files (such as *http://www.shoutcast.com*) and select an appropriate link. Since Konqueror doesn't initially know what to do with this type of file, it will ask whether you want to download it or open it. Just as in the RealPlayer setup, you should click Open. Then, in the next dialog, click Open with

Totem Movie Player. Totem then opens on the desktop and, as shown in Figure 2-21, begins playing the audio stream. If you make the Totem window larger, you'll also be treated to a cool light show.

More than just movies

Don't let the mislabeling of the Totem multimedia program as a "movie player" confuse you. Totem is a complete multimedia application similar to Windows Media Player and it supports most of the media formats you need on a regular basis.

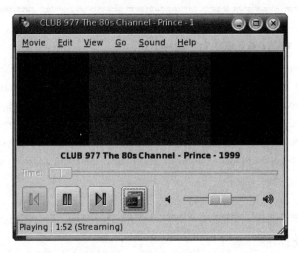

FIGURE 2-21. Playing a streaming audio file with Totem

Accessing FTP Sites

And as if all the other good things in this chapter weren't enough, Konqueror is also a full-featured File Transfer Protocol (FTP) client that supports file transfers, bookmarks, and drag and drop—all the usual stuff. To see Konqueror's FTP capabilities, just connect to the Internet, enter an FTP site into the Location field, and press Enter. For a very popular FTP site that hosts a lot of important open source projects, try *ftp://ftp.ibiblio.org/pub* (Figure 2-22). The FTP site loads, and from this point on acts as if it were a folder on your computer (though it'll probably be slower to respond if you don't have a fast Internet connection). Once you've connected to an FTP site, you can download a file or folder by simply dragging it to a location in your home directory and selecting Copy Here.

FTP: The Linux user's friend

Though FTP is less popular than it once was, Linux users still use it frequently. Often, the best way to get a copy of a Linux distribution is to download a CD image of it (usually called an ISO file) from an FTP site. The installers for many open source programs are also available only on FTP sites.

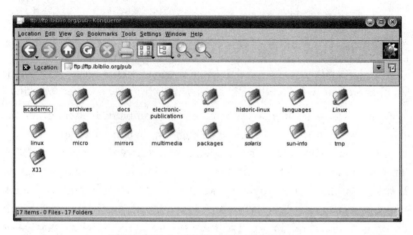

FIGURE 2-22. An FTP site opened in Konqueror

If the FTP site you're trying to access requires a password, enter the location in a format such as:

ftp://accountname@ftp.oreilly.com/

Note that your account name is added to the *front* of the FTP URL. Think of it like an email address for an FTP site.

Enter the correct password into the authorization dialog box (Figure 2-23) and press OK. If the login is accepted, you'll be directed to the FTP site.

FIGURE 2-23. Authenticating yourself for an FTP site

The Mozilla Web Browser

Although Konqueror is the default web browser on the *Move* CD, there is another web browser on the CD as well. This browser is called Mozilla.

Longtime web surfers may remember the company Netscape and its flagship web browser, Netscape Navigator. When Netscape lost the browser wars with Microsoft, it open-sourced its web browser in 1998. That means that all the code for that previously proprietary program became available for anybody in the world to use—and hopefully improve. Since that time, a group of developers has been working on creating a new and innovative browser from the original Navigator source code. This project took a lot of turns, including a ground-up rewrite, but eventually produced the Mozilla Suite, an all-in-one Internet application with a web browser, email client, newsgroup reader, and web page composer.

The *Move* CD includes the full Mozilla Suite, and since this is an application you can use on both Linux and Windows, it is worth taking a look at. The Mozilla browser has most of the features I've already described for Konqueror, including pop-up ad blocking and tabbed browsing. The Mozilla web page composer is covered in Chapter 12.

Reusing good code

The part of Mozilla that determines how web pages are displayed is called the gecko rendering engine. Because it is an open source component, gecko is being used by half a dozen other web browsers, including the incredibly popular, cross-platform Firefox.

Mozilla is also available on Windows. If you want to install it on Windows, visit *http://www.mozilla.org* to download the program. On the Mozilla home page, you will see mentions of the Firefox web browser and Thunderbird email client. These programs are cross-platform as well. They aren't installed on the *Move* CD, but I'll provide more information about them in Chapter 12.

3

FILE MANAGEMENT

Learning where files are on your system and understanding how to manage them is essential to truly mastering the use of a computer. Once you know how to work with files, you can expand this knowledge and learn how to manage files on remote computers, which is useful when you work in a networked environment.

Be sure to read Chapter 11 if you are interested in learning how to manage your files using the Linux command line (a popular method among most Linux users).

Using Konqueror to Manage Files

Though there are dozens of file managers in Linux, this chapter only covers one: Konqueror, the same program you just learned how to use for web browsing. Konqueror can work in two different ways—as a web browser and as a file manager—depending on how you launch, or start, the program.

Since you already know a bit about Konqueror, it should be easy to learn how to use it as a file manager, so let's just dive in and get started. To open Konqueror as a file manager, just double-click the Home icon on your desktop. (As you might guess, it's the icon that looks like a little house.)

Using profiles to control Konqueror

Note that this is a different way to open Konqueror. In Chapter 2, you started the program by clicking the Konqueror icon on the kicker panel, which opened up Konqueror as a web browser. Clicking the Home icon on the desktop opens Konqueror as a file manager. Each icon loads a different Konqueror profile, which determines how the program behaves. You'll learn how to create a new profile and load it from an icon later in this chapter.

Clicking on the Home icon will to bring up a Konqueror window similar to the one shown in Figure 3-1. This window should look familiar to you. There are a few new icons on the toolbar, but basically it's very similar to the Konqueror window you used in Chapter 2.

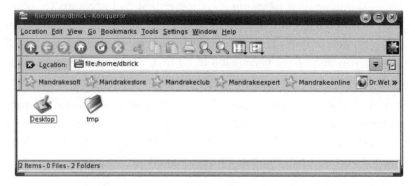

FIGURE 3-1. Konqueror displaying your Home directory

Since you launched Konqueror using the Home icon, it naturally opens up showing the contents of your Home directory. Think of your Home directory like you think of your house—your own private place in an otherwise very public town. Your Home directory belongs to you; everything in it is yours, and nobody else is allowed in unless you give permission. In addition to your data files, your Home directory contains a lot of hidden files that control how programs behave. These files affect only *your* use of the programs; other users have their own hidden configuration files in their Home directories. You can use the techniques described in the section "Making Selections" in Chapter 1 to select files and folders inside the Konqueror window.

Directory or folder?

Directories and folders are two names for the same thing. The term *directory* is older, and came about before there were graphics on the computer. The term *folder* came about when graphical interfaces were created in the early 1980s. The icon that represented a directory looked like a folder.

Basic Navigation in Konqueror

After opening up Konqueror in your Home directory, click the up arrow on your Konqueror toolbar to move you up out of the Home directory. Think of it as walking out your front door and into the neighborhood. When you look around, what do you see? You see the outside of your

Home. If you were working on a computer that had accounts for other users, you would see the outside of their Homes as well. If you double-clicked on one of those Homes and tried to get in, Konqueror would tell you that you don't have permission to do that. This is pretty much what would happen if you tried to walk in through your neighbor's front door.

Now click the up arrow again. Think of this as walking out of your neighborhood and onto the main street of your town, where there are a lot of different kinds of buildings, only some of them homes. If you look in your Location field, you will now see you are at:

```
file:/
```

The single forward slash means that you're at the root of your Linux system, as shown in Figure 3-2. Things are looking pretty busy here, aren't they? There are a lot of directories listed. Some of these directories (the ones that begin with *image*) exist only to allow Linux to run from CD. Others are mainstay directories that you will see on practically every Linux system.

FIGURE 3-2. Konqueror showing the root of your Linux system

While you're using the *Move* CD, you won't need to worry about many files outside your Home directory. But once you install Linux, you will frequently find yourself doing things outside your Home.

There are various ways to navigate to different directories, or folders, in Linux. Here are some different methods you can use:

Click the Home toolbar icon

You can simply click this icon to go back to your Home directory. The icon is on your Konqueror toolbar and looks like a small blue house.

Use the arrow toolbar icons

You can use the arrow icons to navigate from directory to directory. These icons work similarly to the way they do in a web browser. Clicking the up arrow moves you up one directory level. Clicking the left arrow takes you back to the directory you just left; clicking it multiple times goes back to previous directories, just like using the Back button to move back to recently viewed web pages. Once you start moving back, you can use the right arrow to move forward one or more directories (until you get to where you started using the left arrow). Both the left and right arrow icons have small black triangles on them if there are multiple directories you can move forward or back to. Click and hold your mouse on the icon to see a list of the directories, and select a directory from the list to go there.

Click folder icons

You can just double-click on folder icons to get directly into those folders. To go back to your Home directory from the root directory, double-click the Home folder, then double-click your username folder. This is the most commonly used method for moving to different folders.

Type in the Location field

Finally, you can type directions to a folder in the Location field at the top of your Konqueror window. This is called typing in a *path*. A pathname is basically the full name of the directory, starting with the root folder (which is represented with a single forward slash), followed by all the other directories, in order, until you get to where you're trying to go. After you've typed in the full path to your directory, simply press Enter and you'll be taken right to there. So, to go to your Home directory, type **/home/*username*** and press Enter (replacing ***username*** with your actual username on a Linux machine).

Knowing what to type

When you are browsing local files, you don't need to put *file:/* into the Location field every time, just as you don't need to put *http://* in the Location field when you want to go to *www.oreilly.com.* But these designations do matter in some situations, as you will see in the later section "Accessing Network Files."

Creating Files

Since you're just getting started with the *Move* CD, you don't have any files sitting around yet. Let's create some now so that you can experiment with some of the tips in this chapter.

To create a file, start in your Home directory, right-click in the empty space of the Konqueror window, and choose Create New → File → Text File. This opens a window that lets you name your new file. Be original, and call the file *new_file.* An icon representing this file will now appear in your Home directory. Because this is a text file, if you double-click it, it launches the program KWrite, which I talked about in Chapter 1.

You can create new directories in the same way. Right-click in an empty space of the Konqueror window and this time choose Create New → Folder. Just as when you created a file, a window pops up asking you to name the folder. Call this folder *New_Folder.* Although you will often find yourself creating new folders this way, you probably won't often use this method to create a new file. Usually, you'll create new files from within a program you're using, such as KWrite or OpenOffice.org (covered in Chapter 9).

Now that you have a file and a folder to play with, you can try out some basic file management tips in the next section, such as copying and moving files and folders.

Copying, Moving, Renaming, and Deleting Files and Directories

You'll probably find yourself copying, moving, renaming, and deleting files fairly often. Luckily, Konqueror makes this very easy. Let's look at each task, one by one.

There are several ways to copy a file. Let's try the easiest way first. Just right-click on *new_file* and choose Copy (or click once on the file and press Ctrl-C). Then right-click elsewhere in the Konqueror window and choose Paste (or press Ctrl-V). A new window opens, telling you that *new_file* already exists and prompting you to provide a new name for the file. Type in *new_file2*, then click Continue (Figure 3-3). You should now have a new file in your Home directory.

FIGURE 3-3. The file naming window

Another way to copy a file is to double-click your Home icon again to open a second Konqueror window. Now, just drag *new_file2* from one window to the other and drop it. This opens a small menu with several options: Move Here, Copy Here, Link Here, and Cancel (Figure 3-4). For now, choose Copy Here. Again, a window will ask you to create a new name for your file. Call this file *new_file3*.

FIGURE 3-4. The small menu that appears when you drop a file in a new folder

Links and shortcuts

The Link Here option creates a file that points to the file you are linking. Links are just like shortcuts in Windows. Clicking a link to a file opens that file; clicking a link to a directory opens that directory. And like in Windows, if you delete a link, the directory and file are not deleted. A link file simply points to another file or directory; it is not the actual file or directory.

If you hover your mouse over the icons on the Konqueror toolbar, you'll see tooltips that describe what each icon does. Using this method for the scissors icon and the two icons to the right of it, you'll see that these are, respectively, Cut, Copy, and Paste. Using these icons is another way to copy files. To try this, click once on *new_file3* to make it active, then click the Copy icon (which looks like two pieces of paper). This copies the file into memory. Now click elsewhere in the Konqueror window and click the Paste icon (which looks like a clipboard with a piece of paper in front). Again, a window appears to let you give the file a new name. Call this file *new_file4*. (See a pattern yet?)

Resolving name conflicts

These file naming windows pop up only because you are copying the file to the same directory as the original file, and there is a name conflict. When you copy files to a different directory (as you normally will), you won't see this window unless a file with the same name is already in the new location.

Now it's time to move some files. If you still have two Konqueror windows open (if you don't, open up a second one), go into the *New_Folder* directory in one of them. Drag *new_file* from your Home directory to your *New_Folder* directory. When you let go of the mouse, you'll see the same menu as when you tried to copy a file from one window to another (shown back in Figure 3-4). This time, choose Move Here. Your file is now moved into the *New_Folder* directory.

And of course there are other ways to move files as well. For example, you can click a file, press Ctrl-X to cut it from the current folder, go to *New_Folder*, and press Ctrl-V to paste it. You can also right-click the file's icon, choose Cut, and right-click in the new location to Paste it. Or you can use the toolbar icons to move an item—first click on the scissors icon to cut the file, and then the clipboard icon to paste it. (Basically, when moving files you're just using Cut instead of Copy.) As you can see, it's no problem to move files around in Linux. Move all of the files you've created so far into the directory *New_Folder*.

As you might suspect, renaming files is also very easy. Just right-click on a file, choose Rename, and type in a new name for the file. Other ways to do this are to click on the file icon and press F2, or to click directly on the filename itself, which automatically enters renaming mode. Give each of the files you created earlier a new name: *Test, Driving, Linux,* and *Rocks.*

Now let's delete some of these files. I won't say a tidy Home directory represents an orderly mind, but I will say that keeping your files cleaned up makes it easier to find files when you need them, which may help you to maintain an orderly mind. Again, there are several ways to perform this task. Let's try a different method for each file:

1. Right-click on *Test* and choose Delete. A window pops up, asking you if you really want to delete this file. You do, so choose Delete. If you check off the box "Do not ask again," you won't see this window every time you try to delete a file. For now, though, leave it unchecked.

2. Right-click on *Driving* and choose Move to Trash. Again, a window pops up, this time asking you to confirm that you want to move the file to the trash. You do, so click Trash.

3. Click once on *Linux* and then press the Delete key on your keyboard. In the window that appears, click Trash again to move the file to the trash.

4. Finally, position your Konqueror window so that you can see the Trash icon on your desktop. Then drag the last file, *Rocks,* to the Trash icon and drop it. Either the same Move to Trash window will come up, or you will have a blinking icon on your taskbar. If the latter, click on the blinking icon to see the Move to Trash window and answer it by clicking Trash.

So, all your files are deleted—right? Wrong. Double-click the Trash icon on your desktop. This opens the trash in Konqueror, and you can see that three of your files (*Driving, Linux,* and *Rocks*) are still there. The *Test* file, though, isn't. If you paid attention to the warning windows that popped up in Steps 1 to 4, you'll know why. The first window, in Step 1, asked if you wanted to delete the file; the other three windows, in Steps 2 to 4, all asked if you wanted to move the file to the trash. Deleting a file is permanent; the file just disappears at that point. When you move a file to the trash, you are just putting it into another folder—a special folder called Trash.

You can retrieve items from the Trash by using some of the file-moving methods from earlier in this section. (The only method that doesn't work is right-clicking on the file and choosing Cut.) Try moving the files *Driving* and *Linux* back to your *New_Folder* directory. Now, empty your Trash by right-clicking on the Trash icon and choosing Empty Trash Bin. If you reopen the Trash, you will find that the *Rocks* file is now gone for good.

All the file management methods I've described so far apply to directories as well as files. And that's pretty much all you need to know about basic file management in Konqueror. The rest of this chapter deals with more advanced aspects of using Konqueror to manage files.

Changing Your View

Personally, I don't like viewing my files as giant icons—they simply take up too much room. You can control the appearance of the icons to some extent by choosing a view mode from the View menu. Try out different view modes to see which one you like best. I tend to favor the Detailed List view.

If you choose that view, you'll see that it shows a lot of information. Maybe too much. I like to limit this a little by hiding the File Type, Group, and Link columns. To do this, just click View → Show Details and uncheck whatever you don't want to see. You can also resize columns by dragging the column name separators. Figure 3-5 shows my modified Detailed List view.

One of the advantages of choosing a view with multiple columns is that you can sort the files by clicking on the column name. By default, your files are sorted in alphabetical order—folders first, followed by individual files. When you click the Name column heading, the sort order switches to reverse alphabetical order (although folders are still listed before files).

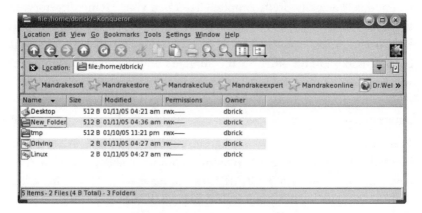

FIGURE 3-5. A modified Detailed List view

Accessing Network Files

Many people use their computers on a network with other computers. If your computer is part of a network, you'll probably want to access files on other computers. It's perfectly possible to do this with the *Move* CD. In this section, when I say *remote computer*, I simply mean any computer on your network other than the one you're currently working at.

Imagine you have a network consisting of three computers, two of which are sharing directories and files. One of these machines runs Windows and is sharing files in the directory *wshared*. Another computer is running Linux and sharing files in a directory called *lshared*. And then, of course, there is your *Move* machine, which isn't sharing any files.

In almost all instances, a Windows computer shares directories with other computers by using the Windows built-in sharing protocol known as Server Message Block (SMB). It's not important to know exactly what this means; just think, "SMB = Windows sharing," and don't worry about the specifics. Windows machines know how to automatically find other computers that are sharing directories using SMB. Usually, all you have to do is look in My Network Neighborhood, and you will see other Windows machines on your network. From there, you can access their shared folders.

Microsoft keeps the workings behind SMB a secret, but some crafty open source programmers have figured a lot of it out. Because of their efforts, you can connect to a Windows computer from Konqueror and view and use the files the Windows computer is sharing.

Doing this is actually pretty simple. First, open your Home directory. In the Location field, type **smb:/** and press Enter. What you are typing is known as a *protocol handler*. With it, you are telling Konqueror to use the SMB protocol to find other SMB computers on the network. Konqueror will search the network for a few seconds and then show you any Windows workgroups it finds. (*Workgroups* are a way to group Windows computers together.)

In my case, I see a Windows workgroup called MSHOME. When I double-click that, I see a single Windows computer called CLAIRE (my wife's laptop). And inside CLAIRE are some shared folders, including one I set up just for this book called *wshared* (Figure 3-6). I can now use Konqueror to manage files on this Windows computer in the same way I would on my *Move* computer.

FIGURE 3-6. The wshared folder on the computer CLAIRE

Connecting to another Linux machine is slightly more complex, but only because there are more ways to share files on Linux. One way Linux can share files is by using SMB, just like Windows. If this is how the remote Linux machine is sharing files, you can simply use the smb:/ method described above to access files on remote Linux computers. If your Linux machine is using another file-sharing protocol, such as the Network File System (NFS) common on Unix networks, you should type **nfs:/** in the Location field instead.

Many Linux machines run a program known as Secure Shell (SSH). You can use this program to do a lot of things, including managing files remotely. If your remote Linux machine runs SSH, you can connect to it by typing **sftp://nameofmachine** in the Location field and pressing Enter.

If you don't know the name of your remote computer, try using its IP address instead of its name. When you use this method, you'll be asked to provide a username and password for the remote system. This information is for your account on the remote machine, not your *Move* computer. When you make the connection to the other computer, you should be dropped right into your Home directory on the remote machine.

Using SFTP to connect to remote machines is great because it works securely, even over the Internet. With this method, I'm able to connect from my *Move* computer on my home network to the remote computer at the O'Reilly office where the files for this book are stored while it is being copyedited (see Figure 3-7). Once I make the connection and get into my Home directory on the work computer, I can move to other folders on that computer.

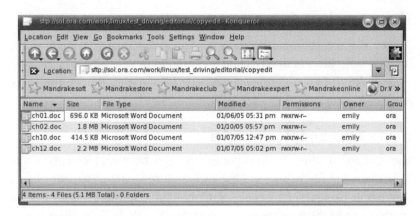

FIGURE 3-7. Making an SFTP connection to a remote machine over the Internet

Misleading acronyms

SFTP stands for Secure File Transfer Protocol. It actually has no relation to File Transfer Protocol (FTP), despite the similarities in their names. SFTP is part of the SSH program run by most Linux computers. SSH allows system administrators to securely control their Linux computers, even from a remote location.

Out of the box, Windows is limited to using only SMB to share files. But Konqueror, KDE, and Linux can use dozens of protocol handlers to connect to remote computers or perform other functions. You can find an interesting article that introduces other protocol handlers at *http://osdir. com/Article2159.phtml*. Be aware, however, that not all of the protocol handlers in this article will work in this version of KDE.

Other uses for protocol handlers

The smb:/, nfs:/, and sftp:/ protocol handlers can even be used inside a File Open or Save window in KDE programs. Test this out in KWrite sometime.

Konquering Advanced Techniques

As you can see, there's a lot more to Konqueror than you might think. It's a core application in KDE and is central to most of what you do with your desktop. In the following section, I'll cover a few of the more advanced features of Konqueror.

Using Tabs and Bookmarks

Some of the features in Konqueror the web browser bleed over into Konqueror the file manager. One such feature is tabs. You can open a new tab in Konqueror by pressing Ctrl-Shift-N, and use it to browse to another part of the filesystem or start surfing the Web. Tabs allow you to keep all your file-browsing windows in one place. If you drag a file from one tab and hold it over another tab for one second, Konqueror switches to that other tab and you can drop the file in the window, using the standard choices to Copy, Move, or Link it. Be sure not to drop the file on *top* of the tab; if you do that, the program just tries to open the file.

You can also use bookmarks to manage files in the same way you use them in the Konqueror web browser. Bookmarks can provide quick links to directories, even on remote systems. To create a bookmark, just go into the directory you want to bookmark and choose Bookmarks → Add Bookmark (or press Ctrl-B). To learn more about managing bookmarks, read the section "Using Bookmarks" in Chapter 2.

Zipping Files

Archives are one or more files that are grouped together and compressed. You probably know of them as zip files. There are different types of archives, because Linux has several methods to compress a file. If you're sharing files with Windows users, select the option Create zip Archive. If you are sharing files with Linux users, use the gzipped or bzipped options instead—these methods are standard in the Linux community, and you'll be much cooler if you use them. Most open source software you download from the Internet will be compressed in one of these two formats.

If you right-click on one of the files you created earlier in this chapter and select Actions from the menu that appears, you'll see that can choose to add the file to an archive, burn it to CD, or to open a Terminal (see Figure 3-8).

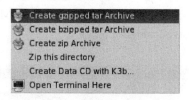

FIGURE 3-8. The Actions menu for a file

So, let's create a zip archive file. Select both of the files in your *New_ Folder* (*Driving* and *Linux*), right-click on the combined files, and choose Actions → Create zip Archive. In the window that appears, type *zipped* in the Location field and click Save. You should now see a *zipped.zip* file in your Konqueror window.

Unpacking, or opening, the zip file is equally easy. But first, delete the *Driving* and *Linux* files so that they won't get in the way. With that done, right-click on the *zipped.zip* file and choose Actions → Extract Here. As you would expect, this extracts the files *Driving* and *Linux* from the zip file and puts them in your directory.

Here's another trick for unpacking zip files. Try double-clicking *zipped. zip*, which causes Konqueror to open it up as if it were a regular directory. This allows you easy access to the zip file, so you can copy one or more items out of it simply by dragging them out of the zip directory.

Splitting Konqueror

Another cool thing you can do with Konqueror is to split the Konqueror window into several different view panes. This allows you to have several file locations open and visible at one time, but still contained within one window. Doing this makes it very easy to copy files between directories or access multiple directories simultaneously without the clutter of having multiple windows. To split the Konqueror window into left and right parts, click on Window → Split View Left/Right. Now, click in either pane, and then click your Home icon. Then click in the other pane and do the same, but then click on your *New_Folder* directory. And voila—you've got a neat, unobstructed view of both directories, and dragging files between the panes to copy or move them becomes even more of a snap. (Note that you can drag the bar between panes to resize them.)

It's also possible to split one of these windows again. Just click inside a window, then click the Window option and choose another split. Using this method and choosing various View → View Mode options, I created the window shown in Figure 3-9.

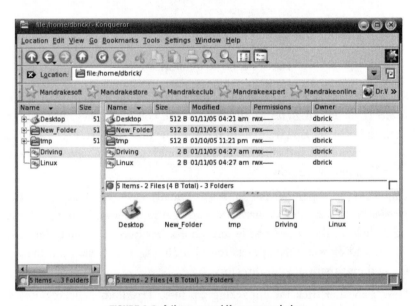

FIGURE 3-9. A three-paned Konqueror window

If you configure a Konqueror view you particularly like, you can save it and reuse it. Remember, Konqueror opens with whatever view profile you choose. To save your setup as a new view profile, click Settings →

Configure View Profiles. In the window that appears, type in **splits** for the profile name, check off the boxes next to "Save URLs in profile" and "Save window size in profile," and then click Save. Close Konqueror when you are done.

Now you just need an easy way to open Konqueror using your new view profile. Right-click on the Home icon on your desktop and choose Copy. Then right-click on the desktop and choose Paste. This opens a window that lets you name the view profile file. Because of a bug in KDE, it doesn't really matter what you name the view profile, as long as it ends in *.desktop* and isn't called *Home.desktop*. Once you name your profile and click Continue, you will have a new icon on your desktop called Home. (I told you there was a bug.) Now you should rename the file using one of the techniques described earlier. This time, call the file *Splitsville*.

Right-click on *Splitsville* and choose Properties. In the window that appears, click on the Application tab (Figure 3-10).

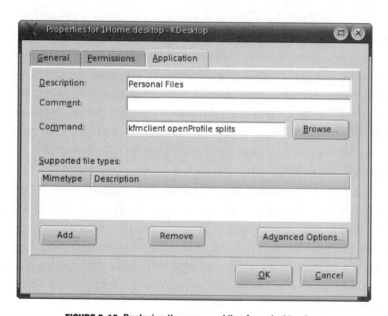

FIGURE 3-10. Replacing the command line for a desktop icon

The Command field contains the instructions the icon runs when it is double-clicked. Replace what is there with **kfmclient openProfile splits**, as shown in , and then click OK to accept the change and close the window. As you can see, all you're really doing is replacing *filemanagement* with *splits*. This new command tells Konqueror (*kfmclient*) to open using the profile named *splits*. Now, you can just double-click *Splitsville* to open Konqueror with your preferred settings.

Accessing Files on Your Windows Hard Drive

Chapters 4 and 7 in this book discuss using multimedia files and editing pictures. Even though the *Move* CD doesn't come with any music to listen to, videos to watch, or pretty pictures to edit, it does let you access your Windows hard drive and use the files you have there.

This might make you a little nervous. But don't worry—really! The *Move* CD will not do anything bad to your hard drive or your files. *Move* only lets you *read* your Windows files—in other words, you can't make any changes to the files or delete them in *Move*. This means that all your data remains safe, and there is nothing *Move* can do to mess up your Windows computer.

Accessing your Windows files is very easy in Konqueror. First, click the Home icon on your desktop to open Konqueror, and click the up button until you are in the root folder (it should take two clicks). One of the directories shown is called *mnt*. This stands for *mount*—in Linux, when you access a storage device, such as a hard drive or USB memory key, you are said to be mounting your filesystem on that device. You access a mounted filesystem through a mount point, which is just a fancy name for a directory. Most Linux users put all of their mount points in one place, the *mnt* directory.

So double-click the *mnt* icon to see what mount points are available to you. In my case, I have only one mount point, called *win_c*. Double-click your mount point, and you should see your entire Windows system (as shown in Figure 3-11). From here, you can navigate to wherever your important files are and use them in *Move*. Windows XP users should find their personal files in *Documents and Settings*, in a folder named for their Windows username.

You can play a music or video file directly from your Windows hard drive, but in order to edit a picture, you need to copy it to your Home directory on *Move*. (See—I told you that *Move* wouldn't let you mess

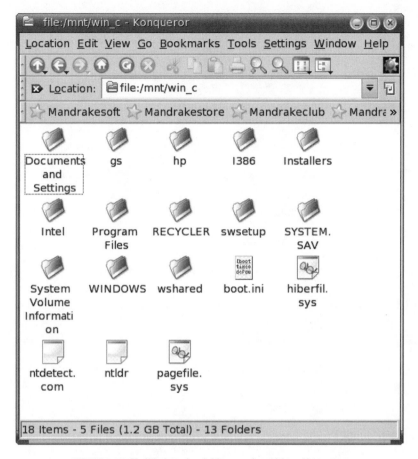

FIGURE 3-11. My Windows hard drive, as viewed from Konqueror

anything up!) Another thing you can do is to drag and drop a photograph from your Windows machine onto your *Move* desktop, then choose Set as Wallpaper to set the picture as your background image.

If you're a longtime Windows user, you know that it is possible for Windows to get so messed up or infested with viruses that it will stop booting. If this ever happens to you, use some of the techniques in this chapter to rescue your important data. You can simply boot with the *Move* CD and access your Windows files using the method I just described. If you have a USB memory key, you can copy important files to it. Or, you can access a shared folder on a remote computer, using the techniques described earlier in "Accessing Network Files," and copy your files there.

4 +

!

MUSIC
AND
VIDEOS

The personal computer is fast becoming the hub of our digital lifestyle. With the emergence of high-speed Internet access, MP3 music files, streaming video, and P2P file sharing, the home computer is often more of an entertainment device than a place to balance your checkbook or write a school report.

A computer running Linux can be a great multimedia machine for your home. It is capable of playing DVDs and most forms of video files, listening to every conceivable type of music format, and creating and editing video and audio content. Many of the people who write programs for Linux are multimedia nuts themselves, so you can rest assured that the capabilities of multimedia software on Linux are second to none.

This chapter covers the common multimedia tasks you'll want to accomplish on your computer. However, because you're running Linux from the *Move* CD, you won't be able to try out some of the things I describe in this chapter unless you have more than one CD or DVD drive in your computer. (Obviously, if you have only a single CD drive, you can't listen to or burn a CD because the *Move* CD is already in the drive.) So instead of trying to work around these limitations, I'll just describe the programs and not worry about whether you can actually test out the features (though of course I'll let you know if there is an easy way to do so).

Booting advice for Move

If you *do* have two optical drives, boot your machine with *Move* in a non-burning drive, i.e., a CD or DVD reader. This leaves the burner device free to make a CD.

Playing Music Files

Besides playing games (which I'll get to in the next chapter), the most common entertainment purpose computers are put to is playing music. Linux has dozens of programs for playing MP3 files and nearly every other digital music format.

Digital Audio Files

A CD, even a music CD, is nothing more than a storage device similar to a hard drive or a floppy disk, designed to hold a certain amount of data. The recording industry standards call for music CDs to hold 650 MB of data. (Recordable CDs for computers can now hold up to 700 MB.) Each song on a music CD takes up a certain amount of space depending upon how long it is—35 MB is pretty typical. So, a 12-song album takes up around 420 MB on the CD, whereas an album with 20 songs usually needs to be put on two CDs because it uses more than 650 MB of space. To make a digital music file you must use a software program to *extract* the song from the CD, a process commonly referred to as *ripping*. This usually produces a *WAV* file that is about 35 MB in size and is an exact copy of the music on your CD.

Since having a bunch of songs in the WAV format can take up a lot of space on your hard drive, people usually compress the files down to something more manageable, such as a 3.5 MB MP3 file. This process is known as *encoding*. Basically, an MP3 encoding tool uses a special algorithm to determine the optimal way to make the file smaller without losing too much of the original qualities of the music. It does this by removing sounds that are out of the range of human hearing, dropping sounds that are masked by louder sounds, and so on. The result is a digital music file that is of lesser quality than the original, but it's much, much smaller and is still good enough for most people's musical tastes. The loss of quality during encoding is why MP3s are known as a *lossy* file format.

There are several problems with MP3 files. First of all, their compression algorithms are no longer the best available—other lossy file formats can produce better quality audio at even smaller file sizes. Also, the MP3 compression algorithm must be licensed if you want to create a legal encoding program that uses the MP3 format. To remedy these problems, the open source community has created its own audio format known as Ogg Vorbis. This format offers superior sound and compression to the MP3, and since it is open source there are no licensing issues surrounding its compression algorithm. You can test the sound difference yourself by visiting *http://www.xiph.org/ogg/vorbis/listen.html.*

The application for listening to music CDs in *Move* is called KsCD. To use it, all you have to do is pop a music CD into the drive, and the KsCD application will load automatically and begin playing your music (Figure 4-1). KsCD is configured to look up the album on the Internet and pull down a list of the album's songs. You have the typical buttons to play, fast forward, rewind, change tracks, pause, and stop. To exit the application, select Extras → Quit.

FIGURE 4-1. The CD player application, KsCD

If the KsCD program did not automatically start when you inserted a CD, it is probably because *Move* is watching the wrong CD drive. When your computer has two CD drives, one is considered the primary and the other the secondary; *Move* is configured to play CDs from the primary drive. To solve this problem, you can either reboot with *Move* in the other drive, or tell the KsCD program which drive to read from. To do this, open KsCD manually by clicking K Menu → Enjoy music and video → Listen to audio CDs. Inside of KsCD, click Extras → Configure KsCD. At the bottom of the configuration window that appears, look for the field labeled CD-ROM Device containing the entry /dev/cdrom. Add a 1 to the end of this entry (/dev/cdrom1) to specify your second CD drive, click OK, and you should now be able to play CDs from that drive.

MP3s and other digital music files are played with the Totem multimedia program (Figure 4-2). Simply double-click an MP3's icon in Konqueror, and Totem will load and begin playing your music. Of course, at the moment this is easier said than done–the *Move* CD doesn't actually have any MP3 files on it. There are a few solutions to this problem. If you have a USB key, you can put a few of your MP3 files on it from within Windows, and then access those files by opening your Home directory in Konqueror. Or, if you have music files stored on your Windows hard drive, you can access them using the method described at the end of Chapter 3.

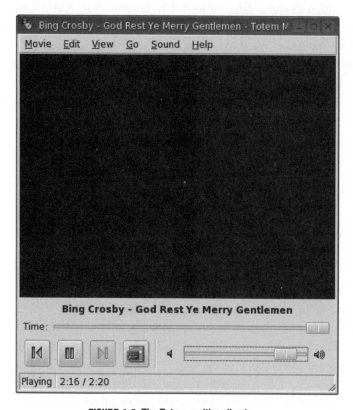

FIGURE 4-2. The Totem multimedia player

Totem's buttons are similar to those of a CD player and are used to control your digital music files. When you change tracks in Totem, you are actually moving through your *playlist*, which is simply a list of songs you select from your collection. This can be a random selection of songs you choose on the spur of the moment, or you can create a playlist and save it so you can use it again and again. You can create playlists to play back albums you have ripped and encoded from CD (many ripping programs do this automatically), or playlists for all the music you like to listen to on a rainy day, or at night, or while driving in Kansas. You bring up the playlist window in Totem by clicking the fourth button in the lower left of Totem's main window. From here you can add and remove music files from your playlist, move files within the playlist, or save the playlist so you can use it later.

Totem is not the only music playback application for Linux; there are several other popular ones as well. My favorites are XMMS and amaroK. XMMS, shown in Figure 4-3, looks and acts a lot like the popular Windows program WinAMP. You can use XMMS to listen to CDs and to play back Ogg files, as well as MP3, WMA, FLAC, and several other audio formats. XMMS has been around for years and is a very mature program; it comes with a playlist manager and a graphic equalizer, and there are dozens of plug-ins available that enhance its features in several ways. Visit *http://www.xmms.org* for more details.

FIGURE 4-3. The XMMS multimedia player

My new favorite music program is amaroK (Figure 4-4). This program provides a lot of features in a cool-looking interface. I like that it can look up my album on the Internet and pull down images of the album cover, that it remembers which songs I've listened to and keeps statistics on my listening habits, and that it can automatically create playlists of the songs I never listen to as well as the songs I listen to most. (It's quite interesting to listen to a collection of songs you haven't heard in a while.) The newest version of amaroK even looks up song lyrics for you! Check out *http://amarok.kde.org* for more information on this neat program.

Watching Video Files

Five years ago most computers were not fast enough to watch a DVD without using special video chips. Today, the typical home computer has enough processing power to run several videos at once while ripping songs off a CD and searching for extraterrestrial life when it gets bored (*http://setiathome.ssl.berkeley.edu*). You can even turn your computer into a TiVo-like device using software included with video capture cards or high-end graphics cards.

FIGURE 4-4. A typical view in amaroK

But even though your *hardware* is powerful enough for almost any video chore, the *software* to actually watch videos isn't always as capable as you'd like. The reasons for this are many and varied, but I'll point out one reason that applies to Linux particularly.

As discussed in the previous section, multimedia files are *encoded* using special software that allows you to create small files while still maintaining most of the quality of the original media. To play back the encoded video, you use a special program called a *decoder*. There are dozens of video encoders and decoders, but most of them are not open source and cannot be distributed without paying a license fee. As a result, Linux is limited in its ability to play back some formats that can be easily played on Windows or a Macintosh, for example, the latest versions of Windows Media Videos (*.wmv* files) and some types of QuickTime videos (*.mov* files).

In addition to playing MP3 and Ogg music files, Totem plays back videos. Think of it as the Linux equivalent of the Windows Media Player, your one-stop program for almost all of your multimedia needs. To play a video in *Move*, just double-click its file icon. If Totem can handle it, it will open the file automatically and begin playing. If you can't see the video, try resizing the window vertically, as sometimes the video window portion of the player is hidden.

The Totem window itself looks exactly the same as it does when playing music, so there are no surprises here. Press F to toggle between full screen and windowed video. Another neat thing you can do is to take a screenshot of your video by going to Edit → Take Screenshot. Unfortunately, this works only while the movie is playing, not paused, so you have to time your selection just right.

The Totem application is actually just a pretty GUI frontend for the open source video playing program xine—the real work of playing the video files is being done by xine and the codecs (video decoders) that it loads. There are several frontends for xine; Figure 4-5 shows another popular one.

FIGURE 4-5. Another xine frontend

Ripping and Encoding Music Files

MP3 files on the Internet come from the hard drive of some person who ripped the music from CD, encoded it in MP3 format, and uploaded it to the Web using any one of a dozen methods for sharing files. It is because of this file sharing on the Internet that MP3 has become synonymous with digital music files.

Besides being able to play back MP3 files, Linux can also be used to create them. Several open source encoders are capable of creating MP3 files; one of them, LAME, is well known even in the Windows world. Many Linux users prefer to use Ogg Vorbis files instead of MP3, because OGG is an open format that produces smaller and better quality audio files than MP3.

There are dozens of tools on Linux that can be used to encode audio files; the one on *Move* is called KAudioCreator. To launch it, click K Menu → Enjoy music and video → Rip audio CDs. You'll probably be greeted with one or two warning windows. The first one complains that "No encoder has been selected"; the second one tells you that "No tracks are selected to rip." Just click OK to close both these boxes.

To rip a CD, launch the KAudioCreator program and insert a CD into the drive. In a few seconds a list of your songs, complete with track titles, should appear in the main program window, as shown in Figure 4-6. *Move* has configured the KAudioCreator program to connect to the CDDB database on the Internet to look up the album information. If the main window displays a list of generic tracks, either your Internet connection isn't working, or the program couldn't find your album information on CDDB.

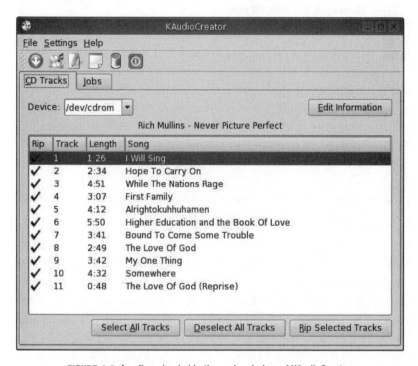

FIGURE 4-6. An album loaded in the main window of KAudioCreator

If there is a successful lookup in CDDB, *Move* has also configured KAudioCreator to automatically start ripping your CD. This is a very bad default behavior for a live CD setup, because each song you rip will take up space on your USB key, and in a matter of minutes the key could be completely full. You should stop the jobs immediately by clicking on the Jobs tab and clicking Remove All Jobs. Not only that, but you'll have to confirm you want to remove each job.

Even if I'm not running a live CD, I still find automatic rips annoying, as I may want to rip only a few songs or change my encoder before ripping. To turn off automatic ripping, go to Settings → Configure KAudioCreator → CD and uncheck the box next to "Automatically rip all songs upon a successful CDDB retrieval." If you choose, you can also disable automatic lookups in CDDB.

Space limitations

All ripped and encoded songs take up space. If you have a USB key, they are written to the key; otherwise, they are put in your computer's RAM. If you rip and encode too many songs, you'll quickly use up all the space on the USB key or in your RAM. To avoid running out of memory, don't rip more than two or three songs at a time (depending upon how large your USB key is), and delete your files before you rip more. (Of course, these limitations don't exist when you have Linux installed on your hard drive.)

By default, KAudioCreator will encode your music files in the Ogg Vorbis format. Since many portable music players cannot decode Ogg files, MP3 may be a better choice for you. To change KAudioCreator's default encoder, go to Settings → Configure KAudioCreator → Encoder, click an encoder from the list at the top, and click Apply. The LAME encoder should be used to encode MP3 files. Choosing "Leave as a wav file" tells KAudioCreator to just rip the CDs, not actually encode them. You can use these WAV files, which have the same quality as the source CD, in a CD burning program to create your own mix CDs. FLAC is a lossless encoder that produces larger files than Ogg or MP3 but smaller than WAV, and with perfect CD quality.

There are some other items of interest on this configuration screen. You can use the Encoded File Location field to enter a command that will determine the naming convention for your file and how it will be stored on your hard drive; for example, it can be stored in a folder named for the album, which is inside another folder named for the artist. The syntax for this command is not particularly complicated, but you may want to click the Wizard button to help you create it. The default should be fine for most people. You also have the option to create an album playlist when you rip the CD. This is particularly useful if you like to put all the music files for one artist in a single directory, as it allows you to play the album by selecting a single playlist file, instead of selecting the songs on an album individually.

It's now time to choose which files to rip and encode. Back in the main window, either click the Select All Tracks button, or click each track you want to rip. A check appears in the Rip column for each song you select. Once you've made your selections, click the Rip Selected Tracks button. The songs you selected are immediately queued up, and the program begins the ripping process. A window pops up to tell you that the jobs have started. Click on the Jobs tab to see the items you are ripping.

That's how the program would work if you were running Linux from the hard drive; now I'll tell you how you can use it within the limitations of the *Move* CD. As mentioned back in "Playing Music Files," if your computer has two CD drives, one is considered the primary one and the other the secondary one. KAudioCreator is configured to look for music tracks on the primary drive; if that's where your music CD is, then you're all set. If not, you can reboot, this time with Move in the other CD drive, or you can go through the same process you did with KsCD to make it see the other drive. Open KAudioCreator without a CD in the drive, and on the main screen click on the entry /dev/cdrom in the Device drop-down list. Add a 1 to the end of the entry to make the program see the second CD drive, then close the program and restart it. KAudioCreator should now be able to detect a CD in this drive, and you can rip some music.

Burning CDs

The *Move* CD comes with the K3b CD burning application, regarded by many Linux users as the best CD burning application available on Linux. Some people find it to be even easier to use and more powerful than the popular Nero burning software on Windows. I've used this program many times to create master copies of the CDs that go into some of

O'Reilly's books. To launch K3b, go to K Menu → Administer your system → Burn CDs-DVDs. When it starts up, K3b should tell you which CD burners it has found. Just click OK to clear this window.

The main K3b program window, shown in Figure 4-7, is divided into three panes. The top left pane presents a typical hierarchal view of your filesystem, and the pane in the top right shows you the files and directories in the selected folder. The bottom half of the screen changes depending upon the actions you are performing. When the program first starts up, this area displays several large buttons that let you start a new project. In this section I'll show you how to burn a data CD and how to make a copy of a CD. As I mentioned previously, you may not be able to follow along if you have only a single CD drive, so I'll just describe how the program would behave if it were installed on your hard drive.

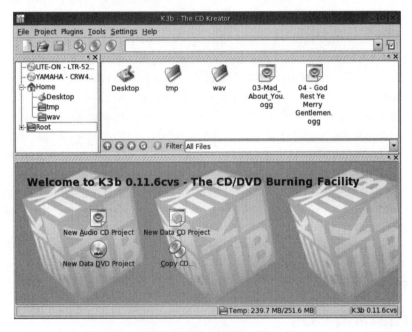

FIGURE 4-7. The main K3b window

Creating a Data CD

One of the most common (and crucial) uses for a CD burning tool is to back up your important files. K3b makes it easy to create archives of your data on a CD or DVD.

To burn a data CD, click the icon called "New Data CD Project" in the main K3b window. Next, select the files you want to add to your CD by dragging a file or folder from either of the top panes and dropping it onto either of the bottom panes. As you add each selection, a bar along the bottom of the screen will tell you how much space your files are taking up and how much space is still available on the CD. This makes it easy to fit the maximum amount of data on each CD.

When you're done selecting files, click on the big Burn button in the lower right corner. This brings up a new window that presents a lot of options to control your CD burning session (Figure 4-8). The default selections are usually fine, so I'll just tell you about a few of your choices.

Only Create Image
Checking this option allows you to create an image file instead of burning a CD. An image file, usually called an ISO, can later be used to burn a CD with just a few clicks, and is a perfect way to share the contents of a CD over the Internet. For example, the Linux distributions you download for free from the Internet come as ISO images.

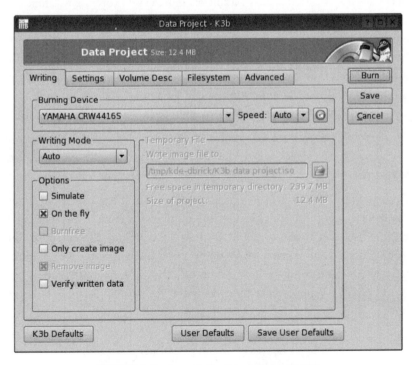

FIGURE 4-8. The burn window for creating a data CD

Multisession

The options for multisession on the Settings tab allow you to burn data to a CD now and add more data to it later. If you check off the "Start multisession" option, you'll be able to add more data later by checking "Continue multisession." When you are ready to finish the disk, check off "Finish multisession" for your final burn session. If you don't check off the "Start multisession" option, the CD will be "fixed" when it's finished burning, and you can't add more data.

Volume Desc

This tab controls the metadata you want on the CD you burn. In most cases I leave this alone, but if you are burning a master CD for work that will be copied and distributed, you'll want to enter information appropriate to your business and the project.

And that's pretty much all there is to burning a data CD. Just click the Burn button and watch K3b's progress.

Copying a CD

Another common task for a CD burner is to copy a CD, for example, to make copies of a Linux distribution. In most cases, copying a Linux distribution and giving it to a friend is not only legal, but actually encouraged. You can freely make copies of the *Move* CD in the back of this book and give it to anyone who is interested in trying out Linux. I also like to make copies of all of my music CDs. I keep the originals safe in the house, and use the copies in the car. That way, if the CDs in the car are ever lost, stolen, or damaged, I've still got the originals in my house.

To start a CD copy session, either click the Copy CD icon at the bottom of the screen or select the option from the Tools → CD menu. Either way, a window pops up that presents you with a few choices (Figure 4-9).

At the top you can select the device to copy from (the reader device) and the device to copy to (the burner device). If your machine has two burning devices you might accidentally make the wrong choices here, but don't worry—your burner won't try to copy a blank CD onto a music CD. At the bottom of the screen you can choose how many copies you want to make. When you're ready to make your copy, just click the Start button.

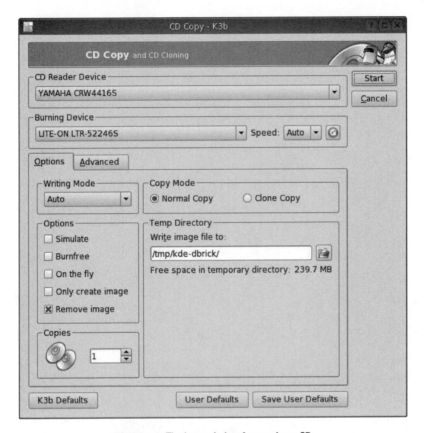

FIGURE 4-9. The burn window for copying a CD

It's even possible to make a copy of a CD if you have only one CD drive, although obviously that drive needs to be a burner. K3b can create a temporary image of the source CD first, then allow you to exchange it with a blank CD, and then continue the burn using the image as the source. Don't try this with *Move*, however; the temporary image will probably be larger than the space on your USB key.

As you can see, K3b is a useful and versatile program. You can use it to create your own custom mix CDs, burn a data DVD, or even create your own video DVDs and CDs that can be played in a DVD player or on your computer.

5 + !

PLAY GAMES

Even with all it has going for it, Linux is a tough sell to some people because of one thing: games. Most kids and teenagers—and many adults, too—are into playing games on their computers. A lot of kids these days take their Playstation with them everywhere and are glued to their Gameboy Advance, and adults from the ages of 20 to 35 often aren't much different. In recent years, these "gamers," as they're called in the computer world, have helped propel the computer gaming industry to sales greater than those of the entire music industry. It was their dollars that took the opening-day sales of Halo 2 for the Xbox to over $125 million, making it the single biggest one-day moneymaker in entertainment history—even bigger than hit movies such as *Spiderman*.

This chapter introduces you to the world of gaming on Linux. It's a fairly mixed bag, with some excellent options in the classic game space, but a dearth of high-end commercial games. That doesn't mean that playing games on Linux can't be entertaining, but it does mean that you won't be able to play all the games you want.

Many Linux users are in the prime gaming demographic—males between the ages of 14 and 35. Linux users who aren't satisfied with their Linux game options sometimes maintain a second computer just to play games, concentrate their game playing on game consoles such as Playstation and Xbox, or set their system to dual-boot Windows and Linux—when they want to play games, they boot into Windows, but when they want to get real work done, they use Linux. Any of these may be an acceptable option for you.

The State of Gaming on Linux

The computer gaming market is a difficult, brutal business, with similarities to the moviemaking business but with none of the glamour. Hundreds of games compete to be the blockbuster title of the season or the year, but this status is achieved by only a few. The remaining games quickly wind up in the discount bins and are written up as a loss on the corporate balance sheet. In this winner-take-all market, it is difficult for a game company to justify the expense, in time and resources, to write a game exclusively for Linux, or to port a Windows game to Linux. Game publishers typically prefer to have their programmers and artists work on the next big hit for Windows, which represents over 95 percent of the computer gaming market, than to port a game to Linux, which represents only a fraction of the remaining 5 percent.

But although Linux users may never have native versions of such hit games as Command & Conquer, Everquest, the Sims, or anything from Microsoft's game division, it doesn't mean that Linux gaming is nonexistent. In fact, in the true spirit of free software, it is very much alive. Not all of the fun to be had in gaming is found in the $50 boxes sold at Best Buy and Electronics Boutique—quite the contrary, in fact. You can find thousands of Java- and Flash-based games on the Internet, and since Linux supports both Java and Flash, it can usually run these games without any problems. These games might not be the next Diablo, but they do provide countless hours of entertainment. This is probably your best resource if you are looking for games for kids.

The open source community has also created a number of games on its own. Although these games lack the professional artwork, sound effects, and musical scores of commercial games, they still offer compelling gaming fun. Also, some commercial game companies have released their game engines as open source, which means that determined programmers can create their own games similar to the commercial games based upon those same engines. Of course, these game engines are open-sourced only after they are no longer commercially useful, so games based upon them are a few years behind current technology.

Through the use of emulators, it is possible to play classic arcade, console, and PC games on Linux. There is even a program that lets you run many of the most recent Windows games directly on Linux. You may run into some minor bugs playing games this way, but usually nothing that ruins your game enjoyment.

Just as with a Windows system, you'll need a good graphics card to play games on Linux. Linux supports ATI and NVIDIA graphics cards with drivers created by the manufacturers themselves. NVIDIA support is usually considered better than that of ATI, but the performance of both manufacturers' cards under Linux is top-notch, and usually on par with the hardware's performance under Windows. There is no technical reason why great games can't run on Linux.

ATI video cards

Unfortunately, the *Move* CD does not come with 3D drivers that allow ATI cards to work in accelerated mode. This means that if you have an ATI card in your computer, you won't be able to enjoy these games from the *Move* CD. However, you can play these games in all their accelerated glory if you decide to install Linux on your hard drive.

Trying Out the Games on the Move CD

Your *Move* CD comes with a small sampling of open source games, but I must admit that I don't think the selections chosen by Mandrakesoft are the best representatives of Linux's gaming ability. (For instance, where's Solitaire?) But let's at least take a look at the games on your *Move* CD. Afterward, I'll discuss some of the other gaming options in Linux.

You'll find K Menu options for games in two places on your *Move* CD, but each set of menus contains the same games (listed below). For the quickest way to launch these games, go to K Menu → Play games.

Frozen Bubble

This Bust-a-Move clone is as addictive as Tetris. The object of the game is to connect three or more colored balls together to make them fall. When you eliminate all the hanging balls, you advance a level. Use your left and right arrow keys to aim the ball launcher, and the up arrow key to launch the ball. Sometimes the better shot is to bounce the ball off a wall. Press Esc to quit the current game, and Esc again to close the program. If you're color-blind, you can launch the game from a Run window (Alt-F2) with the command **frozen-bubble -cb**. Now each of the balls will have a symbol inside it, making it easier for you to match them up.

ArmageTron

This is a 3D version of the classic Tron game. It can be configured for up to four-person play, and has a network setup so you can compete against others, either on your local network or over the Internet. Use the Z and X keys to turn left and right, respectively, and the V key to brake. You can accept the default settings and get right into playing the game, but if you want to set up network or team play, you need to read through the menus and make the appropriate selections. Just use the arrow keys to navigate the menus and the Enter key to accept options. Press Esc, as usual, to get out of the game.

Cannon Smash

The name "Cannon Smash" is a bit deceiving; the game is actually a 3D ping-pong game. It's fairly complex for such a simple idea, because it tries to incorporate real physics into the movement of the ball. Choose "How to play" to learn how to control your player and the ball, and then progress through the Training and Practice menu choices to improve your skills. You can compete with others on your own network or across the Internet.

Chromium

This is a top-scroller shoot-em-up game. As in all such games, the basic objective is to shoot anything that moves or that is shooting at you. Most importantly, don't let any enemy ships get to the bottom of the screen, or you'll lose a life. Some objects give your ship special abilities. Just fly over them to pick up the abilities, or, if you have no use for these power-ups, let them scroll to the bottom of the screen for extra points or extra lives. Use the mouse to control your ship's movements, and the left mouse button to fire. The P key pauses the game, and Esc closes it.

LBreakout2

This is a feature-enhanced clone of the classic Breakout game. This one features explosive and magnetic balls, as well as explosive, regenerative, and indestructible bricks (see Figure 5-1). The objective of the game is to destroy all the bricks on the screen by hitting them with a ball. You control the movement of the ball by deflecting it off a paddle at the bottom. Control the paddle movement with the left and right arrow keys. Use the spacebar to fire the ball at the start of each round.

Tux Racer

This game lets you take on the role of Tux the Linux penguin as he races down a mountainside slalom course, picking up herring along the way. It's a slippery slope, and you have to go as fast as you can while being careful not to miss a single fish. If you cross the finish line before your time limit is up, you advance a level. Use the arrow keys to control Tux's movements. The up arrow increases your speed and the down arrow puts on the brakes. This game is pretty simple, but fun.

Crack Attack

This game looks a bit like a Tetris clone, but it's actually much more difficult. The object of the game is to line up three or more blocks of the same color, either vertically or horizontally, by moving the selection bracket around with the arrow keys and using the spacebar to switch the position of the bracketed blocks. All the while, new blocks are added from the bottom, and occasionally broad red bars are dropped from the top. To make it more difficult, the selection bracket only switches blocks horizontally. The red bars dropping from the top are "junk" bars that you can't eliminate until you change them to normal colored blocks, which you do by removing any blocks that are touching a red bar. In the two-player version of this game, the red bars are dropped when your opponent eliminates four or more blocks at the same time. Press Esc to close out of the game.

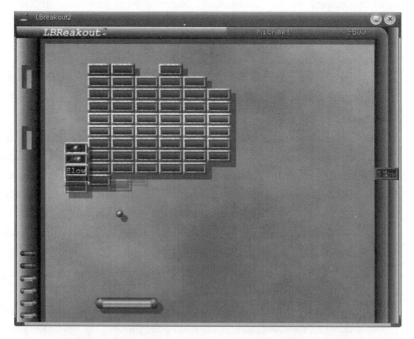

FIGURE 5-1. LBreakout2 is an enhanced version of the classic Breakout

Cannon Smash, Chromium, and Tux Racer all require a video card with hardware 3D acceleration. This functionality should be automatically enabled for any recent NVIDIA card.

Getting Free Games on the Web

The games on the *Move* CD barely scratch the surface of the free games available on Linux. The free software community has created a number of great games that can provide many hours of entertainment. However, there's no getting around the fact that they do not approach the almost lifelike look of today's top commercial games.

One of the best places to get free Linux games is *http://freshmeat.net*, an online database of free open source software. And it is not limited to just games; in fact, it's an invaluable resource any time you are looking for an open source program to fulfill a specific need. From the Freshmeat homepage, click the Browse link to see a selection of categories, and then click Games/Entertainment to see the games available for download. Many of these games run on Windows as well, so you can try them out before you switch to Linux.

The diversity of games available is incredible. There are flight simulators, strategy games, world-class chess programs, and even a remake of Dance Dance Revolution called pydance (shown in Figure 5-2), which is available at *http://icculus.org/pyddr*.

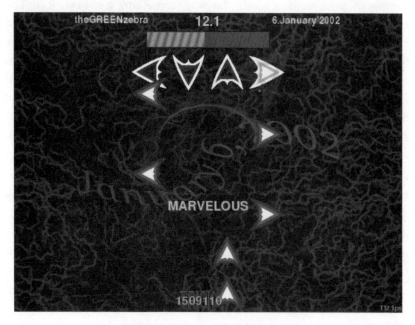

FIGURE 5-2. A dance session in pydance

Trying Out Game Emulators for Classic Games

The 1980s to early 1990s were the heyday of the arcade game. Classics such as Pac-Man and Asteroids gave way to visually stunning games like Dragon's Lair, which were in turn eclipsed by one-on-one combat games like Mortal Kombat and Street Fighter. Arcade games flourished at a time when personal home computers and consoles such as Atari and Nintendo didn't have enough processing or graphic power to deliver fast-paced, visually appealing games.

This situation began to change by the mid-1990s. Consoles such as Nintendo 64 and Playstation were capable of delivering a gaming experience similar to or even better than that of an arcade game. And with the release of Intel's Pentium processor, the PC also became a more capable gaming platform. These days, the classic video arcade is all but gone, and the forefront of gaming technology is on advanced consoles such as the Playstation 2, Xbox, and 64-bit processor PCs with 256 MB of video RAM.

Computer advances have made games such as Doom 3, Halo, and Final Fantasy X possible, but along the way, something has been lost. The new-generation games certainly offer breathtaking graphics and voiceovers from somewhat famous actors, but you often have to wade through 100-page instruction manuals and learn complex key combinations to perform actions. Most new games lack the easy playability of great arcade games of the past such as Donkey Kong, Pac-Man, and Super Mario Brothers, or of classic old PC games such as Tetris or King's Quest. The fact that you can learn how to play these games in just a few seconds is just one reason why old games continue to be fun and popular despite their primitive graphics.

In the fashion world, fashions tend to repeat themselves. What once was old is new again. The same is true in the automotive industry—just look at the Dodge Prowler or the new Ford Mustang and tell me they're not retro. And now the gaming world is starting to see this trend as classic, or retro, games come back into vogue. Not only has the gaming world created new games in the classic style to play on the Web or on cell phones, it is also providing game *emulators* that allow you to play classic games using the games' original code. An emulator is, technically, a re-creation of a hardware device in software. In this case, emulators are re-creations of original arcade machines and game consoles. That means that when you play Pac-Man in a game emulator, you are playing the exact same Pac-Man that was originally available only at the arcade, right down to the software bugs.

XMAME (*http://x.mame.net*) is the program that makes classic arcade emulation possible. This game emulator runs only on X-capable graphic systems such as Linux and UNIX, but it is a port of the MAME emulator written for Windows. XMAME and MAME have identical features, so you don't gain any advantage by using the emulator on a particular platform. Visit the self-proclaimed largest MAME resource on the Web, *http://www.mameworld.net*, or the XMAME homepage to learn more about installing and configuring XMAME. Though the *Move* CD does not include XMAME, you can install it easily once you've put a Linux distribution on your hard drive.

Figure 5-3 shows one of my favorite classic arcade games, Rampage, running in XMAME. There are also emulators for console systems such as the original Atari, Nintendo, Super Nintendo, and Playstation, as well as countless others.

Running Commercial Linux Games

Despite everything I've said previously, there *are* commercial games that run on Linux. In fact, some recent blockbusters, like Neverwinter Nights, Unreal Tournament 2004, and Doom3, have Linux versions. A few small game publishers also develop Linux games—check out Black-HoleSun Software's very fun and highly addictive Bunnies game (*http://www.blackholesun.com*) or the games from Garage Games (*http://www.garagegames.com*). And there are efforts underway to port a few popular Windows games to Linux.

Hardly anything elicits as much excitement in the Linux world as the announcement that an important new game is to have a native Linux version. Linux users anxiously awaited the release of the Linux version of the Dungeons & Dragons game Neverwinter Nights (Figure 5-4). It was eventually released a few months after the Windows version. You won't find a boxed Linux set in the stores, though. Instead, you have to purchase the Windows version and download some additional files from the game publisher's web site to get it to play under Linux. I've spent many happy hours playing this game on my Linux gaming machine.

FIGURE 5-3. Rampage running inside of XMAME

Doom3, one of the most anticipated games ever, offers a Linux version as well. As with Neverwinter Nights, you must purchase the Windows boxed set and download some Linux files in order to play the game. If you want to try it before you buy it, you can get a demo of the Linux version at *http://www.doom3.com.* The game's publisher, iD, provides other Linux games as well, such as Return to Castle Wolfenstein.

Several years ago, a company named Loki Software attempted to make a business out of porting popular Windows games to run natively under Linux. Unfortunately, the company folded, but if you keep an eye out in bargain software bins or eBay, you can sometimes find copies of the games they developed. I own several, and they're all excellent. A list of their games can be found at *http://www.lokigames.com.* You might also check out Linux Central (*http://www.linuxcentral.com*) and Tux Games (*http://www.tuxgames.com*), two resellers that may still have stock of a few Loki games.

FIGURE 5-4. A scene from Neverwinter Nights: Hordes of the Underdark

In place of Loki, another company has now begun porting games to Linux. They're called Linux Game Publishing, and their approach is different from Loki's. Rather than pay high license fees to port the most popular Windows games, they port highly addictive but less well known games. You can purchase these games directly from their web site at *http://www.linuxgamepublishing.com*.

And believe it or not, the U.S. Army has released a free game called America's Army (*http://www.americasarmy.com*) that plays under Linux and is also available for Windows and Mac OS X. The Army hopes that the game will encourage gamers (remember, most gamers are males aged 14 to 35) to enlist in the Army. I don't know if America's Army has achieved that objective, but it has garnered a lot of interest from gamers.

As you can see, the commercial Linux gaming scene is not exactly lively, but it certainly isn't dead. One thing to hang hope on is that most multiplayer games that allow for Internet play require servers to host the games. Often times users can set up their own game servers, and in almost all these cases, there is a Linux version of the game server written by the game company. Perhaps this means the game companies will slowly gain expertise in Linux and eventually start releasing native Linux versions of the game client. Hopefully, as gamers and game companies alike see the merits of Linux, there will be increased demand for true, native Linux games.

Playing Windows Games on Linux

Linux suffers from the classic chicken-and-egg problem. Many people would love to use Linux but won't until it plays all the games they enjoy, and game companies won't write games for Linux until there are a lot of Linux users to buy them. The result is that there aren't many commercial games available on Linux, and many people who would otherwise be interested in using Linux don't do it, because playing games is too important to them.

A company called Transgaming seeks to take advantage of this situation by selling a program that allows Linux users to run their favorite Windows games on top of Linux. This program, called Cedega, does not do the job perfectly, but it may be good enough for people who really want to use Linux and who aren't hardcore gamers. See Figure 5-5 for an example of a Windows game running under Cedega.

FIGURE 5-5. Diablo II running under Cedega

In order to get Cedega, you need to sign up for a subscription to the software. The cost is $5 per month, with a minimum subscription of three months. For your money, you get the current version of Cedega, software updates for the length of your subscription, support from Transgaming, access to forums where other users may be able to help you with your problems, and the ability to cast a vote on which games Cedega should try to support next.

Transgaming maintains a list of the games it supports at *http://www. transgaming.com/searchgame.php*. Games with a rating of 4 or higher are very playable; games rated lower are less so, depending on your tolerance for bugs or display glitches.

You can find several reviews of Cedega on the Internet; I suggest you read them before making a commitment to a subscription (although $15 for three months isn't much, considering the price of a game). What's interesting about these reviews is that the tester often found it necessary to make some manual tweaks to a configuration file in order to get the game to play properly. This may make you nervous, but you could regard it is an interesting challenge, and a chance to learn more about Linux.

Tough installs are good for you!

Old-time gamers like myself often had to manually tweak DOS and Windows configuration files in order to free up enough memory to play games. Doing this is what first made me comfortable with computers, and eventually led to my job as a system administrator.

If you're the type to look on the bright side, you can also regard the lag between the time a new game releases and when it is playable under Cedega as a good thing. Windows games are often discounted months after their release. If you stay well behind the adoption curve, you may be able to purchase twice as many commercial games for the same money. Of course, this also means you have to turn a deaf ear as your gaming friends boast about their latest gaming exploits.

Accessing Linux Online Gaming Resources

Information about gaming on Linux is fairly scattered. Some information can be found at the web sites that each game is hosted on, or in mailing lists or online forums found at those sites. Freshmeat (*http://freshmeat.net*) and SourceForge (*http://sourceforge.net*) are good places to start a search for Linux software, games or otherwise.

General Linux gaming information can be found at:

> *http://happypenguin.org*
> *http://icculus.org*
> *http://www.linuxgames.com*

There are also several places to buy native Linux games. Perhaps the most popular is *http://tuxgames.com.*

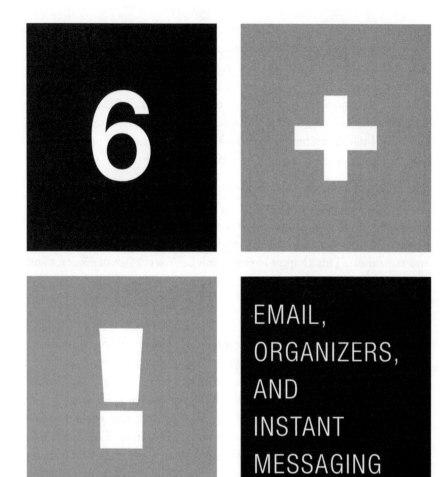

6

+

!

EMAIL,
ORGANIZERS,
AND
INSTANT
MESSAGING

There are dozens of email, chat, and contact programs on Linux. Some of these programs mimic the look and feel of their Windows counterparts so closely that you almost can't tell the difference. *Move* comes with Kontact, a personal information manager that provides many of the same functions as Microsoft Outlook, including email, a contact manager, to-do lists, calendar and appointment management, and even little sticky notes. And because this is Linux, running Kontact does not leave your machine vulnerable to email viruses.

Move also provides an instant messenger client called Kopete, which allows you to connect to practically any instant message network in existence. With this program, you can connect to the AOL, MSN, Yahoo, Jabber, and even IRC networks and chat with friends, family, and coworkers. This chapter explains the basic workings of Kontact and Kopete, along with a few advanced features.

Making Kontact

Kontact is KDE's answer to the personal information manager Microsoft Outlook. Like Outlook, Kontact allows you to manage your email, contacts, calendars, and to-do lists in a single program (Figure 6-1). Kontact actually comprises several individual KDE components; for instance, its email capabilities come from KMail, the organizer and to-do component from KOrganizer, the contact management from KAddressbook, and the newsgroup reader from KNode. All of these programs can be run individually, but the KDE programmers thought it would also be nice to be able to run them through a single, easy-to-use interface. And thus, Kontact was born.

To launch Kontact, just click on its icon in the kicker panel. The icon looks like a calendar, with a globe and pencil in front. For some odd reason, the tooltip that appears when you hover your mouse over the icon reads Popup Notes; just ignore this inconsistency. You can also start up Kontact by going to K Menu → Surf the Internet → Read and send e-mail.

The first time Kontact launches, it asks you to fill out some information so that it can set up your email account to retrieve your email from your ISP or corporate email server. If you want to skip this step for the moment, just click Cancel on the dialogs that appear, but you will need to set up an account at some point if you want to make use of the email component of Kontact.

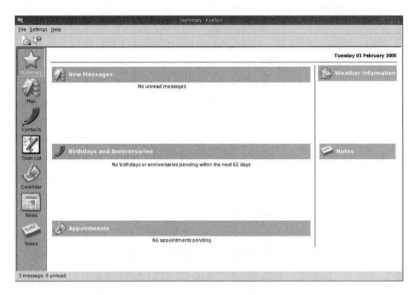

FIGURE 6-1. Kontact, KDE's personal information manager

Be prepared

Setting up Kontact to send and receive email can be a little complicated, but it's nothing you can't handle. You just need to find out the names of your email servers from your ISP or your business. You can usually get this information without calling anyone by looking for the settings in your Windows email client. In Outlook, go to Tools → Account Settings. In Outlook Express, go to Edit → Preferences.

To configure Kontact for email using the first-time startup wizard, just follow these instructions.

1. The first screen asks if you want to enable groupware functions. These functions connect Kontact to a groupware server such as Microsoft Exchange and aren't necessary unless you have such a server. This book does not cover these Kontact functions, so for now, set the screen to "Disable groupware functions" and click Next.

2. In the second screen, enter your name and email address. Entering your organization name is optional. Click Next.

3. The third screen has two tabs. First go to the Sending tab, where you will set up how mail is sent out from your machine. A "sending," or outgoing, mail server is usually referred to as an SMTP server. Click Add to add a new SMTP server connection, and in the next dialog accept the default of SMTP. In the final dialog, fill in a name for this connection and a server (host) to connect to (Figure 6-2). The Name can be anything you want, but the server name is specific to the system that handles your email. If you didn't get these values from your existing Windows setup as described in the previous note, you may need to call your ISP or talk to your IT department at work to find out the name of the server. The other fields usually do not need to be modified, so just click OK.

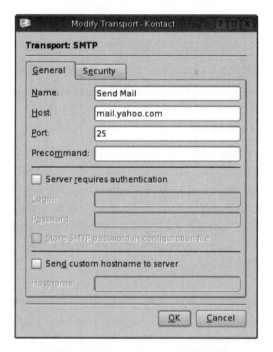

FIGURE 6-2. Setting up your SMTP email server

4. Now click the Receiving tab, where you'll set up a method to get your email onto your computer. Click Add to get started. The first dialog window defaults to POP3, which is the method most people use to receive email, so click OK to move on. In the next screen, enter a descriptive name for your setup, provide your email login name and password, and enter the name of the email server you

want to connect to in the Host field (see Figure 6-3). If you check the box next to "Store POP password in configuration file," you won't have to enter your password each time you start up Kontact. And since you are just test-driving this setup, it's a good idea to uncheck "Delete message from server after fetching." Click OK to continue.

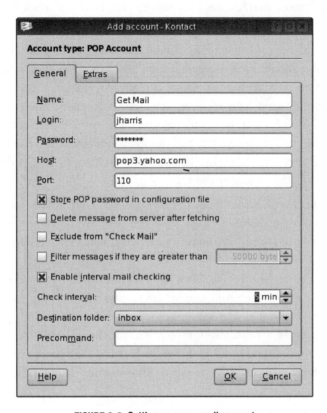

FIGURE 6-3. Setting up your email account

Don't lose your mail!

I really recommend unchecking the box next to "Delete message from server after fetching." If you don't, you may be upset when you download important emails to Kontact and then lose them forever when you reboot the machine. Also, email messages and attachments do take up space on your USB key, and if you use *Move* regularly without deleting messages you could fill up the USB key, which may cause problems while using *Move*.

5. You should now be back at the Accounts screen, so just click Next to finish up. You'll see a message telling you that the groupware functions are disabled; click Finish to finish for real.

6. Kontact now presents you with a new configuration dialog, which sets up a newsgroup reading component called KNode. However, I don't cover the KNode program in this book, so click Cancel to close the screen.

You should now see the main Kontact screen, pictured in Figure 6-1. This screen should look somewhat familiar to Outlook users. Along the left-hand side is a *shortcut bar*, which contains several large icons that link to commonly used Kontact programs. The various menus are located along the top of the screen, and right below them is the default toolbar. The menus, the toolbar icons, and the main portion of the Kontact window all change depending on the shortcut you have clicked in the shortcut bar. I call this changing the *view*.

If you launched Kontact from the kicker icon, your default view is the Summary screen (Figure 6-1). In the main window, you'll see groupings for New Messages, Birthdays and Anniversaries, Appointments, Weather Information, and Notes. These groupings display information based on the preferences and data Kontact has stored for you. For example, the New Messages grouping monitors your inbox; when you receive new email, a number appears next to the folder name to tell you how many messages are waiting for you. The Birthdays and Anniversaries grouping notifies you of all such events based on the dates you enter in the Contacts section. The Weather Information grouping tracks the weather in locales you specify.

You may want to use only some of the components in Kontact. For example, I find the Notes and the Summary programs pretty useless for the way I work, so I like to disable them. To do this, simply go to Settings → Configure Kontact, uncheck the components you don't want, and click OK. You can always add them back again by rechecking the desired items. The restored items will appear at the end of the shortcut bar until you restart Kontact; then they will go back to their original places.

Using Email

Dozens of email programs are available for Linux. This chapter focuses on KMail, which is the email component of Kontact, but Chapter 12 briefly covers two other popular email programs—Evolution, another Outlook work-alike, and Thunderbird, a good replacement for Outlook Express that runs on Windows and Mac OS X in addition to Linux.

To start KMail, click the Kontact icon on your kicker panel, and then click the Mail shortcut from inside Kontact. Alternatively, you can go to K Menu → Surf the Internet → Read and send e-mail.

KMail vs. Kontact

When I refer to KMail, I'm talking about the email component of Kontact as well as the standalone KMail email program. The programs are identical in the way they operate and in their appearance, with the exception that standalone KMail does not have the shortcut bar along the left side.

KMail uses the typical three-pane view often found in email programs (Figure 6-4). Along the left-hand side is a listing of all your email folders, including several default folders such as *inbox, outbox, sent-mail, trash, drafts,* and *Searches.* The *outbox* is where messages are stored until they are sent; once you actually send them, they appear in the *sent-mail* folder. The *drafts* folder is a place to store messages you're still in the process of writing. And the *Searches* folder is a very powerful feature of KMail that is described in the later section "Saved Searches."

The right-hand side of KMail's window is split into top and bottom panes. The top pane, which initially contains only the message "Welcome to Mandrakelinux," is called the message list. It displays all the messages in the currently selected folder. Below the message list is the preview pane. This pane shows you the contents of whatever mail message is selected in the message list. You can also double-click a message to read it in its own window, but the preview pane is so convenient that this is seldom necessary.

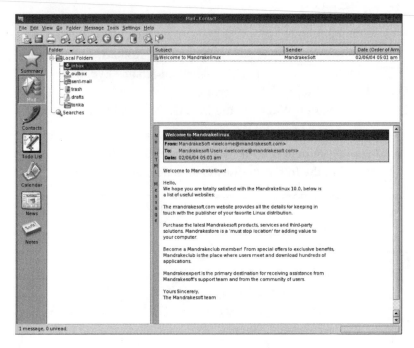

FIGURE 6-4. The KMail component of Kontact

Along the top of the KMail window just beneath the menu bar is the KMail toolbar, which contains icon shortcuts to the most commonly used functions in the program. To see what each icon does, hover your mouse over it and read its tooltip. Here you'll find all the usual email functions such as New Message, Reply, Forward, and Print. As in other KDE applications, the KMail toolbar is completely customizable—simply right-click it and choose Configure Toolbar. The standard KDE toolbar configuration window appears so you can make the desired modifications.

Extra options

You'll notice that several of the toolbar icons have little triangles on them. Click and hold your mouse on these icons to see a small menu of unique actions. This is useful to change the behavior of a Reply or Forward, for example.

Sending email with KMail isn't much different from other email programs. To start a new message, click the New Mail icon on the toolbar (it's the first icon, which looks like a piece of paper and an envelope), or you can use the keyboard shortcut Ctrl-N. Both methods open a blank email in which you can write your message (see Figure 6-5).

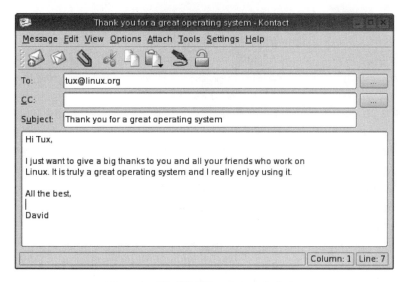

FIGURE 6-5. The KMail compose email window

To attach a file to your email message, just click the paper clip icon on the toolbar and navigate to the file you want to attach. You can attach multiple files at a time by holding down the Ctrl key as you click on each file.

When you're ready to send your message, just click the Send button (which looks like an envelope with a green arrow pointing up) or press Ctrl-Enter. If you want to save your message to work on later, you can put it in the *drafts* folder by selecting Message → Save in Drafts Folder. You can open it up again by going to the *drafts* folder and double-clicking the message.

Selective quoting

If you highlight part of the email in the preview pane before clicking Reply, the new message contains only the highlighted text. This is useful when you want to respond to a specific part of an email.

You can save time and effort by using keyboard shortcuts to move around in KMail or to perform special actions. Using the keyboard is often the fastest way to interact with a program. Table 6-1 lists many of KMail's useful keyboard shortcuts.

TABLE 6-1. Keyboard shortcuts for KMail

Keyboard shortcut	Results
Ctrl-N	Create a new email message.
R	Reply to the message highlighted in the message list.
A	Reply to all recipients and the sender of the message high-lighted in the message list.
F	Forward the message highlighted in the message list as an attachment.
Shift-F	Forward the message highlighted in the message list as inline text.
Ctrl-A	Select all the messages in the message list.
Right Arrow or N	Move down through the message list.
Left Arrow or P	Move up through the message list.
Up and Down Arrows	Move up and down through the message in the preview pane.
+	Go to the next unread message in the current folder.
−	Go to the previous unread message in the current folder.
Shift+Left Arrow and Shift+Right Arrow	Select multiple messages in the message list.
Space	Advance through the message in the preview pane. If you are already at the bottom of the message, this will take you to the next unread message in the current folder.
Ctrl +	Go to the next folder that contains an unread message.
Ctrl -	Go to the previous folder that contains an unread message.
Ctrl-Left Arrow	Move up the folder list.
Ctrl-Right Arrow	Move down the folder list.
Ctrl-Space	Open a folder you've moved to by using Ctrl-Left Arrow or Ctrl-Right Arrow.
Ctrl-J	Apply any manual filters to the current folder.

Configuring KMail

On the surface, KMail looks like a very mild-mannered email application. Almost boring, in fact. This simplicity hides a lot of features that make KMail a truly exceptional email program. You can customize KMail in some pretty powerful ways.

To set up KMail to work the way *you* want, start by selecting Settings → Configure KMail. This launches the KMail configuration window (Figure 6-6). Along the left side of this window are a group of icons. When you click on each icon, it changes the view to the right to a configuration screen. Let's check out some of these configuration settings.

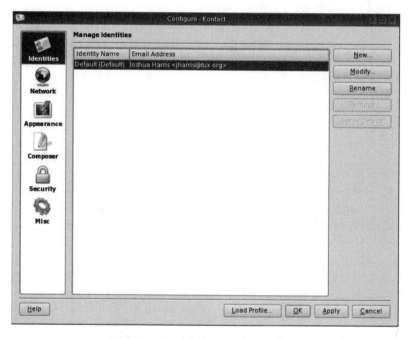

FIGURE 6-6. The KMail configuration window

Creating and Using Email Identities

At the top of the list is the icon for your Identities settings. An *identity* is just a collection of information about you and your email account. Most people don't need more than one, but if you have several email accounts or if you mix your personal and business email in one account, you may want to set up a few identities to help you manage your email. When using an identity you can specify an alternate reply address or email signature, or even a unique sent-mail folder.

When you click on the Identities icon, the configuration screen lists the identities you have set up. There should already be one identity from when you first set up Kontact, as shown in Figure 6-6. To create a new identity, click the New button to bring up a small dialog in which you can give your new identity a name. You can choose whether you want to base your new identity upon an existing profile or to create a new, blank profile. Once you make your selection, the Edit Identity window opens, and you just need to fill out the fields that interest you. Figure 6-7 shows a "work" identity for a fictitious user named Joshua Harris.

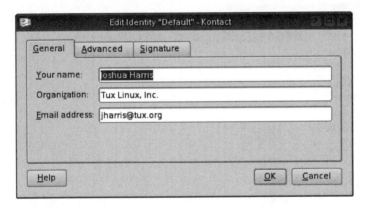

FIGURE 6-7. Creating an alternate KMail identity

You can create as many identities as you need. To set an identity as your default, highlight it in the Identities view of the KMail configuration window and click "Set as Default."

To use a specific identity, just open a new email message (Ctrl-N) or reply to an existing one. Along the top of the compose window, just below the message toolbar, you will see a new field titled Identity. This drop-down list lets you select the identity you want to use when you send your message. Once you select an identity, the From line of your email message will change to reflect the new identity. (If you want to see the From line you must select View → From in the email compose window.)

Specifying Network Email Servers

Now let's look at the Network configuration screen. Click on the Network icon on the left side, and the view to the right displays the configuration window where you can set your computer up to send and receive email. Note that there are two tabs: Sending and Receiving. In the Sending screen, you will choose the email server that will actually send out your mail. In the Receiving screen, you will set up accounts to receive email from. To configure these two parts of your account, refer back to Steps 3–5 in the earlier section "Making Kontact." You can configure multiple email accounts by creating additional sending and receiving email servers.

There's an interesting feature to check out at the bottom of the Sending window. See the "Default domain" field at the bottom of the Sending view? Whatever you enter in this field is automatically appended to the end of any email address for which you haven't provided a domain name in an outgoing message. I normally set this field to *oreilly.com* because that's where I send most of my messages, and it saves me from having to type the whole address each time I write to someone at work.

Giving KMail a Makeover

The next configuration window is Appearance. This panel controls the display of fonts, the colors used for certain types of text, and the layout of the three main windows: the folder list, message list, and preview pane.

The Fonts tab, shown in Figure 6-8, lets you customize the type of fonts and the font sizes that you want to use. To enable the use of custom-defined fonts and sizes, first check off "Use custom fonts." This unlocks the rest of the configuration panel so that you can make changes. There is a lot you can customize here. Many email programs only let you specify changes to the body text, but KMail lets you control the font and size of almost every visible item on the screen. To select the text you want to change, click the drop-down list next to "Apply to," select an option, and choose the font, font style, and font size for that element. Be sure to click Apply after you set up each element; otherwise, KMail won't remember the settings. The various text elements are pretty self-explanatory, but the one I like best is Printing Output, which lets you specify a different font and size for printing. This is convenient if you prefer to view text at one size–maybe larger than normal–but want to print it out at a different size.

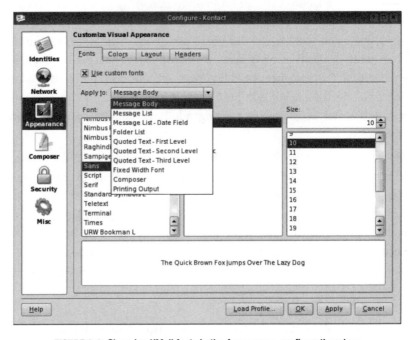

FIGURE 6-8. Changing KMail fonts in the Appearance configuration view

The Colors tab controls the color in which text is displayed. The only adjustment I usually make to the standard colors is to choose different ones for quoted text. When you have a message that has been sent back and forth several times, it can get confusing trying to figure out who said what. By choosing distinctive colors for each level of the conversation, this becomes a lot easier to determine.

The Layout tab has several settings to control the appearance of the main KMail window. You should try out different options and see which ones you like best. For example, you may prefer to have a short folder list, but a wide preview pane. To achieve that effect, you would check off "Short folder list" and click Apply.

The last tab is the Headers tab. There are some interesting settings on this tab under "Message Header Threading Options and Date Display." The Date Display options are pretty self-explanatory. The four options in the "Message Header Threading Options" control the behavior of threaded messages in all folders. The first option always keeps threads open, even when you explicitly tell them to close. The second option keeps threads open unless you tell them to close. The third option is the reverse of the second: it closes threads unless you tell them to be opened. The fourth option, which is the one I find most useful, automatically opens threads when they contain new or unread messages, making it very easy to spot messages that might otherwise be buried in a closed thread. (I'll explain more about email threads in the later section "Sorting and Threading.")

If you look to the left, you'll see three other configuration icons: Composer, Security, and Misc. These configuration screens aren't all that important, so I won't cover them in this chapter. But feel free to check them out on your own.

Now, let's exit out of the Configure screen and go back to your main KMail window.

Getting Notified When New Email Arrives

Back when I was still using Windows, one feature I liked about Outlook was that it displayed a small envelope next to the clock whenever I had a new email message. That was handy because I often had to leave my desk to help others with their computers, and when I came back, I could quickly tell if I had new messages waiting for me without having to bring up the Outlook window.

This feature is even more important on a Linux desktop when you run applications on different virtual desktops. You don't want to have to keep switching back to your email desktop just to see if you have new mail. Happily, you can configure KMail to not only display an icon in the system tray when you have a new message, but also to display a pop-up on all your desktops. This pop-up lasts for just a few seconds and is obviously useful only when you are sitting at your desk, but the icon in the system tray is useful all the time.

For some strange reason, KMail's notification settings are handled by several different windows. Click Settings → Configure Notifications to open one of these screens. Here, you can configure KMail to play a sound each time you receive new email by checking off the box next to "Play a sound" and clicking the folder icon at the end of the field. Then navigate to the location of the sound file you want to use. KMail can play any sound file that your Linux system can handle, so don't be afraid to use WAV or MP3 files. The More Options button allows you to add more options to the Actions section of the existing window. As I mentioned a moment ago, the option I've found most useful to check "Show a message in a pop-up window" and "Use a passive window that does not interrupt other work." By marking these two options, you configure KMail to display a small window on all your desktops that tells you that you have received new email. It displays for only about five seconds and appears on the screen in a non-intrusive manner.

To see some other email notification settings, go back to your main window, click on Settings → Configure KMail → Network, and go to the Receiving tab. There are two options here. One tells your system to beep when a new email arrives; the other configures KMail to put an icon in your system tray that will show the number of unread messages in your inbox. I also check "Show system tray on new mail" so there is only a mail icon there when I have new mail waiting for me, instead of it always being there even when I have zero unread messages.

+

Don't get notified

Versions of KMail that come with KDE 3.3.0 and higher allow you to turn off notifications on a per-folder basis. This means you won't get an icon in your system tray when you receive messages in folders you choose to ignore, like your mother-in-law folder.

Organizing Your Email

Many people who use email never get beyond the basics of their email program. They never learn how to organize their email to make it easier to find old messages, or to create filters that automatically perform an action when email arrives or is sent. KMail offers several features to help you organize your email effectively.

Sorting and Threading

One simple way to organize your email is to sort it in your inbox or any other folder. A sort simply lists your email in a certain, specified way. By default your messages are listed in order of arrival, with the newest messages at the bottom of the list. You can change the sort order by clicking once on a column heading; for example, if you click on the Date (Order of Arrival) column, the triangle next to the column name will change to point up, and your messages will be sorted by Date in descending order, with the newest email at the top instead of at the bottom.

If you click the Date column heading again, the triangle changes to point down. Now the email is again sorted in ascending order, with the oldest email at the top and the newest at the bottom. At first glance, this seems to be the same as the default sort order of Order of Arrival, but it isn't. Many people may send email from computers with incorrect dates or times, so the date and time they send the message is different from the date and time you actually receive it. Also, if you have multiple email accounts but you don't check them all at the same time, you may have an email that has recently arrived from one account but is in fact hours or days older than other email you have already received from a different account. So, if you sort by Date, these messages may appear between other already received messages, and if you sort by order of arrival, they appear at the bottom of the list. It's a subtle distinction, but an important one if you receive a lot of email or have many email accounts.

You can sort by the other columns, too. Sorting by Subject alphabetizes your messages based upon the text in the Subject line; sorting by Sender does the same thing based upon who sent the email. This option is particularly useful when you want to see all the email from a single person. These sorts usually have ascending and descending options as well.

There is also a Size column that tells you how big an email message is, but this column is hidden by default. To display this column, right-click on any column heading and choose Size. This can be useful when you're cleaning up your email folders and want to recover some hard-drive space. By displaying the Size column and sorting the messages in descending order, you can quickly find the messages that take up the most space and remove them.

In addition to sorting your messages, you can also group them using a process known as *threading* (Figure 6-9). Threading groups messages together based upon two criteria: a message ID that most emails have, and a common subject line. The message ID is unique to each email, but messages that are replies to an earlier message also track the message ID of the original email. Therefore, a reply message shares a message ID with the email it originated from. By grouping these messages together, it becomes much easier to follow a particular email conversation. However, some email programs and servers remove the original message ID, which means KMail can't group by that criteria. In this case the second option, to group by a common subject, attempts to catch those messages that lack the message ID. This often works, but if the message ID is not preserved *and* the subject line is changed from the original message, that message will not be threaded correctly and will just show up at the end of your message list.

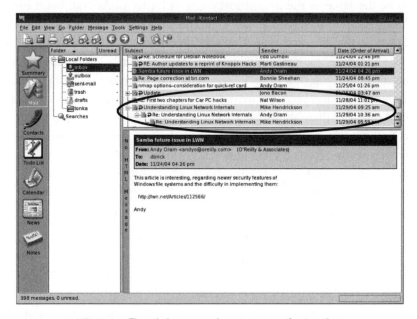

FIGURE 6-9. Threaded messages keep a conversation together

Threaded messaging is enabled on a per-folder basis. To set it up, go to the folder you want threaded and select Folder → Threaded Messages from the main menu. Your messages are now grouped, with all messages that share the same message ID or subject line together. My suggestion is to then sort the messages based upon date and order of arrival, which will sort the threaded conversations by the arrival date of the first message in the thread.

Folders

The most basic way to organize your email is to create folders for your messages. This is no different from organizing your old parking tickets by putting them into paper folders and filing them in a drawer (never to be seen again!). You can move an email message into a folder in several ways: by dragging and dropping it directly onto the folder name, by right-clicking it and selecting a folder under the Move To option, or by creating a filter that automatically moves messages for you. With the first two methods, you can use the Ctrl and Shift keys to select multiple messagesbefore you move them.

To create a new folder in KMail, right-click on Local Folders in your folder list and choose New Folder. This opens a new window that lets you specify all the settings for your folder. Give your folder a name and choose what level it should be on from the "Belongs to" drop-down list. For example, the folder can be a main folder directly under the Local Folder listing, or it can be a subfolder of another folder.

For now, create a main-level folder called Linux, and then go ahead and create a subfolder called Move under the Linux folder. If you forget to select Linux from the "Belongs to" drop-down menu when you're creating the Move folder, you can easily correct this mistake by right-clicking the Move folder, choosing Properties, and selecting a new "Belongs to" folder. In fact, this is the only way you can move a folder from one place to another.

You can also associate a folder with one of the identities you created earlier. This means that if you press Ctrl-N start a new email message from within that folder, it will automatically use the identity assigned to that folder. To set an identity for a folder, bring up the folder's properties and change the value for Sender in the Identity section.

You gotta use the keyboard

You *must* use Ctrl-N to start the new message if you want to use the identity assigned to a folder. Clicking the New Mail icon will not make use of the identity.

Searching

If you're like me, you get a lot of email and you save nearly all of it. The upside of this is that you probably still have the email message in which your wife told you what she would like for her birthday. The downside is that you might have some trouble finding it.

KMail allows you to search through your email based upon criteria you specify. To launch the search feature, just click the search icon on the main toolbar—it looks like a magnifying glass over an envelope. Alternately, just use the keyboard shortcut, S.

The search window is a little complex (Figure 6-10), and with it you can create very flexible searches. The first two options in this window allow you to specify which folders you want to search. The default is to search only the folder from which you opened the search dialog. You can also search all folders, select another folder from the drop-down list, or search a folder in the drop-down list plus all its subfolders. Note that the more folders you specify, the longer your search will take, so choose only the folders most likely to contain the message you're looking for.

For example, let's say I want to perform a search that returns all the email messages in my Inbox that were sent by my boss and that *don't* have the word Linux in the text of the message. This search, shown in Figure 6-10, makes use of the "doesn't contain" parameter to exclude messages that talk about Linux.

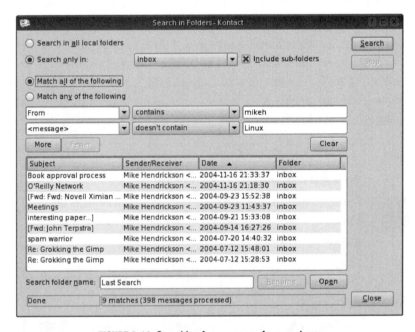

FIGURE 6-10. Searching for messages from my boss

Figure 6-11 shows another search in which I am looking for any messages from the author of the book *Knoppix Hacks* or from anybody I've talked to about the book. This search searches all folders and uses the "Match any of the following" option, which means a result will be returned if any of the criteria is met. This means that this search will return all emails with the words "Knoppix Hacks" in the message body, but will also return emails that are from the book's author but that *don't* include those words. This is useful because not all emails from the author will include the book's title, but nearly all conversations with the author are about the book. If you need to specify even more criteria for your search, click the More button to get another set of fields.

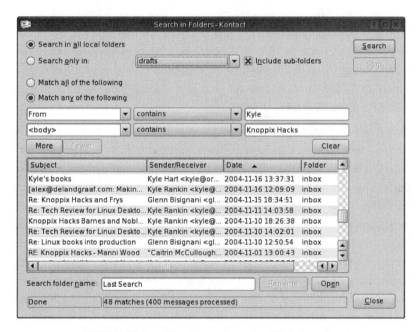

FIGURE 6-11. Searching for messages about Knoppix Hacks

You can open an email returned in the results area by double-clicking it, even if the search hasn't completed yet. You can also sort the results just as you would if the messages were in your Inbox, and you can stop the search at any time by clicking the Stop button. The "Search folder name" field at the bottom of the search window is discussed in the later section "Saved Searches."

Filters

Practically everyone who uses email has a cluttered inbox. And it's not just because people receive a lot of mail—it's also because they don't know quite what to do with it all. If you're on top of things, you've probably already created several folders to store email from particular people or about particular topics. But even though you have a folder for all the email from your boss, and another one for all the email from your spouse, I bet you still don't actually bother to put the messages in their proper place, and they just sit in your inbox, taking up room. Wouldn't it be great if email messages automatically went into the correct folder?

Well, if you learn to use filters, you can make them do just that. A filter is pretty much the same as a search, except that once KMail finds a message that matches your search, it performs an action upon it. For example, you can create a filter that watches all your incoming email, and when you get mail from your boss, it moves the message right to your Bossman folder. It happens automatically, without you needing to intervene. Pretty cool, right?

You can bring up the filter creation window, shown in Figure 6-12, by clicking Settings → Configure Filters. This window is similar to the search window described in the previous section, but also contains some additional elements. Along the left side is a space that shows the filters you already have. Right now, it should be empty. You define the action or actions you want the filter to take in the Filter Actions section, located below the search fields. In the Advanced Options section, you specify when you want this filter to do its work. Most filters are created to apply to incoming messages, but you may sometimes want to create a filter to work on sent messages or that you can apply manually to quickly clean up an email folder.

Most people leave the setting "If this filter matches, stop processing here" checked. Filters are usually applied starting at the top of the filter list and work their way down; therefore, if an email message matches the criteria of a filter at the top, it is never processed by the filters lower down on the list. (If the option is unchecked, all the filters have a go at the message, and usually the last filter wins.) I leave this option checked in all of my filters, and organize my Available Filters list so the most important ones are at the top by highlighting the filter name and clicking the up and down arrows to move them around the list.

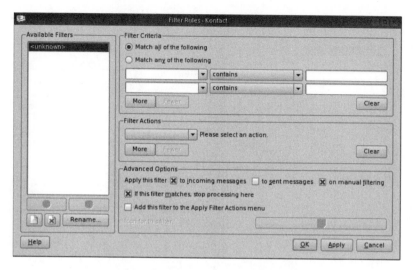

FIGURE 6-12. The KMail filter creation window

To create a new filter, click on the icon in the lower left corner that looks like a blank sheet of paper with the corner turned down. This adds a new entry at the top of the filter list with the title <unknown>. You can give it a new name by highlighting it and clicking the Rename button.

Once you've named your filter, enter your search criteria just as you did for performing a regular search on your existing email. The only difference is that you don't need to specify which folders to search, because filters are always applied according to the criteria you specify in the Advanced Options section.

The next thing to do is to define one or more filter actions by using the drop-down list in the Filter Actions section. If you need more than one action, click More to get another drop-down box. When you select an action, it will usually open an alternate drop-down list where you further define that action. For example, if you choose the action "file into folder," you'll get another drop-down list in which you select the folder to put the email into.

Figure 6-13 shows the settings for a filter that will move all email messages from your boss into a folder called Bossman and flag the messages as important. It applies only to messages that were sent directly to you in the To: or CC: lines (use the <recipients> option to specify both lines). Once you click Apply or OK, the filter will immediately start working on any email that is sent or received.

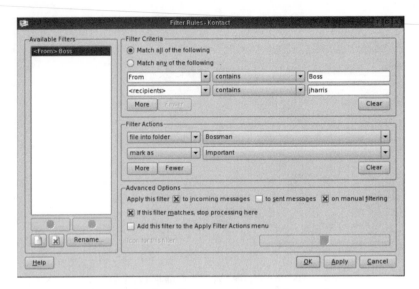

FIGURE 6-13. Creating a filter to move messages from your boss

You can also clean up existing email by applying a filter manually. This is useful when you've created a new filter and already have a lot of email in you inbox that matches the filter criteria. To manually run a filter, go to the folder that has the email messages you want to filter. Because manual filters affect only selected messages, press Ctrl-A to highlight all the messages in that folder, then press Ctrl-J to apply all manual filters.

A quick way to create a filter is to right-click on an email message, select Create Filter from the menu, and choose what criteria you want to filter on. The regular filter creation screen will open with some of the information already filled out. You then just need to specify your action, give the filter a new name, and click OK. I find this method particularly useful when creating filters for mailing lists because it automatically inserts the correct header information into the search criteria. This information isn't always immediately obvious when you create a filter manually, as it's usually buried in an email header.

Saved Searches

A *saved search* is a new feature in KMail that is like a cross between searches and filters. Saved searches are easy to create and can be very useful, but their usefulness is often not readily understood by people who don't already use filters.

If you run email searches often, it can get mighty tedious having to fill out the search criteria each time and waiting for the computer to find all the matching email. However, if you save a search and store it in a saved search folder, you get two immediate advantages: first, you don't have to retype the search parameters every time, and second, searching becomes faster because once you save a search, KMail continually runs that search in the background so it's always up-to-date with its results. If new email that matches your saved search criteria arrives, it becomes visible in the saved search folder immediately.

This may be enough to convince you that saved searches are a useful feature. But there's one more thing that's important, and it's the tricky part to understand. In a saved search, you're actually looking at email that exists in other folders. Some email programs call this a *virtual* folder. This means that while you are looking at the messages in a saved search folder, those actual messages are in another folder at the same time. This is different from a filter, which actually moves the messages around to different folders, or creates copies of a message so it can be in two folders at the same time.

For example, imagine that you have a filter set up to move messages sent by your boss into a Bossman folder. You also have a filter that sends messages about the book *Test Driving Linux* to a Linux folder. So if you get a message from your boss about *Test Driving Linux*, whichever filter is highest on your Available Filters list gets to handle it. That could mean either that a message from your boss might end up in the Linux folder, or a message about *Test Driving Linux* will be in your Bossman folder. You can solve this problem by replacing the *Test Driving Linux* filter with a saved search. This means the actual message can be anywhere—in your Bossman folder or in your inbox—but, because it's related to the *Test Driving Linux* book, it will always be "seen" in the saved search folder.

To create a saved search, just start a regular search as described in the "Searching" section. After you have specified all the criteria, click in the "Search folder name" field and give this search a name—in our example, "Test Driving Linux" would be appropriate. Now run the search by clicking the Search button. If the results are to your satisfaction, click the Open button and look at your KMail window. At the bottom of the folder list is a grouping called Searches, where you should see a new folder/ search named Test Driving Linux. When you click on it, your message list and preview pane will change to show the contents of the saved search (Figure 6-14). The saved search folder acts just like a regular email folder in all ways–you can read the messages and reply to them as usual. Note that if you delete the messages, they will disappear from the folder they are actually contained in as well as from the saved search folder.

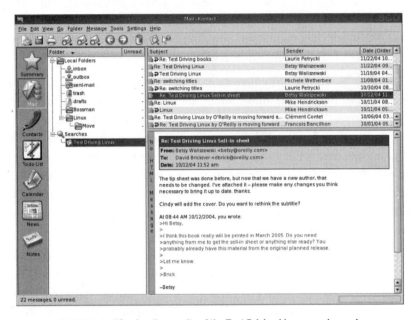

FIGURE 6-14. Viewing the results of the Test Driving Linux saved search

Using saved searches and filters, you can create some very powerful combinations. For instance, you can create a filter that sends all the email from your boss to the Bossman folder, and then create a saved search called Boss Unread that shows you only the messages from your boss that you haven't read yet. Once you read a message, it disappears from the search folder because the search criterion that the message be unread is no longer true. The actual message remains inside your Bossman folder. To set this up, you would create a normal search for messages from your boss, and then select *<status>*, *contains*, and *unread* in the second search criteria.

Organizing Your Time

The *Move* CD contains a personal time organization program called KOrganizer. You can use this program to keep track of your appointments, to-do items, and essential dates such as your wife's birthday.

Launch KOrganizer by clicking the Calendar icon in the Kontact shortcut bar, or go to K Menu → Organize → Organize your time. The main KOrganizer screen is divided into four sections (Figure 6-15). On the left-hand side, from top to bottom, are a small monthly calendar, a to-do item list, and a listing of currently open calendar resources. On the right-hand side is a seven-day view of your appointments, with the weekdays shaded a light purple. You'll notice that the menu items and toolbars along the top have changed to reflect items specific to KOrganizer.

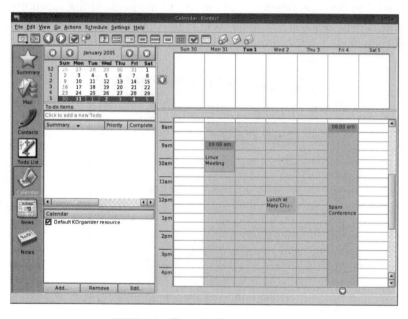

FIGURE 6-15. The main KOrganizer window

Monthly Calendar

There isn't really much to say about KOrganizer's small monthly calendar—just click the single arrows to move around by month, and click the double arrows to move around by year. If you click on a day, the calendar view on the right switches to display only that day. If you click on a week number (the numbers on the left just outside the Sunday column), the view to the right shows the entire week. Days that appear in bold have events scheduled on them.

To-Do List

The to-do item list is just a simple list that helps you keep track of important things you need to do. To add a new item, just type something in the space that contains the message "Click to add a new Todo," or right-click in the empty space and choose New To-Do. Then fill out the relevant information in the Edit-To-Do window. If you want to set a reminder for a to-do item, check the Due box, set a date, and then check the Reminder box and specify how far in advance you want to be reminded. The number you type in is modified by the time interval you specify in the drop-down box at the end of the field. At the appropriate time, a reminder window will appear in the center of all your desktops to tell you about the task you need to do (Figure 6-16).

FIGURE 6-16. A reminder pop-up window

Why reminders won't work

Unfortunately, the *Move* CD does not have the reminder service running, so you won't be notified of upcoming events even when you set the reminder properly. This applies to reminders for calendar events as well. However, the reminders will work if you install Linux to your hard drive.

To-do items can have sub-to-do items that they depend upon. For example, if I create a task called "Throw a party," I can create subtasks to get a cake, invite the guests, and buy a gift (Figure 6-17). The main task of throwing a party cannot be completed until I have finished the subtasks. To create a subtask, right-click upon an existing to-do item and choose New Sub-To-Do.

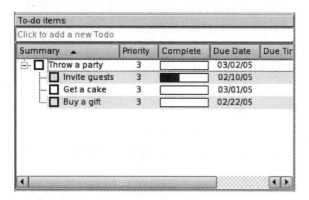

FIGURE 6-17. A main to-do item with several sub-to-dos

When you're finished with a task, just check the box next to it. You can delete finished tasks by right-clicking anywhere in the list and choosing Purge Completed.

Calendar Resource List

KOrganizer lets you have multiple calendars. This feature can be particularly useful if you want to share calendar information with other people. For instance, if three people are working on a project, they can create a calendar for that project and put it in a shared location, such as a file server at work. Then each person can add that calendar as a resource to KOrganizer and see all the events pertinent to the project. They can even modify or add new events as necessary. To manage multiple calendars, use the calendar resource list, located in the lower left of the KOrganizer window (Figure 6-18).

Another way to use multiple calendars is to connect to events calendars on the Internet. For instance, I'm a Notre Dame football fan and I like to have a calendar of the Fighting Irish schedule. By doing a Google search for "Notre Dame Football" and "iCal" (the format that most shared calendars are saved in), I found a web site that hosts the Notre Dame football schedule for 2005.

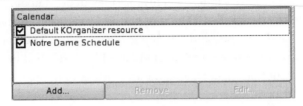

FIGURE 6-18. The calendar resource list with two active calendars

This is how you can add an Internet shared calendar resource:

1. Find the `webcal://` address for a shared calendar. If you can't find that, use the `http://` address that links directly to the *ical* file itself (in my example, this would be *http://ical.mac.com/sports/football/notredame2005.ics*).

2. Click Add in the calendar resource list.

3. In the Resource Configuration window, click Calendar in Remote File, and then click OK.

4. In the second Resource Configuration window, give your new calendar a name, and then enter the address from Step 1 in the Download URL field. I usually mark calendars such as this to reload on startup. When you're finished, click OK.

Now, the next time you start up KOrganizer, it should display the information it's pulled down from the remote calendar. To remove the calendar temporarily, just uncheck it in the calendar resource list. If you want to remove it permanently, select it and click Remove.

Creating Appointments

The main purpose of KOrganizer is to allow you to track events in a calendar. You can use KOrganizer simply to list events, but it's even more useful to have it remind you of upcoming events. KOrganizer is very simple to use; the hardest part is remembering to type in the appointments. (Unfortunately, KOrganizer can't remind you to do that!)

There are several ways to add a new event to your calendar. The first icon in KOrganizer's toolbar, which looks like a small calendar with a sun, represents New Event. Click it to open an Edit Event window, where you can enter all the information for the new event (Figure 6-19). Alternatively, you can press Ctrl-N to bring up the same window. A third method is to right-click in a time slot in the calendar view on the right and choose New Event to create a new event associated with that particular 15-minute time slot. Alternately, you can click and drag your mouse to highlight multiple time slots in a row to make your new event begin and end at the times you highlight.

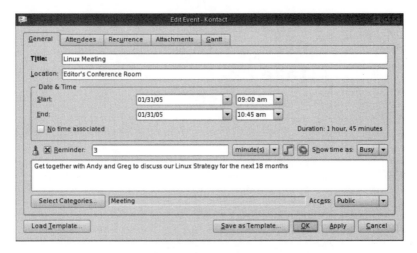

FIGURE 6-19. The Edit Event window, where you create new appointments

Regardless of how you get to it, the Edit Event window is always the same and looks a lot like the Edit To-Do window. Most of the good stuff is on the first tab, and it's pretty obvious what you have to fill out. The Title field is simply a place for you to type a short description of the new event. This description will display in the calendar view on the right side of KOrganizer, so pick something meaningful. The Location field is where you can type the place where the event is occurring. This field is not tied to any sort of resource reservation tool, but it's a useful reminder of where you need to go.

The purpose of the Start and End fields in the Date & Time section should be obvious. If the time fields are grayed out, it is probably because the "No time associated" box is checked, which means that any event you create is assigned to the entire day or days specified by your Start and End dates. When you uncheck this box, you can add specific times to the event.

If you want to set a reminder for the event, check the Reminder box. (Keep in mind that reminders are disabled on the *Move* CD, however.) This enables a few more fields, where you can specify how long before the start time of the event you want to be reminded. The first field contains a number, which is modified by the time interval (minutes, hours, days) specified in the drop-down list. The actual reminder you receive when you set these fields looks like Figure 6-20.

FIGURE 6-20. An event reminder

By clicking the Select Categories button, you can choose a category for the event that will affect its color in the calendar view. You can create new categories by clicking Edit Categories, typing a name in the new window, and clicking Add.

Back in the Edit Event window, you'll notice that there's a big, empty field in the middle of the window in which you can type the details of your event. This information also appears in the event reminder.

Now click on the Recurrence tab of the Edit Event window, as shown in Figure 6-21. If your event will repeat in the future, check the "Enable recurrence" box and tell KOrganizer how often to repeat this event. For example, let's say you want to create an event that repeats every other Wednesday for the next three months. To set this up, click Weekly for your time interval, set the "Recur every" value to 2, and then check off Wed in the days of the week list. Finally, in the Recurrence Range section, check "End by" and specify a date three months into the future.

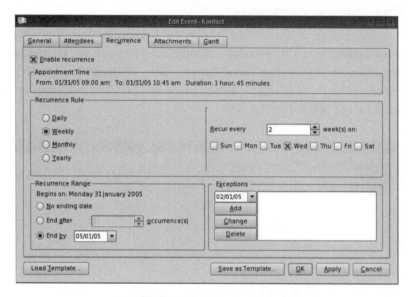

FIGURE 6-21. Setting up a recurring event

As another example, say you have a monthly poker game that occurs the first Thursday of every month, with the exception of the second month. To set this up, click Monthly for your time interval and set it for the next 12 months. There are two options to specify the day this should occur on. For this example, choose the second option and set it to recur on the 1st Thursday. Finally, to exclude the Thursday in the next month, click the drop-down list in the Exceptions section, choose the date you want to exclude, and click Add.

The other tabs

The Attendees and Gantt tabs in the Edit Event window are related to the groupware functions of Kontact and are beyond the scope of this book. The Attachments tab is where you can associate a particular file to an event.

When you're done creating an event, simply click OK to close the Edit Event window and save the event to your calendar.

Customizing KOrganizer

You can customize KOrganizer to a limited degree. To open the config-uration window, go to Settings → Configure KOrganizer. The window that appears looks like most other KDE configuration windows (Figure 6-22). As usual, if you select an icon on the left, it will bring up a related set of options on the right.

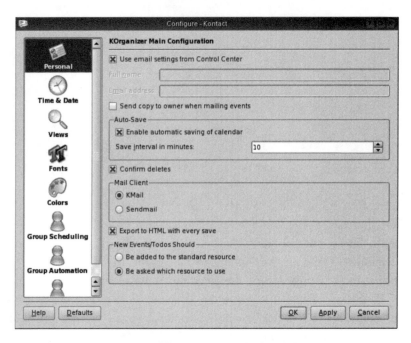

FIGURE 6-22. KOrganizer's customization window

Instead of going through all the options, I'll simply point out the ones I think are the most interesting. In the main configuration window (click the Personal icon), I like to check off the "Export to HTML with every save" option. This creates a web page with your calendar events and to-do items every time you save the KOrganizer calendar, and you can share this page with other people to let them know how busy you are.

If you maintain more than one calendar in your calendar resource list, you should check off the box next to "Be asked which resource to use." Doing this allows you to specify which calendar a new event should be saved in. If you have only one calendar (as most people do), check off the option "Be added to the standard resource" instead.

On the Time & Date screen, you can specify several features related to how KOrganizer handles time. Since most of my events last less than an hour, I like to change the "Default duration of a new appointment" to 1:00 (one hour).

The Views screen controls the actual appearance of KOrganizer. There are a lot of options to play with here. My favorites are to set the "Days begin at" to 9:00 because I start my day later than most. I also like to check the last option, "Time range selection in agenda view starts event editor," which allows you to create a new event just by dragging your mouse over a time range. When you release the button, a new Edit Event window opens with the time range already entered. Very convenient!

The Colors screen lets you specify the colors associated with different items. I usually modify the colors associated with Categories so that different types of events can have different colors. To do this, simply select the category that you want to modify from the drop-down list, then click on the color bar. This opens a Select Color window, where you can choose any color under the rainbow.

Create a Computerized Address Book

Kontact also contains an address book in which you can keep all of your important contact information. Like the email and organizer components of Kontact, this feature actually comes from a separate program known as KAddressbook.

To launch KAddressbook from within Kontact, just click the Contacts button on the shortcut bar on the left of the Kontact window. As usual, the main window, menus, and icon bar change to provide options specific to KAddressbook.

The main window in KAddressbook is divided into three parts. Along the top is a search field to help you find specific information. The left-hand pane displays the list of your contacts (empty now), and the right-hand pane displays the details of a selected contact.

To create a new contact, click the New Contact icon (the one that looks like a small ID card) or press Ctrl-N. This opens the Edit Contact window, where you can fill in all the relevant information about your contact (see Figure 6-23).

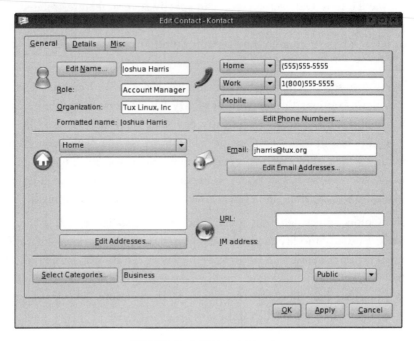

FIGURE 6-23. A KAddressbook entry

There aren't too many surprises here; the data you put into each field should be self-explanatory. Multiple tabs help divide up the information. There are a few interesting features here worth noting:

Select Categories (General tab)

Click the Select Categories button to assign your contact to a category. This makes it easier to find your contacts later and to keep your Aunt Rosie's contact information separate from that of your business associates. You can also assign a contact to multiple categories. For instance, in my job as an editor, I often assign writers to my Authors, Business, and Technical Reviewer categories. You can create new categories as needed by clicking Select Categories → Edit Categories, typing in a new category name, and clicking Add.

Birthday and Anniversary (Details tab)

The birthday and anniversary information for your contacts will show up on your Kontact Summary page. Unfortunately, this information does not integrate with KOrganizer, so you won't get pop-up reminders about your upcoming anniversary. I suspect that this capability will be available in a future release of Kontact.

Photo (Misc tab)

Click on the folder icon to browse to a photo for your contact. Doing this helps you remember what the people you correspond with actually look like.

Once you have entered contacts in KAddressbook, you can use them in KMail. When you create a new email or reply to an existing one, click on the three dots at the end of the To: field to open up the small window shown in Figure 6-24. This window displays the contents of your address book, conveniently grouped into categories (see, I told you categories were handy!). Click the plus sign to expand a category and double-click a contact to add that person to the To: field. You can select multiple contacts, and if you want to put someone on the CC: line, just click once on their name and click the CC >> button. Once you click OK, the window closes and you are back at your email message, with all the addresses entered.

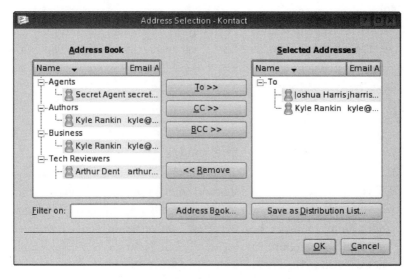

FIGURE 6-24. Selecting addresses in KMail

You can add new contacts from within KMail by right-clicking on the contact's email address in the preview pane and selecting Add to Address Book or Open in Address Book. I usually choose the latter because it lets me enter full contact information right away.

Instant Messaging with Kopete

These days it seems like more and more people are using instant messaging. If you have teenagers in your house, you already know that having IM is more important than having a second telephone line. Fortunately, the *Move* CD comes with its very own instant messenger program, Kopete. This handy little program lets you connect to all the major messaging networks such as AIM, MSN, Yahoo, and Jabber—and it lets you do it all at the same time! That means you can chat with any of your friends without worrying about which network they're on.

To start Kopete, just click K Menu → Surf the Internet → Chat. The first time you launch Kopete, it displays a contact window (just like a buddy list in AIM) and a Configure window, where you can make several choices that affect Kopete's behavior. Just click through the Appearance and Behavior choices to see what options are available to you. The default choices are pretty good, and I seldom find the need to change them.

To set up your chat accounts, click on the Accounts icon and then click New. This launches a wizard to help you add a new account. The following steps illustrate how to connect to the AIM service; connecting to any other service is pretty much the same.

1. The first window is just introductory, so click Next to continue.

2. In the second screen, labeled Step One, select the service your account is on—in this case, AIM—and click Next.

3. In Step Two, you enter your AIM screen name, and your password if you want it to be remembered. The Connection tab allows you to specify whether you want to automatically log onto the AIM service each time you start Kopete. After you've made your choices and entered the account information, click Next to continue. Finally, click Finish in the last screen.

At this point, the KDE Wallet Wizard may launch. KWallet is a program that remembers all of your passwords for you. To keep things simple, I recommend that you simply click Next and then Finish, to make KWallet go away. You may get a warning that Kopete could not save your password to the wallet and that offers to save your password in the unsafe configuration file instead. Go ahead and click Store Unsafe for now. You should now be back at the manage accounts window; if you wanted to edit an account, you can simply select it and click Modify. If you're ready to start using Kopete, click the OK button to close the configuration window.

Now you're back to just the contact window (Figure 6-25). To connect to the account you just set up, click the icon that looks like a plug with a lightning bolt on it, or go to File → Connection → Connect All. Now comes the annoying part. A new screen will come up, and despite any settings you made when you configured the account, you will now need to enter your password again, specify whether you want it saved, and state if you want your account to auto-connect in the future. This is the last time you'll have to do it, though—the choices you make here will really stick.

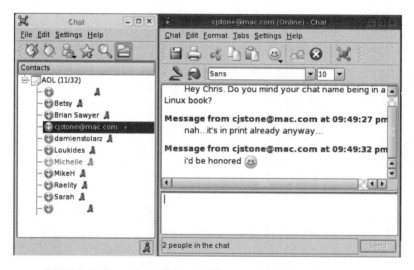

FIGURE 6-25. The contact window of the instant messenger program Kopete

Once you connect, all of your buddies should start showing up in the Contact window, with indications of their status. I like to hide my offline buddies by unchecking Show Offline Users from the Settings menu.

From this point on, chatting in Kopete is a lot like using any other instant message program. (One gotcha is that you need to press Ctrl-Enter to send your message; pressing Enter just gives you a new line in the chat window.) Kopete supports smileys, tabbed chats, sharing files, and other advanced chat features. Though it isn't identical to the chat clients of AOL or MSN, it should enable you to do just about anything you want to do. Happy chatting!

7

EDIT DIGITAL IMAGES

These days, it seems like everybody has a digital camera. If they don't have a digital version of a traditional film camera, they have one built into their cell phone or PDA. The increasing popularity of digital cameras naturally leads to more digital pictures, which in turn leads to the need to store, manage, and manipulate those pictures. That's where this chapter comes in. It shows you the programs included on *Move* that will help you get your images off your digital camera, view them on your computer, and edit them to your heart's content.

The crown jewel of this small collection of software is the GNU Image Manipulation Program, known as the GIMP. This handy program is considered by some to be a capable alternative to Adobe Photoshop, and considering that the GIMP is free and Photoshop costs more than $600, it is probably worth your time to find out if this is true for you. Though the GIMP was originally developed for Linux and Unix systems, there is now a Windows version you can try out as well. Visit *http://www.gimp.org* for more information.

Getting Images

Before you can view or edit your digital images, you first need an image to edit. Though *Move* does come with a few wallpaper images, they aren't particularly interesting to work with. You can download all kinds of images off the Web, but you may prefer to work with pictures that have more personal value to you.

If you already have digital photos on your Windows hard drive, you can access them using the method described at the end of Chapter 3. Since *Move* cannot write data to your hard drive, you need to copy the file to your Home directory on a USB key if you want to save any changes to an edited image. Reading and writing changes to your USB key takes time, so be prepared to wait several seconds for changes to happen to very large images.

You can also work with images stored on your Compact Flash, Secure Digital, or other camera storage medium. To do this, you need to have a media reader on your computer—usually, a USB device that you can stick the flash-based memory card into. When you plug in your media card reader, *Move* should add an icon on your desktop, usually labeled Hard Disc, to let you access the device. When you double-click the icon, it opens in Konqueror and you can navigate to where the images are stored. Though you can view the images directly from the flash media, you have to transfer them to your Home directory before you can edit them. For your own safety, *Move* does not allow you to edit the file directly.

Viewing Images

Once you can access your images, you'll probably want a convenient way to view them. There are dozens of programs on Linux for viewing images, but *Move* comes with just a few. You have probably already noticed that Konqueror shows you thumbnail views of any image in a directory. To see this in action, type the following into Konqueror's Location field and press Enter:

```
/usr/share/wallpapers
```

When the *wallpapers* directory loads, it generates thumbnails of all the images in the directory (Figure 7-1). To view an image full-size, simply double-click its icon to load the image inside of Konqueror. Though this is a convenient way to view an image quickly, you cannot manipulate your view of the image, such as rotating it or zooming in or out.

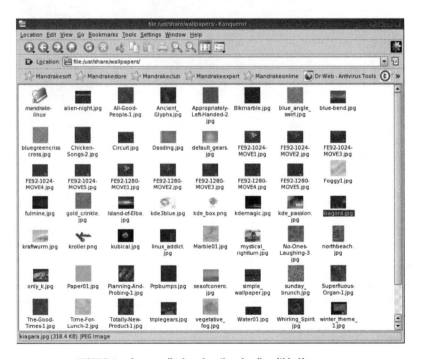

FIGURE 7-1. Images displayed as thumbnails within Konqueror

For more control over how you view your images, you need to use an external viewing program such as GQview. To open an image with this program, simply right-click on the image icon inside Konqueror and choose Open With → GQview (Figure 7-2). The GQview program window is divided into three panes: the top left pane allows you to navigate to the directories where your images are stored, the pane below that lists the image files in the currently selected directory, and the large pane to the right displays the chosen image. A small toolbar and the programs menus are located in the upper-left corner.

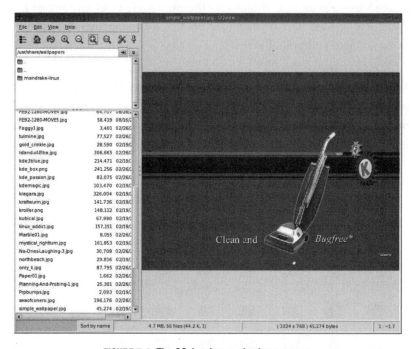

FIGURE 7-2. The GQview image viewing program

Press F to view the image full-screen. You can press the spacebar to see the next image in the directory, and the backspace key to see a previous image. This is an easy way to rapidly view all the files in a directory—it's kind of like a digital photo album. GQview can also perform a slide-show for you. To do this, exit the full-screen mode by pressing the F key again, and in the image list on the left, select the images you want in your slideshow. (Use the Shift-click and Ctrl-click methods described in Chapter 1 to select multiple images.) Once you've selected your images, right-click on one in the view pane on the right and choose "Start slideshow" (or just press the S key). The slideshow will change images every 15 seconds; to change the time interval, click View → Options and make the adjustment in the "Slide show" section at the bottom.

Right-clicking on an image in GQview gives you several other options. You can zoom in and out, autofit the image to the window size, and, under the Adjust menu, you can rotate, mirror, or flip the image. This is useful for rotating images that appear sideways because you held the camera vertically when you took the picture.

Getting to Know the GIMP

The GIMP is not the only image editing program on Linux, but it is the best known. Though it's not as full-featured as Adobe Photoshop, the GIMP should be able to handle the image editing chores of most non-professional users. Using the GIMP, you can resize, crop, color-correct, and combine images, fix blemishes, and perform hundreds of other tasks.

Timeless instruction

Move comes with version 1.2 of the GIMP, which is actually quite dated. Though the current version 2.2 looks different, what I write here still applies.

To launch the GIMP, go to K Menu → View, modify, and create graphics → Edit images and photos, or simply click its icon on the kicker (it looks like a cartoon dog with a big nose). Alternately, you can right-click on an image file and choose Open With → The GIMP. When the program launches for the first time, it will ask you several configuration questions. Unless you have reason to do otherwise, just accept the defaults by clicking Continue on each screen.

Managing memory

If your USB key is smaller than 64 MB, pay attention to the third configuration screen. This screen asks you how large a Tile Cache Size you want, which determines how much hard disk space (or USB key space) the GIMP reserves to hold its image data. The setting defaults to 32 MB, and you should adjust it depending upon how much space is actually available on your USB key.

The GIMP displays several small windows when it opens, including an image window if you opened it by right-clicking an image file. If you're not familiar with image editing tools, these windows could use some explanation:

GIMP Tip of the Day

This is the typical Tip window you see when many programs start up. You can click through the available tips with the Previous Tip and Next Tip buttons, click Close to make it go away until the next time you start the GIMP, or uncheck "Show tip next time GIMP starts" and click Close if you want to get rid of it for good.

Tools Palette (labeled The GIMP)

This is the GIMP's main window (Figure 7-3). In addition to the main menu, this window holds all the tools you use to edit your image. When you close this window, the entire program closes.

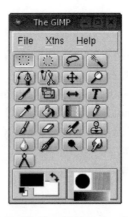

FIGURE 7-3. The GIMP's tools palette

Tools Options

This window displays a set of options that affect the tool selected in the tools palette. Each time you click on a new tool, check this window to see what features are available for it. If you accidentally close this window, you can bring it back up by double-clicking a tool's icon in the tools palette.

Brush Selection

This is the digital equivalent of an artist's paintbrush collection. The brush sizes you choose here affect the tools in the main window. For instance, if you're using a line drawing tool, the choices in the top row of this window affect the width of the lines you draw.

Layers, Channels & Paths

This palette controls the *layers* in an image. You can think of image layers like layers of clothing, but unlike layers of clothing you can manipulate any layer, not just the top one. Imagine being able to take off your t-shirt without needing to take off your sweater and coat first. In an image, if the t-shirt is on a different layer than the sweater and the coat, you can remove the t-shirt and leave the other two pieces of clothing in place with a single click.

Image

The image window is where you view and edit an open image. The GIMP auto-adjusts the size of your image to fit the screen; if you look at the title bar of this window, you can see what percentage of the actual size the GIMP has set your image to.

If you look at the menu choices in the main GIMP menu, you may be surprised at how little is actually there. There are two reasons the menus are sparse. One is that many of the functions that are normally assigned to a menu in other software interfaces are handled in the GIMP by icons and options in the various palettes. The other is that most options are assigned to the menu that appears when you right-click an actual image. This might seem like a weird place to put so many options, but when you think about it, it does make sense. It's useful to have the menu choices close at hand so that you don't have to drag your mouse all the way to the main menu bar just to select a new action.

The GIMP supports multiple levels of Undo. If you make a mistake, you can press Ctrl-Z to remove your most recent changes, or Ctrl-R to redo a recent change. The GIMP is configured to allow five levels of Undo; you can increase this number using the GIMP's preferences panel, which is opened by clicking File → Preferences. This configuration window has a lot of useful settings to manipulate the GIMP's behavior; click on the Environment category to reach the Undo setting. Because each additional level of Undo requires more system memory, I suggest you don't set this value higher than you typically need. Within the memory-constrained environment of the *Move* CD, it's probably best not to change it at all.

Many image editing programs offer built-in functions that can do interesting things to your photos. In the GIMP, you can access these functions by right-clicking on an image and making a selection from the Filters or Script-Fu menu. I would normally encourage you to play around with all these options, but because accessing an image from a USB key is very slow, this kind of experimentation will take a long time—many of the menu choices may take a minute or more to affect your image.

Obviously, I can't cover everything that the GIMP can do in this chapter, but the following sections describe a few basic things that I find myself using the GIMP for fairly often.

Rotate Images

I don't imagine myself an expert on photographic technique, but every now and then I realize that a particular picture is best taken as a portrait rather than a landscape, so I turn my camera on its end and click away. Of course, this produces pictures that are turned 90 degrees in one direction. When thumbing through a stack of printed pictures, it is easy enough to turn a picture 90 degrees to view it properly. But when looking at digital photos you usually have to select a menu option to rotate the picture, which can get awfully tedious when viewing a large number of photos and sharing them with friends. However, using the GIMP you can rotate the image permanently, so you won't get a crick in your neck the next time you view your photos.

To begin, go to File → Open and select the image you want to rotate from the file browser. (You may notice that this window is a bit different from the ones you've seen so far in KDE. This is because the GIMP is not a KDE application, so it doesn't share the common KDE Save and Open dialogs. One thing to note about this particular Open window is that if you want to move to a directory above the one you are in, you must double click on the ../ in the Directories pane.)

Once you've got the image open, right-click it, choose Image → Transforms → Rotate from the menu, and select the appropriate degree of rotation. Remember, because of slow USB key access speeds this rotation may take quite a bit of time to complete, so give it a couple of minutes before you give up on it. To save the rotated image, right-click it and choose File → Save. Figure 7-4 and Figure 7-5 show a picture of one of my cats before and after I rotated the image.

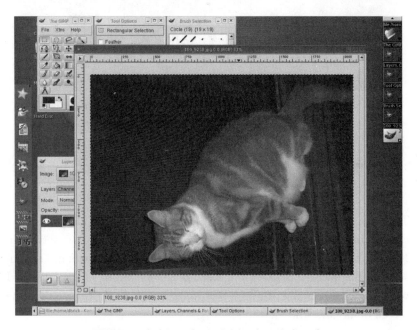

FIGURE 7-4. A picture of my cat, taken in portrait mode

Resize Images

Another common task you'll perform when working with digital photos is resizing the images. Modern megapixel (MP) cameras produce really outstanding images, but the files are several megabytes in size and not suitable for sending in email or displaying on a web page. Using the GIMP, you can easily resize the picture so that it takes up less space and isn't 20" wide and 15" tall.

To understand the best way to resize a picture, you first need to know a few things about digital images, so I'll explain the important concepts here. If you go back to the picture of my cat in Figure 7-5, you'll see on the titlebar that the image is being displayed at 33 percent of its full size.

FIGURE 7-5. The picture after it has been rotated 90 degrees clockwise

To see just how big an image really is, you need to right-click on it and choose Image → Scale Image. This brings up the window shown in Figure 7-6. By looking at the Print Size & Display Unit section, you can see that this picture is 21.444" wide and 28.889" high. That's huge. If I were to put this image up on a web page, it would be bigger than the screen of anyone who viewed it.

The size of an image is determined by its width and height in pixels combined with the dots per inch (DPI) at which you are viewing it. When I first launched the GIMP, I accepted the default setting of 72 DPI. This used to be a very common setting on most computers, and means that 72 pixels take up exactly one inch of display on the computer screen. If you look at the Pixel Dimensions section of the Scale Image window, you'll see that my image takes up 1544×2080 pixels. If you do the math and divide these two numbers by 72, you'll get the dimensions I mentioned earlier. If I sent this image to a computer user whose screen was set up for 96 DPI (a common setting on many new computers), the picture wouldn't be quite so huge—16.083"×21.667"—but it would still be much too large.

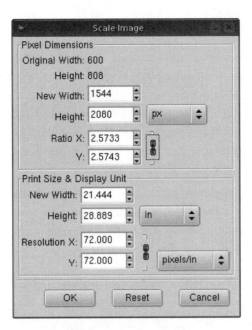

FIGURE 7-6. The Scale Image window

In addition to the size of the image on the screen, you have to take the size of the image file into account. This picture of my cat, taken with a 3MP camera, is currently 675 KB in size. Though this is small enough to email to most people, if the recipient is on dial-up it could take a minute or more to download. Thankfully, when you scale down the size of the image, the file size is reduced as well.

Reducing the image size is easy. In the Scale Image window, just type in a new value for any one of the dimensions—either the width or the height in either pixels or inches—and click OK. The GIMP auto-adjusts the other values to keep the image properly scaled (i.e., it won't stretch out your cat and make him look even fatter than he already is). I usually set the width of a portrait picture to 600 pixels, which sets the height to around 800 pixels. (In a landscape portrait, the two numbers would be reversed.) In the case of my cat, the pixel dimensions 600×808 give the picture a size of $8.333" \times 11.222"$.

To save your new settings, right-click on the image and choose File → Save. Now when I check the size of the file, it is only 46 KB—less than one-tenth the space it took up before I resized it. My email correspondents will be grateful. And as long as the picture is viewed at 100% actual size or less, there shouldn't be any noticeable quality change.

Crop Images

When my wife and I were in Vienna a few years ago, I took a lot of pictures of her in various gardens and palaces using a regular film camera. I thought I had framed each picture perfectly, but when I developed my pictures I realized I had not zoomed in closely enough. In almost every picture my wife was too small, and there was a lot of background material that wasn't particularly interesting. I'm sure I'm not the only person who makes this mistake, but thankfully it is easy to correct in the GIMP by *cropping*, or cutting out, the unwanted parts of the picture.

Figure 7-7 shows a picture of my other cat crouching underneath the coffee table. It's not a great picture, partly because there are some distracting elements around the edges that just don't need to be there. This is a good example of an image that needs to be cropped.

FIGURE 7-7. A picture of my cat that needs to be cropped

To select the cropping tool in the GIMP, click its icon in the main palette. (It looks like a small scalpel, and the tooltip "Crop or resize the image" will appear when you hover your mouse over it.) Now, when you move your cursor over the image, you'll see that the cursor has changed to a small crosshair with a strange symbol in the lower right. To use the cropping tool, left-click on the image and drag your cursor to create a box around the part of the picture you want to keep. Once the box is in place, you can tweak it by using the handles at the corners—the handles at the top right and lower left let you move the whole crop box, while the ones at the top left and lower right let you move the bounding lines horizontally and vertically. Once you have the crop box positioned exactly the way you like, click once inside the box to perform the actual crop (or click the Crop button in the Crop & Resize Information window that appeared when you started the cropping process). Voila! You now have a new image without any unwanted parts in it. As usual, to make the change permanent, you need to save the image by right-clicking on it and choosing File → Save. (Or, if you don't want to over-write the original figure, select File → Save As.) Figure 7-8 shows the newly cropped image of my cat, without any stray feet in the picture.

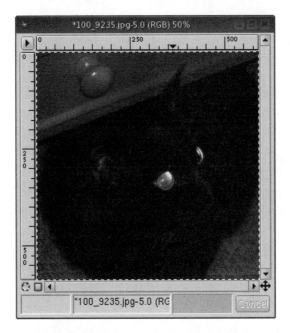

FIGURE 7-8. The same picture after cropping out some unnecessary elements

Remove Red Eye

I expect that everyone has a photograph in their collection that is per-fect in every way, with the exception of the subject's glowing red eyes. Red eye is caused by the light of the camera's flash reflecting off the subject's retinas. Though many cameras come with a red-eye reducing flash, it doesn't always work. As a result, removing red eye is one of the most common tasks you'll use an image editing tool for.

There are several ways to remove red eye using the GIMP. The method I'll cover here is not only easy to use, but it will introduce you to a few tools we haven't gotten to yet. For this example, I'm going to use the cropped image of my red-eyed cat shown in Figure 7-8.

With your picture loaded, zoom in on the troublesome eye by clicking on the image window and pressing the = key on the keyboard (press the – key to zoom out). For my particular image, a zoom level of 500 percent worked well. You will have to center the image on the eye after you zoom by using the slider bars in the image window.

Now bring your Layers, Channels & Paths window to the front and click on the Channels tab. There are three entries here: Red, Green, and Blue. Every color in an image is a combination of varying amounts of these three colors. By adjusting these channels, you can affect only certain colors in an image; and since your goal here is to remove red eye, you obviously will be working only with the Red channel. Click once on the words Green and Blue to remove the highlighting and deactivate those channels. Now, when you use a color tool on the image, it will affect only the color red. (Be careful not to click on the iconic eye next to each channel name; this will hide that color in the image and make it more difficult to work with.)

To remove red eye from your image, you're going to use a technique known as *burning*. Select the burn tool from the main tools palette—the icon looks like a small wand with a black circle on the end, and it has the tooltip "Dodge and Burn." The Tool Options window will change to show you the options available for this tool. Set the tool to burn by checking the Burn box, and then set the Mode to Highlights. There is no need to click OK or Apply for these changes to take effect.

Now you need to select a brush size in the Brush Selection window. This will determine the size of the area that is affected when you perform your "burn." For reducing red eye, you'll probably want to select a brush with fuzzy edges; such brushes apply a change 100 percent at the center of the brush and to a lesser amount around the edges, which gives your changes a softer and more natural look. As you click on each brush, you will see a description of the brush and the number of pixels affected by it at the top of the window. For close-up work like this, you'll want to use a brush size of 11 or less. You might need to switch to an even smaller brush when you work near the edges.

Now all you need to do is click on the red portions of your image and the burn tool will remove the red. You'll probably need to click a specific spot multiple times. It will look like you are painting black on the image, but you're actually removing all the color of the active channel, and of course the absence of color is black. Keep in mind that this can be time-consuming and delicate work, so be patient. If you make a mistake, press Ctrl-Z to undo the change. Figure 7-9 shows you the results of my red-eye removal attempt. I think you'll agree that my cat looks much less demonic now.

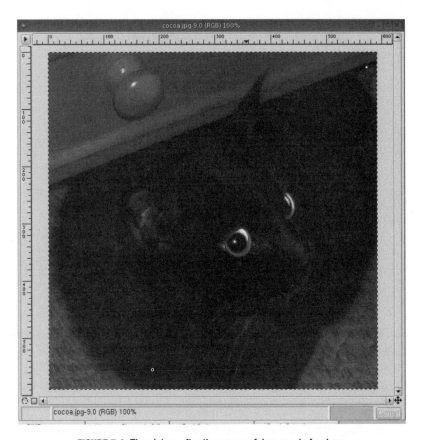

FIGURE 7-9. The picture after the successful removal of red eye

Taking Screenshots

Linux users love to share screenshots of their desktops and applications—perhaps because Linux is so highly customizable and it is interesting to see how someone has personalized their desktop. (You'll learn all about customizing KDE in Chapter 8.) In order to share your screenshots, you first need to learn how to make them. To this end, *Move* includes the program KSnapshot, which can take screenshots of specific windows, the entire screen, or a selected portion of the screen.

1. To launch KSnapshot, click K Menu → View, modify and create graphics → Create a screenshot. Figure 7-10 shows you the only window in the program. Taking a screenshot is a fairly simple process. Select the type of screenshot you want to create from the "Capture mode" drop-down list.

FIGURE 7-10. The screenshot program KSnapshot

2. Select a time in the "Snapshot delay" field, which determines how long KSnapshot will wait before it actually takes the screenshot. Setting a delay of a few seconds gives you enough time to open a program window or expand a menu you want to be in the screenshot.

3. Click the New Snapshot button to take the screenshot. The KSnapshot program disappears until the screenshot is taken, to ensure that it does not appear in the final image. If you selected the Fullscreen

capture mode, you just have to wait for the screenshot to be taken. If you chose Window Under Cursor, you need to click on the window you want in the screenshot before the Snapshot delay expires. And if you selected Region, you have to use your mouse to draw a box around the portion of the screen you want to capture. When you release your mouse button the screenshot "snaps."

4. Once the screenshot is taken, click the Save As button to save it. KSnapshot saves images only in PNG format, which is an open standard that combines some of the best qualities of GIF and JPEG images.

And that's all there is to it. All of the screenshots in this book were taken using this tool (with the exception of the one of the program itself, of course, for which I used the GIMP).

8

CUSTOMIZE
YOUR
DESKTOP

Visit any car dealership and you'll see rows upon rows of cars that all look the same except for the color. But looks can be deceiving—many of those cars are actually very different inside, in the way they're configured and the options they come with. Some cars have leather seats; others have cloth. Some have six-cylinder engines; others have four-cylinder. Some come with the mega-bass six-CD-changer stereo system; others only have FM radio. Buyers can decide what options they want based upon their practical needs, their aesthetic preferences, and their budget.

Linux and KDE have a lot of options as well. For example, you can configure your interface to look like Windows or the Macintosh. There are a hundred different icon sets you can use. Even the look and location of the buttons that control program windows can be changed. This customization is all built-in, it's all free (unlike the pricey options on cars!), and it's part of what makes using Linux such a fun experience.

However, having all these options can also be confusing. There are literally hundreds, if not thousands, of things that you can tweak on a Linux desktop. This chapter explores some of the most popular customizations that users like to make to KDE.

Basic Customization

Perhaps the first and most basic thing you'll want to do is change the desktop background picture. I discussed how to do this at the end of Chapter 1, but let's revisit the configuration window where you make the change. It has several other options that may be of interest.

To bring up the Configure Desktop window, simply right-click on your desktop and choose Configure Desktop. You'll see five icons on the left-hand side of the configuration window that appears. Clicking on one of these icons changes the configuration options displayed on the right side of the window.

See "Setting Your Desktop Background" in Chapter 1 for a review of the Background icon (Figure 8-1). The configuration panels of the remaining four icons—Behavior, Multiple Desktops, Paths, and Screen Saver—are described in the following sections.

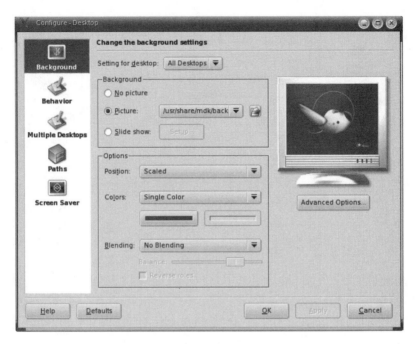

FIGURE 8-1. The Background configuration window

Behavior

The Behavior configuration screen, shown in Figure 8-2, contains an odd collection of settings. Feel free to go ahead and experiment with all of them, but the most useful ones are in the Mouse Button Actions section. The choices you make here affect how your mouse buttons behave when you use them to click on your desktop. Try making a change here and clicking Apply, and then click on the desktop to see if you like the change. I prefer the default settings for the Left and Right buttons, which make your mouse buttons act exactly like they do in Windows. But I like to change the Middle button to Custom Menu 1 and click the Edit button to add programs to the list. By doing this, I'm creating a quick way to launch programs that I use frequently but that I don't tend to run for very long, such as *kdict* (a dictionary), *kcalc* (a calculator), and *ksnapshot* (a screen capture program). Once you configure a custom list for the Middle button, you can launch the programs simply by middle-clicking on the desktop and choosing a program from the list. If you have only two mouse buttons, you can middle-click by clicking both buttons at the same time.

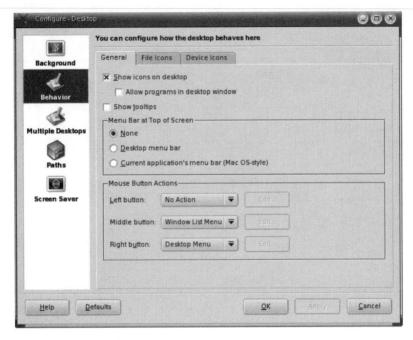

FIGURE 8-2. The Behavior configuration window

I tend to avoid the options that allow me to put a menu bar at the top of the screen, but if you're used to the desktop layout of the Mac you may like this option.

Multiple Desktops

The Multiple Desktop icon controls how many virtual desktops you have on your computer. The *Move* CD defaults to just 2, but by moving the sliding lever at the top, you can have up to 16 virtual desktops! In addition, you can give each desktop a name to make it easy to remember. Naming desktops also encourages you to use desktops for specific purposes, as I suggested in Chapter 1. The last option in this window gives you the ability to change desktops using the scroll wheel of your mouse when the cursor is over the desktop background. To set your changes to this window, just click Apply.

Paths

There are only four options available on the Paths window, and only one of them (Document path) is something you'll likely want to change right now. But let's look at all four options anyway:

Desktop path

Icons and documents you put in this directory will appear on your desktop.

Trash path

This is where KDE stores items until you delete them for good. (Refer back to Chapter 3 for more on the Trash.)

Autostart path

This is a folder containing programs or documents that run automatically when you log into KDE. If you place a link to a document or program here, it will load when you log in. You can do some very clever things with the Autostart folder, particularly if you know how to program. (You'll notice that the path includes a directory with a dot in front of it (*.kde*), which means this folder is inside a hidden folder. To view hidden folders, you need to click View → Show Hidden Files in Konqueror.) Try going to the Autostart folder and dragging an icon for a program, such as Konqueror, from your kicker panel to your Autostart folder. The next time you log into KDE, Konqueror should load automatically.

Document path

This is simply the default location used by the Save and Open dialog boxes in KDE applications such as KWrite or KMail. It might be a good idea to point it to a directory inside your Home.

Screen Savers

Now, click on the Screen Saver icon to open its configuration window (see Figure 8-3). You will see a list of available screen savers you can use.

To keep the list of screen savers tidy, *Move* places them in several groups. To open a group, click the plus sign once or double-click the group's name. You can then choose a particular screen saver by clicking once on its name. When you do that, the monitor to the right previews the screen saver for you.

Some screen savers have a lot of configuration options, which you can access by clicking on the screen saver name and then clicking the Setup button at the bottom of the list. Just to experiment, let's set up the Banner screen saver now. Expand the Banners & Pictures grouping, select the Banner screen saver, and then click on Setup.

Wallpapers or screen savers?

People often get confused about the difference between desktop backgrounds (wallpapers) and screen savers. A wallpaper is the picture or color you see on your desktop all the time as you are using it. A screen saver appears after your computer has been sitting idle for a while, and usually hides everything on your screen and puts on an animated show for you. You've probably already noticed that if you leave *Move* sitting alone for more than five minutes, a screen saver kicks in.

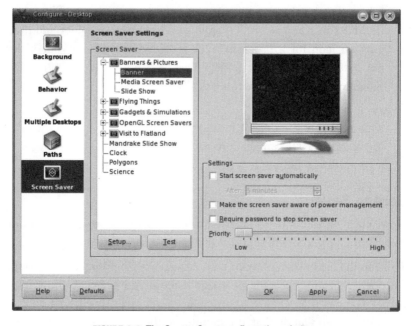

FIGURE 8-3. The Screen Saver configuration window

The Banner screen saver simply scrolls some text of your choosing across the screen. You can use the Setup window to change the font, font size, and color of the text, as well as setting the text that you want to display and how fast it should scroll. The *Move* CD provides a lot of fonts to choose from, and if you don't like the font sizes listed, you can type in one of your own.

The first thing you want to do is pick the color of your text, so start by clicking the red bar. This opens the Select Color window shown in Figure 8-4. This window appears all the time when you are picking colors in KDE, so you might want to take this opportunity to familiarize yourself with it; you'll probably find it much better than the limited color selector available in some Windows programs. My favorite feature is the icon that looks like a medicine dropper. To see how this works, click on the icon and notice that your cursor changes to a crosshair. Position the crosshair over a color on your desktop that you like, such as a spot of color in your background image or an icon on the kicker. When you click your mouse, the color window captures the color you clicked on and makes it the selected color in the window. Click OK to accept this new color choice. By using colors common to other elements in your desktop, you can create a pleasing color scheme for all your programs. Later in this chapter you'll have the chance to experiment with this color selection window a little more.

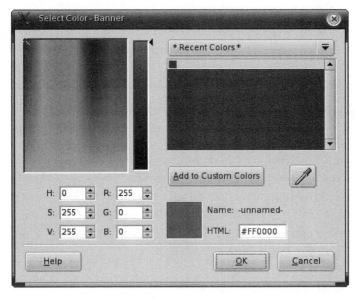

FIGURE 8-4. The Select Color window

Now that you have a color selected, you need to type some text into the Message field. You can also move the slider left or right to adjust the speed at which the text scrolls across the screen. After you've made all of your selections, click OK to apply them and close the window, and click

Test at the bottom of the screen saver list to see the results. If you press any key while the screen saver is running, the test will close and you'll be back at the Screen Saver window.

In the Settings portion of this window, you can do things like disabling the screen saver by unchecking "Start screen saver automatically," or configuring it to run more or less often by changing the time interval. I usually uncheck the "Require password to stop screen save" option so that I don't need to enter a password to get back to work after the screen saver kicks in. If you check the box related to power management, you are telling the screen saver not to run if power management has kicked in. The Priority slider simply tells the screen saver how much of the computer's processing power to use while it's running. Some of the prettiest screen savers, found under the OpenGL grouping, require quite a bit of horsepower to run well.

Securing your desktop

Instead of using a screen saver with a password to secure my machine when I'm away, I use the keyboard shortcut Ctrl-Alt-L.

Customizing the Kicker Panel

Throughout this book, you've been making extensive use of the kicker panel at the bottom of your screen, but I haven't told you much about how you can customize it. Well, you shouldn't be surprised to find out that there is quite a lot you can do with this little panel, so prepare to be amazed. Figure 8-5 shows how I like to configure my kicker. As we explore the options below, I'll point out which ones I used to make my screen look like this.

Location, Location, Location

You can move the kicker panel anywhere you want along the edge of the screen. To do this, just click in the taskbar area and hold down the left mouse button while you move your cursor to another edge of the screen. Once you see an outline of the panel appear on the new edge, release the mouse button, and the kicker will appear in the new location.

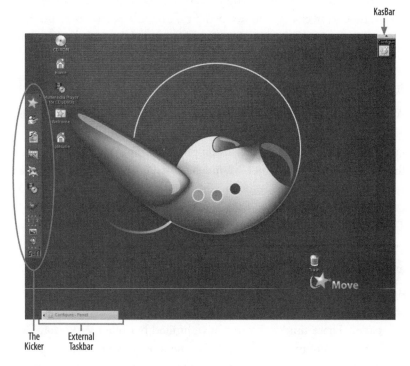

KasBar

The
Kicker

External
Taskbar

FIGURE 8-5. My desktop after customizations to the kicker panel, taskbar, and KasBar

My preference is to put the kicker along the left side of the screen. I think it has to do with reading things left to right, so I consider the left side of the screen the location where I start new things, like launching a program.

On the edge of the kicker, near the clock, you'll see a small rectangle with a triangle in its center. When you click this, the whole panel slides away and hides. Click the button again to bring it back. The speed at which the panel hides itself can also be controlled, which I'll show you how to do in a minute.

If you don't like the positions of the various elements on the panel, you can move them around very easily by right-clicking on an icon and choosing Move to move it along the panel and drop it in a new location. Alternately, you can simply left-click and drag an icon to a new location. To move applets on the panel such as the clock or the virtual desktop pager, you need to click on the small bar next to the element that contains a dot and a triangle (let's call it a handle) and drag that to the new location. You'll know you're clicking the right part of the applet when the cursor changes to a crosshair. A handle is always to the left of the applet it controls (or above it if you've moved the kicker to the left or right edge).

Adding More Items to the Kicker

As I mentioned in Chapter 1, you can create quick-launch icons by dragging program icons from your K Menu and dropping them onto the kicker panel. Another way to accomplish the same task is to right-click the K Menu, choose Panel Menu → Add → Application Button, and select the program you want to add from the menu that appears. You can also choose to add the entire menu or submenu by selecting the Add This Menu choice at the top of each menu listing.

There are several other items on the Add menu, including Applet, Panel, and Special Button. Let's take a look at these options:

Applet

> Applets are mini-programs that can be embedded in the kicker panel. These mini-programs have limited but often very useful functions. Two of my favorites are the Dictionary, which is a simple field that lets you query the *kdict* dictionary program, and the Klipper, a tool that remembers text you have previously copied. Click on the Klipper icon to choose from a number of past "copies" and select them for reuse. This is much better than the Windows clipboard, which limits you to only one item. To remove an applet, right-click on its handle and choose Remove. Most applets also have configuration options on this same menu.

Panel

> The kicker is actually a parent program that holds several panels. And a panel's purpose is to show running programs, hold icons to launch new programs, or act as a container for other applets. I like to place an External Taskbar along the bottom of the screen, and remove the taskbar that is already inside the kicker. You can move the External Taskbar by grabbing its hide button and dragging it to a new location. My wife likes to use the KasBar because it shows small representations of her running programs. When I use the KasBar I place it along the right side of the screen.

Don't mind the mess...

If you've been following along and selecting the same options that I use, your screen probably looks pretty odd right now. Don't worry—as you complete the steps in the next section, everything will start to clean up.

Special Button

The choices in this menu add special function buttons to your kicker. Some of them, like Desktop Access and K Menu, are on your kicker by default. I like to add multiple Quick Browser buttons, which I configure to point to various directories. This creates a quick-access menu to the files in those folders so that I can load them with just a single mouse click.

Configuring the Kicker

It's now time to perform some serious customization of your kicker panel. This is where you'll discover just how customizable some parts of KDE can be. To begin, right-click on the kicker and choose Configure Panel from the menu. This will launch a new window with a lot of options, as shown in Figure 8-6. If you didn't add the External Taskbar and KasBar panels, as I suggest in the previous section's discussion on Panels, your Configure Panel window will look slightly different.

Like other configuration windows, the icons on the left side determine the available options on the right. For now, we're going to ignore the Taskbar icon and focus only on the Layout.

I have three items in my panel list: Main Panel, External Taskbar, and KasBar. The options for each panel are divided into several tabs and apply only to the active item in the list. Let's go through these tabs one by one.

The Arrangement tab

The Arrangement tab is pictured in Figure 8-6. The Position section allows you to place the panel in one of nine positions around the edge of your screen. This accomplishes the same thing as dragging the panel to a new location. The Length section lets you specify how much space the panel should take up and whether it should get larger as more items are added to it, and the Size section lets you specify how "thick" the panel is. The Screen section on the far right gives a preview of how your choices will affect the selected panel.

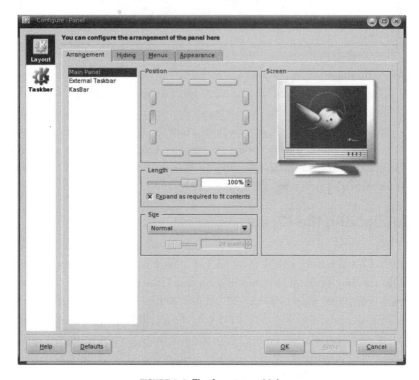

FIGURE 8-6. The Arrangement tab

Let's start with the Main Panel, since it should already be the active item. To position your Main Panel the same way I have it, click the center screen position on the lefthand side and choose a length of 50%. To make the Main Panel icons a bit larger than the default set up in *Move*, choose a size of Normal. As always, click Apply for your changes to take effect.

Now, click the External Taskbar entry. To duplicate my setup, select the leftmost of the positions along the bottom of the screen, a length of just 15%, and a size of Tiny. Click Apply to see the results of these changes.

Finally, click the KasBar entry, put it in the top position on the right side, and give it a length of just 1%. This reduces it down just to the hide button when you don't have any applications open, but it will grow as you open more programs. Once again, click Apply.

Supersize it

If the box "Expand as required to fit contents" is unchecked, your External Taskbar and KasBar will get filled up very quickly with program icons and become pretty much unusable.

Your screen should now look considerably cleaner, but there is still much to be done–after all, there are three other tabs to explore in the Configure Panel window. The last two, Menus and Appearance, only apply to the Main Panel and the K Menu.

Don't lose your changes

Once you start making changes to your kicker, avoid clicking on the Defaults button in the Configure Panel window. The Defaults button will reset everything pertaining to the active panel back to the default, not just the settings on the current screen. Of course, if you mess things up beyond recognition, the Defaults button is a good way to get back to square one.

The Hiding tab

The settings in the Hiding tab affect how various panels can be hidden (see Figure 8-7). I'm not a big fan of hiding panels, so I usually disable all these settings. However, many people like the extra screen space they can get by hiding some of these elements automatically, so I'll show you how to do that. Just like on the Arrangement tab, you have to select a panel from the list on the left to change its settings. Here's how to hide something automatically, using the Main Panel as an example:

1. On the Hiding tab, click on the Main Panel to make it active.

2. Click the radio button for "Hide automatically" and choose a delay time, which specifies how long the panel should wait to hide after your cursor is no longer over the panel.

3. Uncheck the box next to "Show bottom panel-hiding button."

4. Use the slider to modify the panel hiding speed. I slide it to "Fast," all the way on the right. If you want hiding to be instantaneous, uncheck the box next to "Animate panel hiding."

5. Click Apply to apply your changes to the panel.

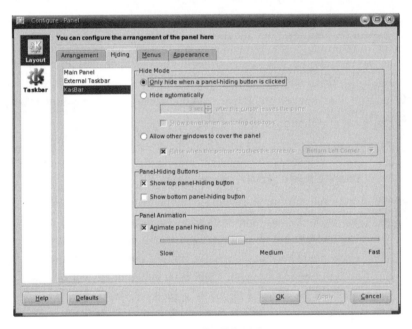

FIGURE 8-7. The Hiding tab

Your Main Panel will hide itself a few seconds after you click Apply. To get it back, move your mouse to the edge of the screen where the panel was, and the panel will appear. You can now select an item from the panel, move your mouse away, and the panel will hide again. Repeat this process to customize hiding behavior for your other panels.

The Menus tab

The Menus tab normally allows you to change the appearance of the K Menu and the items on it. Because of the way the *Move* CD is built, though, you can't actually configure any of the menus right now, so I won't cover these options.

The only thing I usually do on this tab is set the "Maximum number of entries" in the QuickStart Menu Items to 0. Doing this means that the programs I run will not show up at the top of my K Menu list in the Most Used Applications area. I don't find having program launchers in this part of the K Menu useful. If I run a program often, I just put an icon for it on my kicker so that I don't need to go hunting for it or hope that it shows up as a Most Used Application. This way, I don't clutter up the K Menu with the Most Used Applications area.

The Appearance tab

The Appearance tab is where you can put the final tweaks on the appearance of the Main Panel (see Figure 8-8). In the General section, you can specify whether icons on the kicker should grow larger when you hover your mouse over them (similar to the effect you see on the Mac OS X Dock, but not as nice) and whether icons should show a tooltip. Since I'm an experienced KDE user, I don't usually need tooltips, but you might want to keep them on for a while.

The Button Backgrounds section lets you specify a background look to your panel icons. I don't find the effect of multiple colors on my panel very appealing, so I always turn off all background effects.

My favorite part of this tab is the Panel Background section. Here, you can pick an image to display behind your panel icons. Any image with a gradient to it is usually quite nice, especially when you check the box "Colorize to match the desktop color scheme." Using this option really makes the panel seem to "belong" with the rest of the desktop. Another cool trick is to make your panel transparent by checking the box "Enable transparency"; in my opinion, this is even better than using a background image. Your Main Panel icons will now appear to float on top of your desktop.

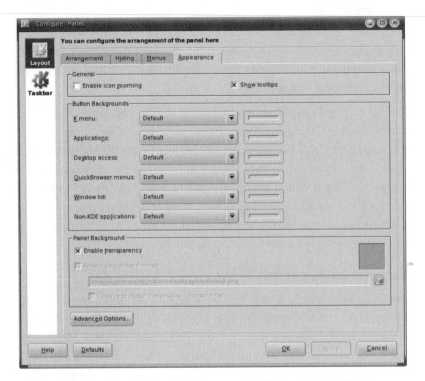

FIGURE 8-8. The settings on the Appearance tab affect only the Main Panel

I actually find 100% transparency to be a little bit disconcerting, but it's easy to change it to something a little more opaque. Click on the Advanced Options button and, in the window that appears, adjust the slider to the right and click Apply. Keep making adjustments until you get to a tint level you like. You can also select a color for the tint by clicking the Tint color bar. The transparency effect isn't complete until you make your virtual desktop pager transparent. To do this, right-click on its handle and choose Pager Menu → Show → Transparent.

External Taskbar

There are a few final tweaks you can make to your External Taskbar. Click the Taskbar icon in the Configure Panel window, or right-click the hide button of the taskbar and choose Configure Taskbar, to display the configuration window shown in Figure 8-9.

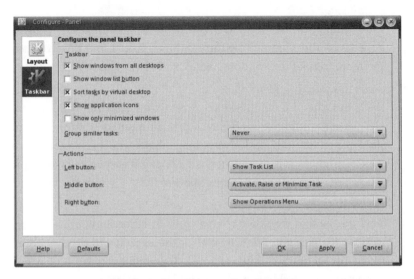

FIGURE 8-9. The taskbar configuration window

The taskbar displays a number of options; from top to bottom, they are:

Show windows from all desktops

> With this option checked, the taskbar displays icons for windows running on any desktop. When it is not checked, the taskbar shows only programs running on the current desktop. I always leave this option checked.

Show window list button

> With this checked, a small, rectangular button appears on the taskbar next to the hide button. You can click on this button to see a list of open windows and which desktop they are on. I don't find this information useful, so I always leave this option unchecked.

Sort tasks by virtual desktop

> With this checked, programs are grouped on the taskbar according to which desktop they run on. Items running on Desktop 1 appear first, followed by items on Desktop 2, and so on. Within a desktop, icons appear based upon which program was launched first. If this option isn't checked, program icons appear in the order that they were launched, regardless of which desktop they're running on. I always leave this box checked because doing so means the programs I run all the time will almost always appear on the same place on the taskbar. This is because I always run specific programs on each desktop, and usually only one or two programs per desktop.

Show application icons

This simply means that a small icon representing the program appears on the window's button on the toolbar. I find this breaks up the monotony of the window names, so I always leave it checked.

Show only minimized windows

With this checked, the taskbar shows icons only for windows that are currently minimized. That means an opened window will not show up on the taskbar. I always leave this unchecked so that all my windows have icons on the taskbar, making it easy to see which programs are running on different desktops.

Group similar tasks

This means that windows related to each other show up as a single icon on the taskbar. When you click the icon, it will display a small menu of windows to choose from. Using this feature is a way to unclutter your taskbar, and it's similar to a feature introduced in Windows XP. You can test it out by setting the drop-down list to Always, clicking Apply, and then launching several instances of KWrite. I always set this drop-down to Never, because I find the grouping disruptive to my work habits, but I admittedly didn't give the feature much of a chance to grow on me.

The Actions section controls what your mouse buttons do when a button is clicked on an empty area of the taskbar. There are a lot of options to choose from, so it's probably easiest just to try out the different settings using one mouse button, see if you like what any of them offer, and choose which button should use which setting. Personally, though, I'm just fine with the defaults.

KasBar

The final thing we'll configure here is the KasBar. This program really just duplicates the function of a taskbar, but it does so in such a cool way I would be remiss not to tell you about it.

Right-click on the KasBar's hide button and choose Configure Kasbar to bring up its very limited configuration window. There are two changes I think you should make. First, click on the Thumbnails icon and drag the Thumbnail-size slider about three quarters of the way to the right. Then click on the Behavior icon and uncheck the box next to Group Windows. Click OK to close the window.

Now the fun begins. Open up Konqueror and go to a web page, and then launch some other program. The KasBar now shows two icons that represent your running programs. Place your mouse over one of the icons, and a small "thumbnail" of the window of that program will magically pop up (see Figure 8-10). Cool, huh? This feature makes it easy to keep track of multiple open documents (very important when you're a book editor).

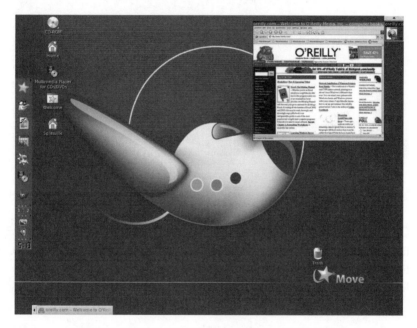

FIGURE 8-10. A thumbnail of a web page displayed in the KasBar

Changing the Look of KDE

The KDE Control Center is the granddaddy of configuration programs in KDE and contains hundreds of settings to control your environment. Click K Menu → Administer your system → Configure your desktop to get to the main window (Figure 8-11). As you can see from the list of icons on the lefthand side of this window, there are an awful lot of options to configure. We'll cover only the LookNFeel section here, but feel free to poke through all the other options. I would recommend, however, that you do this *without* the USB memory key. That way, if you mess something up, you can just reboot to get back to your normal settings.

FIGURE 8-11. The KDE Control Center with the LookNFeel grouping expanded

Click once on the LookNFeel item to expand the grouping. There are fifteen items here, but we've already covered six of them in earlier sections. Here are brief descriptions of how to use the nine options that we haven't gotten to yet:

Colors

Set the colors used by the windows, menus, and widgets in KDE. ("Widget" is just a term used to describe things like buttons, scrollbars, checkboxes, and other standard elements of the GUI.)

Fonts

Quickly choose which fonts and font sizes to use for toolbars, menus, and icons.

Icons

Select the icon set you want to use. An icon set is a group of icons that share a common look. By choosing a new icon set, you can quickly change the look of all the icons on your desktop and in program toolbars.

Launch Feedback

Control the type of notification you receive while a program is loading. The Busy Cursor selection lets you choose whether your regular mouse cursor should indicate that a program is loading. The taskbar notification controls whether there should be any indication that a program is loading on the taskbar.

Splash Screen

Determine what your login screen looks like. Simply select a screen from the list and click Apply. Click Test to see a simulation of what the screen looks like while loading.

Style

Set the shape and size of buttons, scrollbars, tabs, lists, and checkboxes. (A style defines the way widgets look.) Styles can enable effects like transparency and fade for menus.

System Notifications

Determine how your programs will notify you of events. This is similar to the settings you configured for KMail in Chapter 6 (and those settings are here as well).

Window Behavior

Control how your windows behave under all sorts of different conditions. Among other things, you can define what happens when you double-click the titlebar of a window, how windows position themselves on-screen, and whether or not you can drag a window off one desktop and onto another. There are dozens of settings in this screen.

Window Decorations

Control how the decorative frame of a window looks; i.e., the size and shape of the titlebar; the icons to minimize, maximize, and close windows; and the appearance of the window's border.

Now let's look at some of these configuration panels in more detail. The Launch Feedback and Splash Screen panels are fairly simple, so I won't go into more detail about them or the System Notifications panel here. I will, however, cover the other panels.

Colors

The Colors configuration panel is divided into three sections (see Figure 8-12). The top part of the panel shows you various GUI elements and how they appear using a specific color scheme. The list on the left lets you choose a color scheme, and the Widget Color section on the right allows you to change the color of specific widgets. These tools give you everything you need to create your own color scheme.

FIGURE 8-12. The Colors configuration panel

First, choose a color scheme in the Color Scheme list. Try to pick a color scheme that's a big contrast with the current theme so that you can clearly see the difference between them. Dark Blue is a good choice. You can also use the Contrast slider bar in the lower right to modify the contrast for any color scheme you choose. Note how the top view changes to reflect your new colors, and click Apply to see the color scheme applied to all of your windows. To change back to the default Move colors, select the Galaxy color scheme.

Next, choose a widget from the drop-down list in the Widget Color section and click on the color bar to select a new color for the widget. The color bar opens a color selector window just like the one described in the

"Screen Savers" section earlier in this chapter. Once again, as you select new colors for each widget, the view at the top changes. Once you're satisfied with your colors, click Apply to see them on your desktop. If you *really* like what you see, you should save it as a new color scheme. To do this, click the Save Scheme button and give the new scheme a name.

The checkbox at the very bottom of the Colors screen allows you to apply your color choices to non-KDE applications. However, Linux is made up of a lot of independent programs, and not all of them adhere to the suggestions made by the desktop environment. Checking this box means that KDE will attempt to change the colors of those programs that do listen to suggestions (which should include all the KDE applications), but there's no guarantee that you'll get a unified look.

Fonts

The choices you make in the Font panel affect the look of the entire KDE desktop. Choosing fonts here is just like choosing fonts in other applications. Simply click on the Choose button to select the group you want to change, and select a font, style, and size in the window that appears.

The Adjust All Fonts button is a little more interesting. It opens a Select Font window similar to what the Choose button brings up, but the difference is that you have to enable a particular list before you can change it (Figure 8-13). This makes it easy to change only the font size for all fonts, for example, or only the font family.

You probably won't see a lot of font names that you recognize in these lists. Fonts need to be licensed from their creators, and few Linux vendors are willing to pay the fees necessary to include commercial fonts in their software. They also wouldn't be allowed to distribute their software at no cost over the Internet if they included licensed fonts. Instead, most distributions do what Mandrake has done with the *Move* CD, which is to include a lot of community-developed, free fonts. Some of these fonts are quite nice, but others leave something to be desired. My personal favorites are the Bitstream fonts, which used to be commercial but were donated to the open source community by the company that created them.

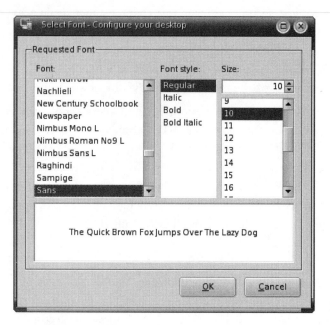

FIGURE 8-13. The standard KDE font selection window

At the bottom of the Font Configuration panel are some options that control anti-aliasing of your fonts. Anti-aliasing is a technique to remove the jaggedness of fonts. The side effect is that at small sizes, some fonts look a little blurry. You can use the options in this screen to turn anti-aliasing on or off, and specify if some font sizes should not be affected. The sub-pixel hinting options may improve the quality of font display on LCD monitors and laptops. You have to restart KDE for changes to anti-aliasing to take effect.

Icons

The icons you've been using in *Move* are from the default KDE icon set known as Crystal SVG. KDE icon sets can contain anywhere from a few to several hundred icons in various sizes. You can easily change icon sets by clicking on the set's name in the Icon screen and clicking Apply. Just for fun, click on "Kids beta1" and click Apply. Now look at your desktop and notice how different the icons for your CD-ROM drive and Trash look. Not all the icons have been changed, however, because the Kids theme doesn't include all the fonts necessary to replace the Crystal SVG icon set.

When you install Linux on your hard drive, you can also install more Icons themes. The "Eye Candy on the Web" section at the end of this chapter tells you where you can find these.

Style

Your choice of style affects the look of most of the widgets you see on the screen. The Preview section of the Style configuration window (shown in Figure 8-14) shows you which elements of the GUI are affected by your style choice. Each time you select a style from the drop-down list, the Preview pane changes to show you how it will look. The default style on the *Move* CD is called Thememdk.

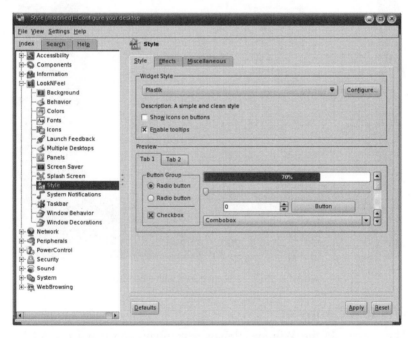

FIGURE 8-14. The Preview section of the Style configuration panel

Let's now test out a couple of the features that are unique to some of the styles. Switch to the style called Plastik, and once it's loaded, click on the Effects tab. On this tab, you can specify which features of a style you want to use. Not all styles have all features, so you may not see any change, or you may be told that the feature is not supported. One feature that is supported by Plastik, and is enabled by default, is the Make Translucent option for the Menus. Click on the K Menu and notice how you can now see through the menu. The slider at the bottom of the Effects tab controls the opacity of the menus. Don't make them too translucent, or you'll have a hard time reading the menu text.

Another nice effect to enable is the Menu drop shadow. This adds a small shadow to each of your menus, giving them a slight 3D effect. Figure 8-15 shows you how these two effects look when applied to the Plastik theme. Note that you can read the Style tab label through the menu I've expanded in the upper-left corner.

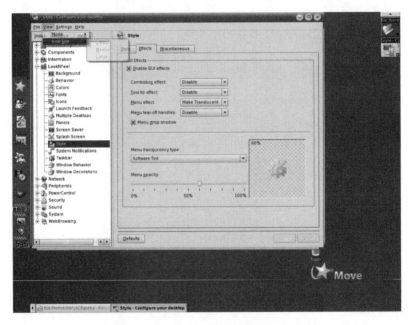

FIGURE 8-15. Translucent menus with drop shadows

Window Behavior

The options in the Window Behavior configuration panel control how windows behave when you click and drag them. As you can see in Figure 8-16, there are a lot of options available here, and the best way to learn about them is to experiment. I'll just point out a few of the most interesting ones in this section.

You might recall from Chapter 1 that if you double-click on a window's titlebar, the window rolls up into it. This is called "shading" the window (like a windowshade), and is a quick and easy way to get a window out of the way without minimizing it. To enable a useful addition to this feature,

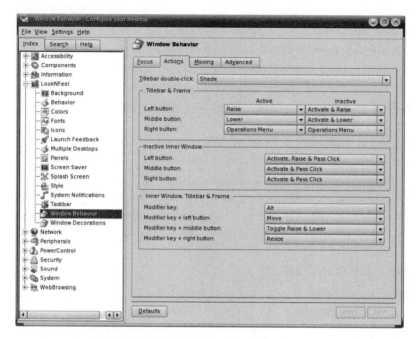

FIGURE 8-16. The Window Behavior configuration screen

go to the Advanced tab, check the box "Enable hover," and then click Apply. Now, double-click the titlebar for the Control Center window; when the window rolls up, move your mouse off the titlebar and then back onto it. The window unrolls for you automatically; when you move your mouse away from the window, the window rolls back up. This is a great way to manage an application that you use occasionally but that you don't want hanging around when you aren't using it. I use this feature all the time for the dictionary program *kdict*. I keep it shaded just behind my main writing window and slightly above my current titlebar, so that I can easily get to it whenever I need it. Double-click the titlebar to make a shaded window behave like a normal window.

Another feature you might want to enable is the ability to drag a window from one desktop to another. To do this, check the box "Only when moving windows" on the Advanced tab and click Apply. Now drag the Control Center window to the right edge of the screen, and keep dragging. After a slight pause (which is controlled by the "Desktop switch delay" slider), the window will move to Desktop 2. This can be a very convenient way to place windows on different desktops.

Finally, I like to disable a couple of options that affect KDE's performance, particularly on computers with slow processors. On the Moving tab, you'll see two options: "Display content in moving windows" and "Display content in resizing windows." Before you disable these choices, try a little test on your computer. Drag the Control Center window around on your screen and notice how you can see everything in the window as you move it around. The same is true when you grab the edge of a window and resize it. Now, uncheck the two display options and click Apply. When you move the Control Center window now, you're moving only the outline of the window—the original window stays in place until you release the mouse button. The nice thing about moving a window this way is that it eliminates the jaggedness you see when you move a window with the default setting.

Window Decorations

I explained earlier how styles can change the look of widgets inside a window. Window decorations, on the other hand, change the look of widgets on the *edge* of a window. Making a decoration change is as simple as selecting a new decoration from the drop-down list in the Window Decorations panel. As you can see in Figure 8-17, the default decoration is Galaxy 2, which was developed by Mandrake and is used in the *Move* CD. People usually match their window decorations to their style, but not always. For the past year or so I've been using the Plastik style and window decoration. When you select a new decoration, the preview image shows you what your selection will look like. As always, click Apply to make the actual change.

The Buttons tab lets you control the placement of the buttons in the titlebar. Not all window decorations allow you to move the buttons—the only way to know for sure is to try it out. Check the box "Use custom titlebar button positions," and then start dragging buttons around in the preview image below the checkbox. If you don't want a button to appear, just drag it off the titlebar completely. Click Apply to finalize your changes.

Creating Keyboard Shortcuts

Using the keyboard is often the fastest way to perform a function, and throughout this book I've made a point of showing you as many keyboard shortcuts as possible. The more familiar you are with shortcuts, the more you'll use them and the more efficiently you can get things done.

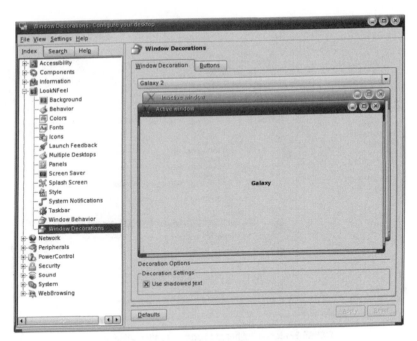

FIGURE 8-17. The Window Decoration selection screen

You can modify some of the keyboard shortcuts used by KDE, as well as assign new shortcuts of your own to launch and control programs. To modify and create shortcuts, click Accessibility → Keyboard Shortcuts in the KDE Control Center. This opens the Keyboard Shortcuts control panel, shown in Figure 8-18.

As you can see, this panel has three tabs along the top. The Shortcut Schemes tab allows you to control the keyboard shortcuts used by the KDE desktop. The Command Shortcuts tab allows you to add shortcuts to programs in the K Menu so you can launch them with just a keystroke. And the Modifier Keys tab tells you which keys map to which internal X Windows function. This is for informational purposes only, and you needn't worry about it.

If you go to the Shortcut Schemes tab, you'll see a long list of actions you can modify and the keyboard shortcut that performs each action. As you can see, most actions don't have shortcuts assigned to them, so we'll have ample opportunity to create them.

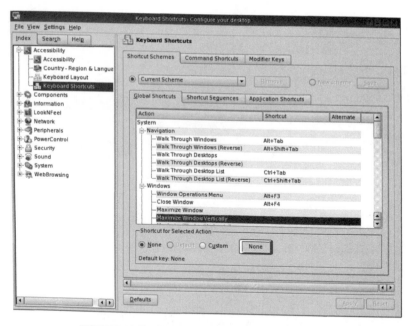

FIGURE 8-18. The Keyboard Shortcuts configuration screen

Let's modify a function that I find somewhat useful: Maximize a Window Vertically. To assign a shortcut to this function, click on the action in the list and click on the None button in the section below. This opens a small window in which you can "type" the shortcut you want to use. We want to assign Alt-Shift-M to the action; to do this, hold all three keys down at the same time, starting with Alt, then Shift, and finally M. When you release the keys, the window disappears and you're back at the configuration window, where the new keyboard shortcut should now appear in the Shortcut column. Press Apply to make KDE aware of your change.

Now let's see if it works. First, make sure the Control Center window is active and smaller than the screen. Then press Alt-Shift-M. Voila! The Control Center window should stretch to its full height.

Nothing happening?

Only the left Alt key works for these keyboard shortcuts. Using the right Alt key has no effect.

You can modify an existing keyboard shortcut by performing the exact same steps. You can remove a keyboard shortcut by clicking on the action, clicking the None radio button, and clicking Apply. You can modify more actions on the Shortcut Sequences tab, and you can also save your changes as a new scheme. (The Save button becomes active after you've made at least one modification.)

The Command Shortcuts tab lets you specify keyboard commands to launch programs in the K Menu in the same way you did in the Shortcut Schemes tab. Simply expand the groups in the Command column, select the item you want to create a shortcut for, and click None to open the window where you can type your shortcut. When you're finished, click Apply to make KDE aware of your new command.

Avoiding conflicts

Be careful when assigning shortcuts—you don't want to create a KDE shortcut that conflicts with a keyboard shortcut that's already in the program. For example, if you assign the shortcut Ctrl-Shift-N to launch Konqueror, you won't be able to use that shortcut to open a new tab in Konqueror (as you normally would).

Eye Candy on the Web

Eye candy is a term that computer geeks use for all the gee-whiz, pretty features of a software program that don't serve any useful purpose beyond making things look cool. Transparent kickers, fading menus, pretty icons, and wacky window decorations are all eye candy.

KDE is known for its eye candy, and I must admit, it's much of the reason I like it so much. Others in the Linux community feel the same way, which is why an entire web site, *http://www.kde-look.org*, has been created just to provide eye candy for KDE. This site has it all: wallpapers, styles, window decorations, icons, sounds, screen savers, and even add-on programs that enhance KDE in significant ways. All these things have been donated by users from around the world who are eager to show off their artistic skills or who just want to enhance KDE in whatever small way that they can.

Although you can't really do anything with the items on this site while using the *Move* CD (because you can't write any files to the CD), you can make use of them once you install Linux on your hard drive. In the meantime, browse around and look at the various contributions. Nearly every item comes with a screenshot showing you how your desktop will look if you use it. Take some time to browse the Screenshots section to see how people have put together all the different pieces of eye candy to create something truly unique.

9

+

!

A
FREE
OFFICE
SUITE

Have you ever purchased car accessories from a dealership? If so, you know that these can be some of the most expensive items you ever get for your car. Floor mats can cost several hundred dollars, a rear spoiler on your trunk close to a thousand, and a stereo system can run from a few hundred to more than a thousand, depending upon its features.

What some people don't realize is that they can get the same accessories elsewhere, for far less money. Those floor mats will cost only $30 or so from an AutoZone. An aftermarket rear spoiler, painted to match your car's color, is half the price you'd get from the dealership. And as for the stereo, you can get better quality and brand selection from Circuit City or Best Buy at a fraction of the cost.

As you might guess, the same is true in the world of computers. Just like with cars, there are alternatives to purchasing from the computer dealer. For example, you can buy your memory from a third party such as Crucial (*http://www.crucial.com*) and get a low-priced, high-quality product. But what's the alternative to the ubiquitous Microsoft Office suite that comes with so many new computers?

The answer is the OpenOffice.org office program. This office suite is entirely free, both in price and in the openness of its code. You can use it right now on the *Move* CD, or download it from *http://www.openoffice.org* for use on another computer. It runs on Windows, Linux, Mac OS X, and Solaris (a Unix operating system). It may have a strange name, but that doesn't mean it isn't a very capable office suite. It can even open Microsoft Word, Excel, and PowerPoint documents, and save back as those formats.

An odd name

OpenOffice.org sounds more like a web site than an office suite–and actually, it's both. The reason it isn't just called OpenOffice is that some other company already claimed that name. By the time the OpenOffice.org people realized that, everyone was used to the name, and the project didn't want to switch. You will often see the name abbreviated as OOo.

The OpenOffice.org Office Suite

Just a few years ago, OpenOffice.org wasn't free at all. It was a product called StarOffice, sold by a German company called StarDivision. The big Unix company Sun Microsystems bought the code for StarOffice in 1999, and some time afterward they open-sourced as much of it as they could and named the resulting project OpenOffice.org. (Sun continues to sell a version of OpenOffice.org called StarOffice, which is basically OpenOffice.org plus some pieces that couldn't be open-sourced—some fonts, a database component, some templates, and a lot of clip art.)

OpenOffice.org contains several programs that are similar to the applications in Microsoft Office. Although it lacks a personal information component like Microsoft Outlook (see Chapter 6 for a discussion of Kontact, an alternative open source program), it has pretty much everything else in the standard Microsoft Office Suite, in addition to a few unique features of its own. The programs in OpenOffice.org are:

Writer

Writer is a word processing program that you can use to create all kinds of documents, from simple letters and resumes to complex documents such as books or a college thesis. Writer also includes a component that lets you create web pages of mid-level complexity.

Calc

The Calc spreadsheet program is a very capable replacement for Excel. It supports hundreds of functions to perform complex calculations, charting, and integration with outside data sources. However, note that although Calc has its own macro language, it cannot run Excel macros.

Impress

Impress allows you to create presentations in a similar manner to PowerPoint. It lacks PowerPoint's diversity of effects, but it is still capable of creating very nice presentations. One useful feature is that you can save presentations to a Flash file, which lets you easily put your presentations on the Web.

Draw

The Draw program is a handy tool to manipulate images or create artwork. Its capabilities fall somewhere between those of Paint and Photoshop, and it makes a nice complement to the GIMP, a photo editing program covered in Chapter 7. If you like using WordArt in Word, you'll love this program.

Math

The Math component of OpenOffice.org ties in with the other programs, particularly Writer, and allows you to display complex mathematical formulas, which makes it useful when writing scientific or engineering papers.

This chapter covers only Writer and Calc, the two most commonly used components in OpenOffice.org. But these are big, feature-rich programs, and though I'll provide an overview that should answer all your basic questions, you may well want to research them further after reading this chapter. For more information about Writer, check out *OpenOffice.org Writer: The Free Alternative to Microsoft Word* (O'Reilly). For more information about the entire office suite, pick up a copy of *The OpenOffice.org Resource Kit* (Prentice Hall).

Give it away

If you download a copy of OpenOffice.org to use on your Windows or Linux computer, feel free to make copies for your friends. It's perfectly legal to make a hundred copies and give them away to whoever you want. You could install copies on every machine in your office and never have to pay a dime. (But of course, you'll want to make sure your system administrator is okay with that.)

Writer Basics

In most ways, you'll find that Writer operates a lot like Microsoft Word. It has many of the same features; they're just in different places. This section will familiarize you with the basics of Writer.

You can launch Writer by clicking K Menu → Use office tools → Create a text document. Be prepared for a wait—Writer takes a long time to open not only when it's launched from a live CD, but it takes about 10 seconds even when it is installed to your hard drive. Happily, though, load times are improving with each new release.

When Writer comes up, you'll see a window that looks a lot like Word: menus along the top, icon bar just below that, and a large space just waiting for you to start typing.

Open and Save Files

To open a file, select File → Open or use the keyboard shortcut Ctrl-O. In the Open window, browse through the filesystem, select the desired file, and click the Open button. This browse dialog is similar to what you see in KDE applications, but not identical. This is because OpenOffice. org is not a KDE application, and therefore doesn't use KDE's built-in methods to open and save files.

To save a document, just select File → Save or use the keyboard shortcut Ctrl-S. If it's a new document, Writer asks where you want to save the file. If it's an existing document, Writer just saves on top of the previous version.

If you want to put the file in a different directory or change the filename or file type, select File → Save As. Make the appropriate selections in the Save As window and click the Save button. You can save a document in Microsoft Word format by simply choosing Microsoft Word from the "Save as type" drop-down list before you click Save.

Scary warnings

If you save a document in MS Word format and then close Writer, you will get a warning that "Saving in external formats may have caused information loss." Don't worry about this too much. If anything is lost, it will just be some formatting, not actual text. This warning is really just a last chance to also save the document as an OpenOffice.org document.

Compare Features of Writer and Word

One of the most common complaints lodged by new OpenOffice.org users—or by people trying to delay a forced migration to a new OpenOffice.org—is, "It doesn't have my favorite feature. It's missing the one thing I need to get my work done!"

But the truth is that Writer has most of the features offered by Microsoft Word. Not only that, it has a few significant features that Word lacks and that make Writer more suitable than Word for large and multi-chapter documents. However, the problem is that corresponding features may be located in a different place or labeled under a different name than in MS Word, so you might just need a little help to find your favorite feature.

Table 9-1 familiarizes you with the new terminology and layout of Writer.

TABLE 9-1. Feature comparison of Word and Writer

Feature name	Word 2000	Writer
AutoCorrect	Tools → Autocorrect	Tools → AutoCorrect/Auto-Format
AutoNumbering	Format → Bullets and Numbering	Format → Numbering/Bullets...
Compare Documents	Tools → Track Changes → Compare Documents	Edit → Compare Document...
Envelope	Tools → Envelopes and Labels	Insert → Envelope...
Go To	Edit → Go To	Edit → Navigator
Header and Footer	View → Header and Footer	Insert → Header → Default Insert → Footer → Default
Insert Clip Art	Insert → Pictures → Clip Art	Tools → Gallery
Labels (create)	Tools → Envelopes and Labels	File → New → Labels
Master Document	View → Outline	File → New → Master Document File → Send → Create Master Document
Mail Merge	Tools → Mail Merge	Tools → Mail Merge View → Data Sources
Page Numbers	Insert → Page Numbers	Insert → Fields → Page Number
Record Macro	Tools → Macros → Record New Macro	Tools → Macros → Record Macro
Styles	Format → Styles	Format → Styles → Catalog Format → Styles → Load Format → Stylist
Table (insert)	Table → Insert → Table	Format → Autoformat... Insert → Table
Track Changes	Tools → Track Changes	Edit → Changes → chk 'Record,' chk 'Show'
Word Count	Tools → Word Count	File → Properties → Statistics

Writer's Toolbars

The important toolbars in Writer are the Main Menu, the Function Bar, the Object Bar, and the Main Toolbar. Figure 9-1 shows the main Writer window with the various toolbars labeled.

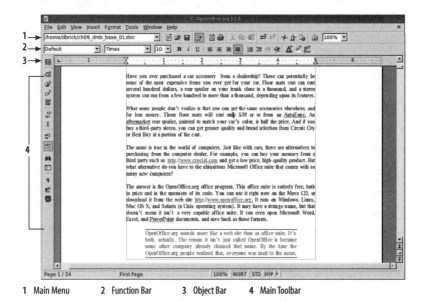

| 1 Main Menu | 2 Function Bar | 3 Object Bar | 4 Main Toolbar |

FIGURE 9-1. The Writer toolbars

Main Menu

Contains the File, Edit, View, Insert, Format, Tools, Window, and Help menus. You can also view each menu by pressing the Alt key along with the first letter of the menu name (Alt-F for the File menu, for instance).

Function Bar

Contains the Open a Recent Document drop-down menu, the Open New Document, Open File, Save Document, Edit File, Export to PDF, and Print File icons, and other handy icons for one-click execution of common functions.

Object Bar

Contains the Document Styles drop-down menu, the Fonts & Font Size drop-down menus, and options for bold, italic, underline, indents, bullets & numbering, and character coloring.

Main Toolbar

Contains Insert Table, Insert Fields, Insert Objects, Spellcheck, Data Sources, and other tools. This toolbar lies along the left edge of the Writer window.

And these are merely the default toolbars that are visible out of the box. You can display other toolbars by customizing your setup, as described in the following section.

Additional toolbars in Writer include:

- Table Object Bar
- Numbering Object Bar
- Frame Object Bar
- Draw Object Bar
- Control Bar
- Text Object Bar/Graphics
- Bezier Object Bar
- Graphics Object Bar
- Objects
- Text Object Bar/Web
- Frame Object Bar/Web
- Graphics Object Bar/Web
- Object/Web
- User-defined no.1

To hide any of the toolbars (except for the Main Menu), right-click in the empty space within the toolbar and uncheck the toolbar's name. You can also rearrange elements in a toolbar and redesign it to your personal preference by right-clicking in the toolbar and choosing any of the four options in the bottom half of the right-click menu:

Visible Buttons

Check (to display) or uncheck (to hide) specific buttons/icons that appear on that toolbar.

Configure...

Customize and allocate which toolbars are available.

Customize...

Call up the Customize Toolbars dialog, which offers a grand array of buttons to add to any toolbar.

Reset

Restore the default configuration for all toolbars.

Changes made using the first three commands apply only to the specific toolbar on which you right-clicked to call up the context menu.

Document Formatting

When writing documents you often want to use special formatting, such as bold, italic, underlining, special fonts, different font sizes, and indentations. The Object Bar in Writer provides basic character formatting buttons. These buttons can help you execute quick formatting changes with one click.

Figure 9-2 shows the available formatting buttons, which allow you to make fancy changes such as coloring text and creating bulleted or numbered lists. And you can use the B, I, and U buttons to set text as bold, italic, and underlined, respectively. (You can also do this using the familiar keystroke combinations Ctrl-B, Ctrl-I, and Ctrl-U.)

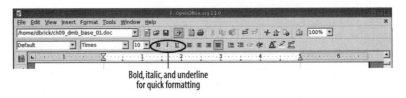

Bold, italic, and underline
for quick formatting

FIGURE 9-2. The formatting buttons on the Object Bar

In Writer, there's no need to highlight a whole word in order to format it. As long as your cursor is somewhere within the word when you apply formatting changes, Writer will change the format of the whole word. This saves extra mouse maneuvers or keystrokes. Direct changes can also be made to sequences of characters or to whole paragraphs:

Character formatting

The Object Bar buttons allow you to make simple formatting changes, but if you have more unusual needs, such as applying advanced font formatting, you'll need to use the Character window. To do this, highlight the character or characters you want to change and go to Format → Character.... You can then make more advanced formatting changes in the Character window.

Paragraph formatting

You can also indent, align, set borders, and manipulate paragraph formats by going to Format → Paragraph.... The Paragraph window is shown in Figure 9-3. If you highlight multiple paragraphs first, changes will be applied to all selected paragraphs; if you don't highlight anything, paragraph changes will affect only the paragraph in which the cursor is currently placed.

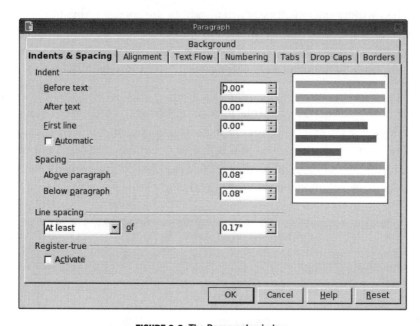

FIGURE 9-3. The Paragraph window

Headers and Footers

Headers and footers are the text or other content that you wish to appear at either the top (header) or bottom (footer) of every page of a document or section.

To insert a header, select Insert → Header → Default. This opens a header frame in the document, where you can type or enter the content that should appear at the top of every page. To insert a footer, select Insert → Footers → Default.

Most documents use headers or footers to display page numbers. To generate automatic page numbers, insert either a header or a footer and click once inside the header or footer frame. Go to Insert → Fields and select Page Number in the drop-down menu. This inserts the page number automatically at the location of the cursor.

You may sometimes want to use page numbering that states both the page number and the total number of pages in the document, giving you a footer that reads "Page 16 of 96," for example. To use this format, place the cursor in the target location in the header or footer and type **Page** followed by a space. Then insert the Page Number as shown previously, type **of** followed by a space, and insert Page Count from the same drop-down menu.

Print Documents

You can print a document in one stroke by simply clicking the printer icon on the Function Bar. It looks just like the print icon in MS Word and most other programs.

You can also print documents from the Print window (Figure 9-4), which you can bring up by selecting File → Print or simply pressing Ctrl-P. Here, you can choose a non-default printer (if one is set up), a limited page range, or the number of copies for your print job.

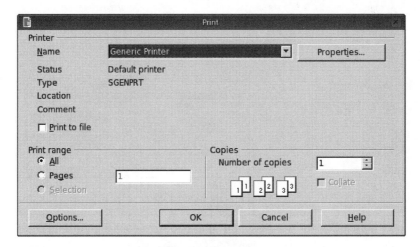

FIGURE 9-4. The Print window

Save or Export to Common File Formats

OpenOffice.org facilitates saving files in several different file types, including some very useful document standards such as PDF. By choosing the format in which you save a document, you can ensure that your work is viewable and editable by people who don't have OpenOffice. org. (Of course, they could always just go and download OpenOffice. org—it *is* free, after all!)

To save your document as a Microsoft Word file, choose File → Save As..., open the File Type drop-down menu, and select the desired MS Office file format version. Choices include:

- Microsoft Word 97/2000/XP (.doc)
- Microsoft Word 95 (.doc)
- Microsoft Word 6.0 (.doc)

To create a PDF of your current document, click the small, red Export to PDF icon on the Function bar. The Export window will open with the file format preselected to Adobe PDF, as shown in Figure 9-5.

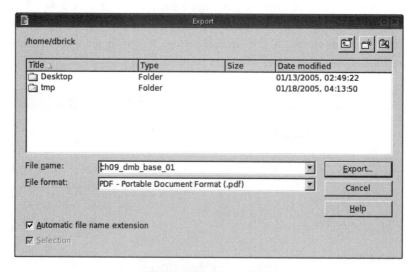

FIGURE 9-5. The Export window

Enter a filename for the new PDF file, choose a folder in which to save it, and press the Export button. You can also bring up the Export window by selecting File → Export as PDF.

Advanced Formatting with Styles

Styles are one of the most powerful and important features of word processing. Using styles, you can create consistency of appearance and formatting in a document or across documents. A style is simply a saved set of formatting choices that you can then apply with just a few mouse clicks. As an example of using styles, imagine that you've created a 100-page document with a lot of headings, and you later decide that you need to make the headings bigger so they will stand out more. If you originally applied your heading font sizes manually, you would need to go through each heading one at a time in order to change its font size. However, if you used a heading *style* to create all your headings, all you'd need to do is change the font size in the style, and all of your headings would update automatically. It's easy to see how this could save you a lot of time and prevent a lot of formatting errors. Styles even make it possible for a group of people to maintain a consistent look in all of their documents, which is useful in a business setting.

The Stylist

In Writer, the interface to the Styles toolset is a floating palette called the *Stylist*. You can open the Stylist by pressing the Stylist on/off button on the Function Bar (the button looks like a page with a tiny hand in the corner). Alternately, you can press the function key F11.

The Stylist lets you toggle among five different style types or categories, each of which applies to a specific type of text or element, as described in the following list:

Paragraph Styles
> Set formatting for a whole paragraph, note, sidebar, list, frame, table, or other collection of set-off text.

Character Styles
> Apply to a word, single character, or selection of characters.

Frame Styles
> Set formatting for frames that might include such content as text, a bulleted list, graphics, charts, or other frames.

Page Styles

Apply an entire set of Styles to a whole page. This is the tool you use to apply style sets to chapters and title pages.

Numbering Styles

Apply a numbering format to numbered lists.

The default state of the Stylist is to open in Paragraph Styles with the Automatic mode, as shown in Figure 9-6. To switch from one style category to another, simply click the corresponding icon at the top left of the Stylist's toolbar.

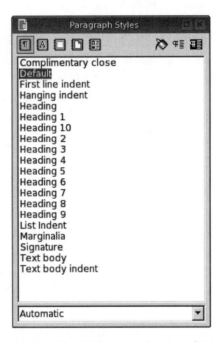

FIGURE 9-6. The Stylist opens to Paragraph Styles

Apply a Character Style

One of the simplest things you can do with the Stylist is apply one of its default character styles. To do this, click on the Character Styles icon at the top of the Stylist (the second icon from the left, showing an A). This reveals all the default character styles available, as shown in Figure 9-7 (the window is in All mode by default).

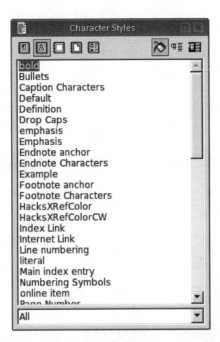

FIGURE 9-7. The Stylist in Character Styles, ready to paint bold

For example, to apply a bold style, highlight the bold character style (at the top of the list by default) with a single click and then click once on the paint-can icon at the top right corner of the Stylist. When you click the paint can, your cursor turns into a little paint-can tool that makes it easy to apply your chosen style with precision. Click on the word you want to set in bold or drag the paint-can cursor across some text. As you can see, the paint can gives you a Midas touch, turning everything you click into bold. You can turn off the style by pressing F11, by clicking on the X icon at the top right of the Stylist box, or by choosing a different style.

Modify Styles

You can also modify the behavior of a built-in style. For instance, if you want list items to be indented differently than the default, you can edit that list style and make it indent all your lists the way you want. Note that when you modify an existing style, it immediately takes effect on all items in the document that are tagged with that style, as well as items you create in the future.

To modify a style, select Format → Styles → Catalog... to bring up the Style Catalog, as shown in Figure 9-8. The Style Catalog displays different styles depending on the style used at the cursor's current location. Highlight the style you want to alter ("Default" in the figure) and click the Modify button on the right side of the window. This opens the Style Settings window for the Default style, as shown in Figure 9-9; here, you can change any characteristic that is available for modification.

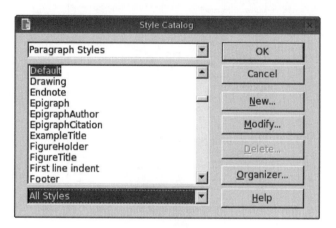

FIGURE 9-8. The Style Catalog

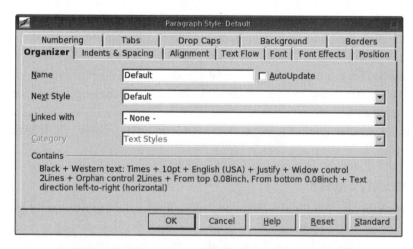

FIGURE 9-9. The Style Settings window for the Default paragraph style

Alternately, you can modify a style by right-clicking on the style in the Stylist and choosing Modify to open the Style Settings window.

Borrow Styling

Writer also makes it easy for you to quickly change an existing Style by applying the format of a selected character, paragraph, or page. To update a particular style, press the function key F11 to open the Stylist and click the icon of the style type you want to update: Paragraph, Character, or Page. Then, click once in the document in the place from which you want to copy/update the style—for example, you may be "borrowing" paragraph formatting that you had previously applied manually. Next, click on the style name you wish to update in the Stylist, and then click the Update Style icon at the far right of the Stylist toolbar.

Add or Create New Styles

Although Writer comes with many predefined Styles, you may have specialized documents that require an entirely new Style. Writer makes it easy to create new Styles, too.

To add a new style to the Stylist, first open the Stylist by pressing F11 and select a style category. Highlight an existing style upon which you want to base your new style; it should be as similar as possible to the one you wish to create. Right-click that style and select New... to open the Style Settings window shown in Figure 9-9. Here, you can set all the characteristics you want for the new style, including its category.

Work with the Navigator

The Navigator is a floating panel, like the Stylist, that adds horsepower to your movements within a document. You can turn on the Navigator by clicking the Navigator button on the Main Menu (just to the left of the Stylist button) or by pressing the function key F5.

Figure 9-10 shows the Navigator panel with the major categories, Headings, Tables, Bookmarks, Hyperlinks, and Notes, collapsed. If you click the plus sign in front of the Headings category, for example, all headings within your current document will be revealed. Double-click on one of these entries to move to that place in the document.

You can also use the Navigator to easily move sections of the document. This is a great way to quickly reorganize a document, without having to do a lot of cutting and pasting in the main window. To move things around, click on a section name to highlight it, and then click one of the icons in the top right of the Navigator window to promote or demote the section (which Writer calls a chapter).

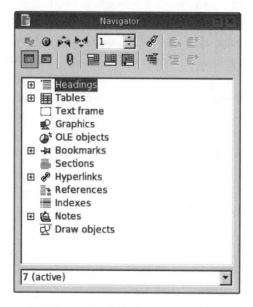

FIGURE 9-10. The Navigator in collapsed view

In addition to the major categories, Navigator displays a variety of different object types in its panel, allowing you to move quickly among sections and types of elements in a document.

Other Features in Writer

There are hundreds of features in Writer. What I've written so far barely scratches the surface, but it should be enough to get you started. This section describes several other features you might find useful.

Use the Changes Tracking Feature

In business situations you often want to have someone else review one of your documents. For example, perhaps you've written a proposal and want to have a coworker look it over before you submit it to your boss. Wouldn't it be useful to be able to see your coworker's comments and edits in the document? Like MS Word, Writer offers a great tool that allows you to do just that. When you track changes onscreen, each person's edits appear in a different color, which makes it easy to tell who changed what. To turn on Changes Tracking in Writer, select Edit → Changes and single-click both Record and Show. Now you'll be able to track and see any changes made to the document. Keep in mind that once turned on, these settings "travel" with the document when it is saved, and will stay on until someone unchecks them and saves the document again.

As a writer, I use the Changes Tracking feature all the time when reviewing documents with my editor. If you need to have other people review your documents for any reason, you'll find this feature an invaluable tool.

Save Time with Keyboard Shortcuts

Keyboard shortcuts can be enormously helpful in speeding up your work. I use them all the time—in fact, I couldn't live without them! You'll find that it's often faster to use keyboard shortcuts than to use mouse clicks and drop-down menus, because using keystrokes allows you to keep both your hands on the keyboard at all times. This can also help you to avoid repetitive stress syndrome, which often develops through excessive use of the mouse. Table 9-2 lists some common keyboard shortcuts that you can use to do various things quickly within a document.

TABLE 9-2. Common keyboard shortcuts

Function	Keyboard shortcut
Copy text	Ctrl-C
Cut text	Ctrl-X
Paste text	Ctrl-V
Bold text	Ctrl-B
Italicize text	Ctrl-I
Underline text	Ctrl-U

Use Find and Replace

To find and replace characters in a Writer document, press Ctrl-F to open the Find & Replace dialog (see Figure 9-11). Alternately, you can access this dialog by selecting Edit → Find & Replace.....

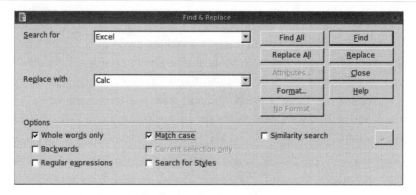

FIGURE 9-11. The Find & Replace window

Enter the term you want to find in the "Search for" field; if you want to change this term to another word, enter the new word in the "Replace with" field. Then press the Find button at the top right of the window. Starting from the current location of your cursor, Writer will locate the next instance of the term you're searching for.

Once you find the term, just press the Replace button to put in the new word. If you come to an instance that you *don't* wish to replace, just press the Find button again to advance to the next example of the search term.

It's usually a good idea to place your cursor at the beginning of the document before commencing Find & Replace. You can also go from your current point to the end of the document, and then let the search process start over from the beginning of the document when you are prompted to do so.

Calculate Word Count

Journalists, authors, and editors depend on this feature for their daily bread, so they can be forgiven for their oft-reported anxiety that Writer doesn't include a word count feature. In fact, word counting is indeed available in Writer—it's just in a mysterious location. It's under File → Properties → Statistics, whereas in MS Word it's under Tools → Word Count. (See the Feature Comparison chart in Table 9-1.)

Change Unpopular Default Settings

By default, OpenOffice.org is set to automatically complete words, replace certain characters, and capitalize initial letters in a new sentence. If you find such autocorrection intrusive while you're typing, it's easy to adjust the settings or turn them off completely.

Word Completion

Writer's Word Completion feature is turned on by default. If you like to have Writer complete your words, simply press the Enter key when its recommendations are good and press the space bar to reject the suggested word.

On the other hand, if you find Word Completion annoying and want to turn it off, select Tools → AutoCorrect/AutoFormat → Word Completion and uncheck the box before the phrase "Enable word completion" near the top of the window. Then click the OK button.

Auto-Replace

If you find Auto-Replace annoying—such as when you try to type (c) and it keeps replacing it with the copyright symbol ©—you have two options: edit the replacement list, or turn off Auto-Replace altogether.

Editing the replacement list is straightforward. Select Tools → Auto-Correct/AutoFormat, go to the Replace tab (Figure 9-12) and highlight the offending element. Then, either press the Delete key or enter a different target result in the With: field.

To turn off the Auto-Replace function entirely, select Tools → Auto-Correct/AutoFormat and click on the Options tab. The topmost option is "Use replacement table," with two checkboxes in front. By unchecking both boxes in the [M] and the [T] columns, you can turn off the specific substitutions listed in the replacement table. You can also turn off any other specific automatic replacement actions by unchecking the respective boxes under [M] or [T] as you go down the list.

Before you disable Auto-Replace entirely, note that the list of default replacements in the Replace tab is based on the OpenOffice.org developers' extensive knowledge of common keystroke errors and frequently used symbols (such as the copyright symbol). Leaving Auto-Replace

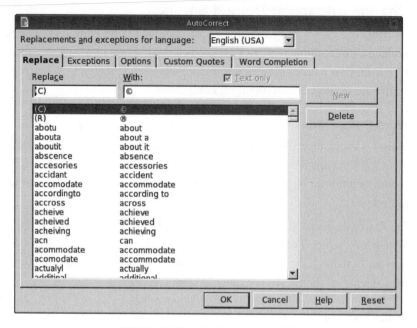

FIGURE 9-12. The default replacement list

turned on can aid your productivity, especially if you customize the replacement list with your own most frequent word, character, or symbol replacements.

Auto-Capitalization

Writer is set to automatically capitalize the next character you type after a period and to lowercase a second uppercase character typed in a sequence. This is beneficial most of the time, but it can be annoying when you try to type abbreviations or acronyms that include two initial capitals.

You can turn off the Auto-Capitalization feature by selecting Tools → AutoCorrect/AutoFormat and clicking on the Options tab. Uncheck the two boxes under the [M] and [T] columns in front of the second option, "Correct Two Initial Capitals," and the third option, "Capitalize the first letter of every sentence."

However, Auto-Capitalization can be very helpful when you integrate it into your typing repertoire. Consider keeping the feature turned on and tweaking its exceptions to make it work for you instead of against you. You can adjust the Auto-Capitalization exceptions by selecting Tools →

AutoCorrect/AutoFormat and going to the Exceptions tab (see Figure 9-13). Here, you can add abbreviations you use frequently to the "Abbreviations (no subsequent capital)" list in the upper window. These entries tell Auto-Capitalization not to automatically capitalize the first letter after any of the abbreviations listed. You can also add to the list of words or acronyms that demand two initial capitals. The default entries already there serve as examples.

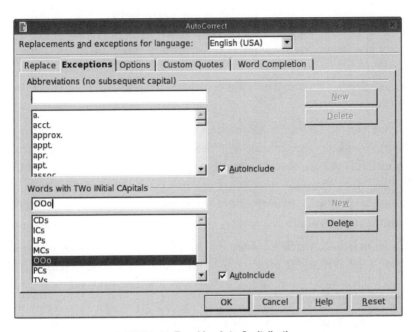

FIGURE 9-13. Tweaking Auto-Capitalization

Open Documents Created with Other Programs

Conveniently, Writer has the ability to read or open documents in non-Writer formats. Perhaps most significantly for many people, it can open most documents written in Microsoft Word. A 2003 study conducted by Hal and Christopher Varian at U.C. Berkeley called "MOXIE–Microsoft Office–Linux Interoperability Experiment" indicated that StarOffice 6.0 opened MS Word documents with no noticeable formatting problems 93 percent of the time. That's a pretty good percentage. In fact, because Word users face incompatibilities trying to share files amongst themselves across the different versions of Word, OpenOffice.org is actually more compatible in opening Microsoft Office files than

Microsoft Office itself! This is because OpenOffice.org opens *all* MS Office versions automatically. Meanwhile, users of Word 6.0 (an older version) cannot open or read files in the native MS Word 2000 file format, so it is 100% incompatible with Word 2000.

Calc

Calc is the spreadsheet program in OpenOffice.org. In its basic features and functions, Calc is comparable to Microsoft Excel, so if you're familiar with recent versions of Excel you'll feel quite at home in Calc. However, just as in Writer, you may sometimes have trouble locating a familiar old command in Calc. You may also occasionally have a problem importing an Excel file, although most Excel files should open fine in Calc.

If you are an advanced spreadsheet user, you will be disappointed to learn that Calc cannot run Microsoft Office–originated Visual Basic macros. (There are workarounds, but these are beyond the scope of this book.) More than the other programs in OpenOffice.org, Calc calls for adjustments from Microsoft Office users. However, if you are a basic- or intermediate-level MS Excel user, Calc will probably meet your needs.

To launch Calc, click K Menu → Use office tools → Create a spreadsheet. Like Writer, the program may take quite some time to start up.

Open and Save Files

First things first. To open a file in Calc, select File → Open, choose the desired file in the dialog window, and click the Open button. You can also press the keyboard shortcut Ctrl-O.

To save the currently opened file to its current folder location, simply select File → Save or use the keyboard shortcut Ctrl-S. If you want to put a file into a new folder (as you need to do when saving a file for the first time), select File → Save As.... Choose the folder location, enter a filename in the dialog, and press the Save button.

To export your current spreadsheet into PDF format, select File → Export as PDF.... . Select the target destination folder in the Export dialog, enter or change the filename if you choose, and press the Export button. Alternatively, you can export directly to PDF using the dedicated Export to PDF icon on the toolbar.

Enter Simple Formulas

Just as in Excel, calculations in Calc are performed by entering formulas into the spreadsheet cells. All formulas begin with an equals sign (=). For example, to calculate the result of 1+1, you would type =1+1 and press Enter.

To calculate a result based on other cells, type = in the cell where you want the result to appear, then click on the first cell in the formula. This will highlight the cell in a red outline. Type an operator such as + and click on the second cell, which again will highlight that cell in a red outline. You can enter as many operators followed by cells or other values as you like. Finally, press Enter, and the result will appear in the target cell.

As an example, set the cursor in cell B9 and type =. Next, click on cell B5 and then type -. Click on cell B7 and press the Enter key. The result now appears in cell B9, as shown in Figure 9-14.

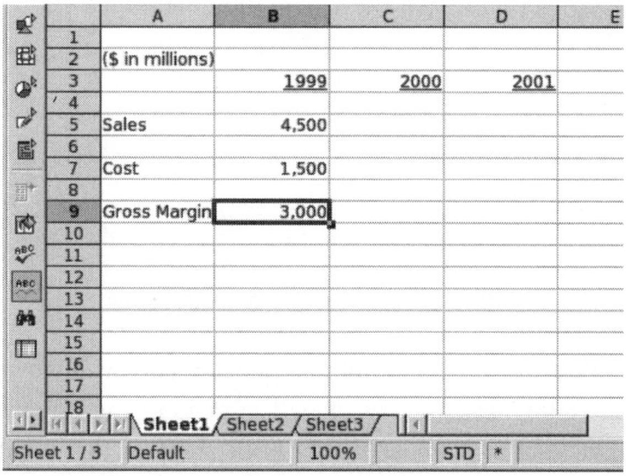

FIGURE 9-14. The formula appears in the Formula Field

Note that the Formula Field now contains the formula I just described, =B5-B7. As you might have guessed, an alternative way to create the same formula would be to simply type it directly into the Formula Field. First, click once on cell B9; then click once on the empty Formula Bar, type =B5-B7 into it, and press the Enter key. The result is the same.

Sum a Column of Numbers

To quickly sum an existing column of numbers, highlight the target result cell with a single click and then click the sigma icon (it looks like a cross between an S and a Z, and has a tooltip of "Sum") on the Formula Bar. This automatically highlights in blue the most likely nearby column of numbers to be summed (see Figure 9-15).

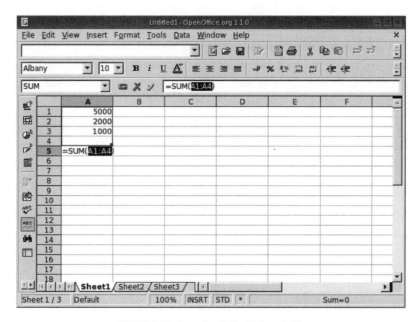

FIGURE 9-15. Summing fields A1 though A4

If the highlighted group of numbers is what you want to add up, just press the Enter key and the result will appear in the target cell. If not, grab the small blue square at the bottom right of the highlighted column, adjust the grouping to the precise numbers you wish to sum, and press Enter.

Adjust Column Widths and Heights

To change the width of a column, bring the mouse pointer up into the grid's column headings, which are labeled A, B, C, and so on. The mouse pointer will change to a double horizontal arrow when it rolls over any column divider. When the arrow becomes visible, click your left mouse button and simply move it to the right or left to change the width of the column to the left of the divider. (Use the same procedure to adjust the height of a row, but position the mouse cursor on the top or bottom of a row heading at the left edge of the page.)

To put a column back to its default width, right-click on the column heading to call up the Column Width dialog. Check the empty box labeled "Default value" and click OK. The column will now snap back to its default width (0.89 inches). (To restore a row's default height, use the same technique but apply it at the left edge of the page, on the desired row heading.)

Use Autofill

You can use the Autofill feature to speed up common repetitive tasks. Autofill permits you, in one stroke, to fill in either a column or a row with incrementing numbers. This can be useful when you first create a new table or spreadsheet. In the case of labels, Autofill will simply repeat the label across the cell range you specify.

As an example, enter the numbers 10, 20, and 30 in cells A1, A2, and A3 respectively. Then click and drag your mouse over all three cells to highlight them. You'll see a small black square at the bottom right corner of cell A3, as shown in Figure 9-16. Grab the small square with a left click, and with the left mouse button held down, drag the square down for as many cells as you wish to fill in with numbers. Release the mouse button, and the numbers will fill in consecutively.

I particularly like to use this feature to fill in months. Just type January in a cell, grab the square at the bottom right, and drag down. When you release, all the months will be filled in.

Merge Cells

A properly formatted spreadsheet has a lot of text labels to describe the contents. These labels are often long and span across multiple cells. You could enlarge these cells to fit the entire label, but that expands the entire column, which usually looks bad. Instead, it is often better to merge multiple cells together so the label will fit. To do this, first highlight the group of cells you wish to merge and select Format → Merge Cells → Define. This will create one single cell that combines the contents of the cells in the range you highlighted.

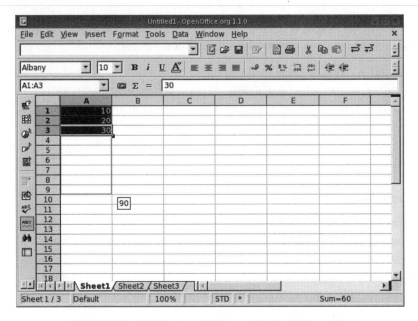

FIGURE 9-16. Autofill can save time-consuming, repetitive work

Calc's recognition of data can be quite sophisticated. For instance, if one column contains Jun and another contains 3, the date 06/03, followed by the current year, appears in the merged cell. However, you'll need to watch out for things like this when you merge cells, as the changes may not always be desirable.

Format Cell Contents

Most spreadsheet users find that a few cell formatting commands carry them through most of their work. The quickest way to format numbers and labels in the cells of a spreadsheet is to use the formatting buttons across the Object Bar shown in Figure 9-17. Calc offers Bold, Italic, and Underline buttons, as well as buttons for justification and simple number formatting.

FIGURE 9-17. The Object Bar

If the formatting choices on the Object Bar prove too limiting, you can apply more customized formats by going to Format → Cells.... This brings up the Format Cells dialog box, which offers a bewildering range of formatting options. I'll discuss just a few of these here.

Underline a cell or cell label

Underlining an entire cell or range of cells is called adding a *border*. To do this, highlight the range you wish to underline and click on the Borders icon (it looks like a four-paned window) on the Object Bar to open the Borders palette. Click on the underline button in the palette, as illustrated in Figure 9-18.

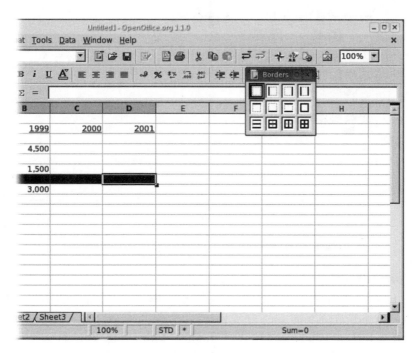

FIGURE 9-18. Underlining cells using the Borders palette

Note that this is a completely different process from underlining the actual text in a cell. To do this, simply highlight the text you wish the underline and click the Underline icon on the Object Bar (just as with typical word processors).

Change the cell background color

Sometimes you want to dress up a simple table of numbers or make the bottom line stand out by giving the cell backgrounds a little color. You can do this easily in the Format Cells dialog. First, highlight the range of cells you'd like to color. Then select Format → Cells... and click the Background tab, as shown in Figure 9-19. Choose a color on the color palette with a single click and then click the OK button.

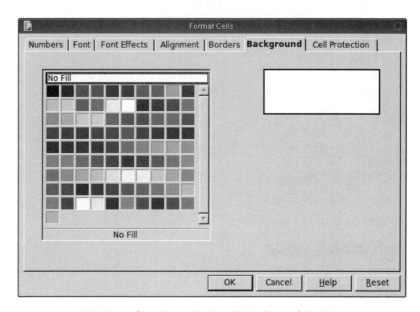

FIGURE 9-19. Choosing a cell color with the Format Cells dialog

Format numbers

When you first enter numbers in a cell, they have no formatting. If you'd like to indicate a unit, such as dollars ($12), dollars and cents ($12.43), or a date format, you'll need to apply number formatting. You can also format data with commas to separate thousands.

To format number data, first highlight the desired range to format and then select Format → Cells.... In the Format Cells dialog, go to the Numbers tab by clicking on it, as shown in Figure 9-20.

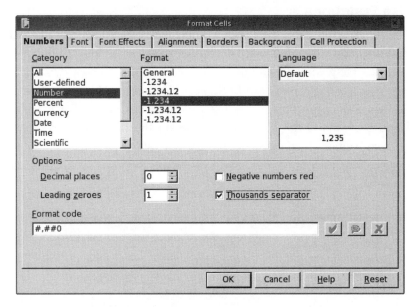

FIGURE 9-20. Formatting numbers with the Format Cells dialog

To format data in thousands, select Number in the Category list at left and choose the desired number format from the Format list in the center. For example, if you want numbers in the thousands to appear with a comma, choose -1,234. Click the OK button, and the numbers in your designated range will appear with the new formatting.

Set the Print Range

When you create a new spreadsheet from scratch, no print range is set. To set a print range for your spreadsheet, turn on Page Break View (View → Page Break) and highlight the full area you wish to print by clicking on the cell in one corner and dragging the mouse pointer across the entire range. Finally, select Format → Print Ranges → Define. Any spreadsheet content that is outside the range you set will not be printed.

If there is a print range already defined and you need to adjust it, simply grab the corner of the blue outline (or just grab a side) with the mouse and stretch it to include all the desired cells of your new print range. To "grab" the blue outline, move the mouse pointer over the outline until you see it turn into a bidirectional arrow. This arrow permits you to drag the outline to a different place simply by clicking and dragging to the desired location.

Use Functions

The functions in Calc, their syntax, and their required formats are well documented in the Help drop-down menu. Select Help → Contents to open the Help window, and in the Index tab at the "Search term" field, type **functions** and press the Enter key. Now, you can double-click on the name of a function in the left pane to learn about that function. Figure 9-21 shows the Help information on the financial function PV (present value), which calculates the present value of a stream of regular payments or cash flows and is understandably popular with MBAs and bankers.

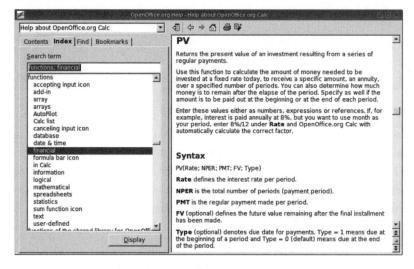

FIGURE 9-21. The Help window for the PV function

Calc has a full array of function types, including:

- Financial
- Database
- Temporal (Date & Time)
- Array
- Statistical
- Informational
- Logical
- Mathematical
- Textual

When entering a function into a cell, always start your entry with an equals sign (=). Figure 9-22 shows what the PV function formula looks like in the formula field when it's correctly typed into a cell and the necessary information for the function is properly cell-referenced:

```
=PV(B1;B2;B3)
```

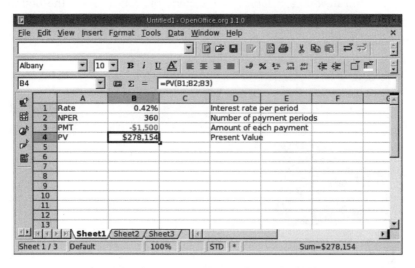

FIGURE 9-22. A common mortgage problem, solved with PV

It is also possible to enter numbers as well as cell references into the body of a function. In the formula field, this would look like:

```
=PV(.0042;360;-1500)
```

However, using cell references instead of actual numbers makes it easier to try alternative inputs or generate a sensitivity analysis using a range of choices for one variable.

Create Graphs

In terms of overall quality, Calc's ability to create and render graphs needs improvement, but its functionality is adequate for the simplest types of graphs. In the following example, we'll create a simple bar graph from a table of numbers.

The table we'll be using consists of a column of labels (the different operating systems employed by users of OpenOffice.org) and a column of numbers (the number of responses indicating use of the respective operating system). Since we want to show the relative scale of responses for each category, a bar graph is a good choice. In general, the graph type you select is determined by the type and amount of data you are portraying and by the important points you need to communicate.

The first step is to highlight the range of data to be included in the table, as shown in Figure 9-23. For this particular graph, you want to include the column headings as labels, but exclude the totals row at the bottom because its inclusion isn't necessary for the type of comparison we are making.

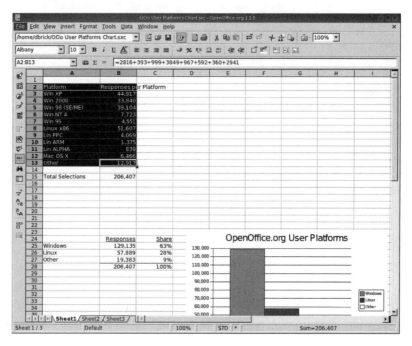

FIGURE 9-23. Highlighting the data to be included in the graph

Next, select Insert → Chart to open the AutoFormat Chart wizard (see Figure 9-24). Here, you want to check the two checkboxes labeled "First row as label" and "First column as label" to enable the wizard to reference the proper axis labels automatically. Note that your predefined range is already displayed in the Range field, so you don't need to enter or adjust it. Click the Next button.

Let's now adjust a few additional settings to allow the AutoFormat Chart wizard to create an accurate and informative chart. This particular table offers data series in rows (it's a series of *one*, so don't be confused), so

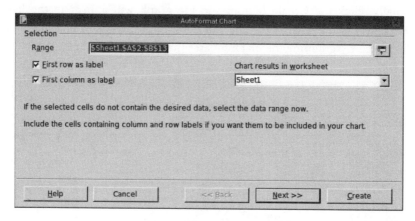

FIGURE 9-24. The AutoFormat Chart wizard

click the radio button for "Data series in: Rows." You should also check the box for "Show text elements in preview." This provides a WYSI-WYG (What You See Is What You Get) preview of the bar graph in progress. If the graph or text looks incorrect in the preview, you can click the Back button to adjust your settings or pick a different chart type if necessary. When you've made these changes, click the Next button.

The next dialog allows you to label the main chart title and the axes, and provides a checkbox to include or exclude the legend (see Figure 9-25). Leave the Legend box checked so that you'll know which color bar in the graph represents which OS platform.

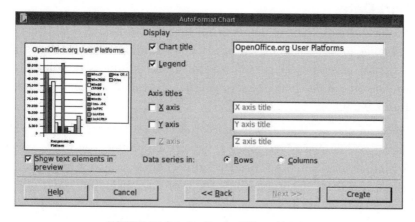

FIGURE 9-25. Entering the chart title and labels

Finally, click the Create button, and the graph will appear in the live worksheet (see Figure 9-26). You can now adjust the size or placement of the graph by grabbing the black squares that border the graph.

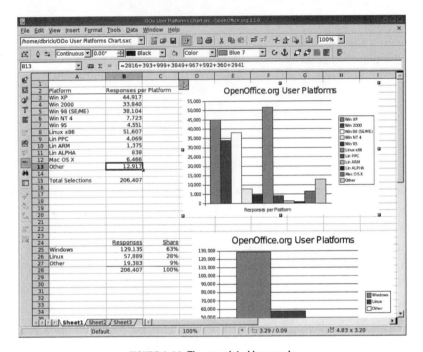

FIGURE 9-26. The completed bar graph

Sort Data

To sort a list or chart of numerical or textual information, highlight the full range to sort (including the labels, but excluding unwanted data such as totals) and select Data → Sort. This brings up the Sort dialog box, where you can designate the sorting order, among other parameters (see Figure 9-27).

For example, say you want to reorder the data to put the category with the largest number of responses at the top. To do this, you would select to sort by the "Responses per Platform" column and click Descending. Then click the OK button. You'll see how rearranging the order of the source table automatically registers that new order in the bar graph (see Figure 9-28).

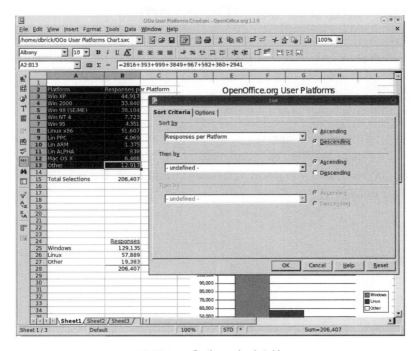

FIGURE 9-27. Sorting a simple table

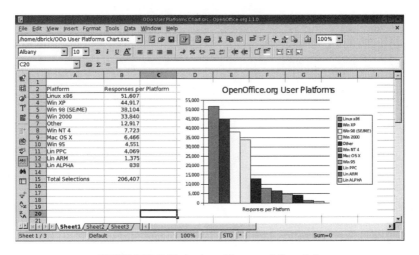

FIGURE 9-28. Table (and graph) successfully sorted

The Future of OpenOffice.org

OpenOffice.org 2.0 should become available in the spring of 2005. This version promises decreased load times, overall improved speed, and the addition of a database component similar to Microsoft Access. On top of this, there will be a slew of bug fixes and feature enhancements that will make this already outstanding office suite even better.

Many governments, businesses, and schools are already evaluating the use of OpenOffice.org as a replacement for Microsoft Office. The lack of a license fee and its open document format make it a very attractive program.

10

MANAGE
YOUR
FINANCES

By now you may have noticed that there is an open source application for just about anything you could want to do with a computer. Managing finances is one of the most common computer tasks, so it should not come as a surprise that an open source application exists to do just that; it's called *GnuCash.*

GnuCash is the open source world's answer to popular personal financial applications like Microsoft Money and Intuit's Quicken. While it doesn't have all the bells and whistles of those applications, GnuCash has everything you need to keep track of your money. You can keep tabs on your income, expenses, checking and savings accounts, debts, investments, and assets like cars and houses. Once you master GnuCash's easy interface, a simple investment of a few minutes each day will keep you on top of your financial life. You will be able to see into the past to figure out where your money has been going, keep an eye on your balances in the present to make sure you don't suffer any nasty surprises, and forecast your financial well-being into the distant and not-so-distant future.

If you use an off-the-shelf application like Money or Quicken, you're in for a few surprises when you try GnuCash. Compared to those applications, GnuCash's interface is extremely straightforward. There are no fancy embedded web pages or advisors. You won't find endless options dialogs and wizards, and you can't pay your bills electronically from inside GnuCash. Instead, when you start GnuCash you are presented with a simple list of accounts. Double-clicking on an account opens an *account register*, which looks exactly like the one in your checkbook. You enter transactions in the account register, and the balance of each account is shown in the accounts list. You can view several reports to get an at-a-glance view of your financial life. And that's almost all there is to GnuCash. When it comes to finances, simpler is better, so this simplicity is an asset, not a liability. The other major difference between GnuCash and those other applications has to do with the way you keep track of your money. I'll cover that in detail in "The Account" later in this chapter.

Getting Started

Starting GnuCash is easy. After logging into KDE, just select K Menu →
Organize → Manage your finances. The GnuCash splash screen appears,
showing you which modules are loading. The splash screen is then
replaced by the Tip of the Day screen and the Welcome to GnuCash!
dialog box.

The Tip of the Day screen presents a different piece of information each
time you start GnuCash. You can also peruse the tips one at a time by
clicking the Prev or Next button. It might be a good idea to keep this
screen around for a while because the information can be useful, but if
you prefer not to see it you can disable the feature by unchecking the
"Display this dialog next time" checkbox. You can close the window by
clicking the Close button, but not until you answer the question in the
Welcome dialog.

The Welcome dialog (Figure 10-1) is only displayed the first time you
use GnuCash. It gives you the option of creating a new set of accounts,
importing data from Quicken (via QIF files), or opening the new user
tutorial. You are going to create a new set of accounts. This should be
the default option, so just click OK.

This launches the New Account Hierarchy Setup druid. A *druid* in Linux
is analogous to a wizard in Windows, and lets you click through a series
of questions and setup screens to perform a complicated task. The first
screen you see is an explanation of the druid; click Next to go on to the
important parts.

FIGURE 10-1. The GnuCash Welcome dialog

Choosing a Currency

Figure 10-2 shows the dialog for currency selection for new accounts. The default currency is USD (US Dollar). If you use a different currency, select it from the available options in the drop-down list. Click Next to continue.

FIGURE 10-2. The Choose Currency page

Choosing Accounts

Figure 10-3 shows you the list of preset account structures. Each of these options creates one or more accounts for you. You can select multiple options (for example, if you want both a checkbook and a car loan), but for now just select A Simple Checkbook. Once you select that option, you'll see a description and a list of the accounts that will be created. Don't worry about the number of available accounts; it may look confusing, but all will become clear by the end of this chapter. Click Next to continue.

Entering Opening Balances

The dialog in Figure 10-4 allows you to give each account an *opening balance,* that is, the amount of money in the account when you first begin tracking it in GnuCash. If you want to put an opening balance in your checking account, just click that account to select it and enter the opening balance in the textbox to the right. Click Next to continue.

Finishing Your Account Setup

And that's all there is to setting up an account hierarchy in GnuCash. Just click Finish and the druid will close.

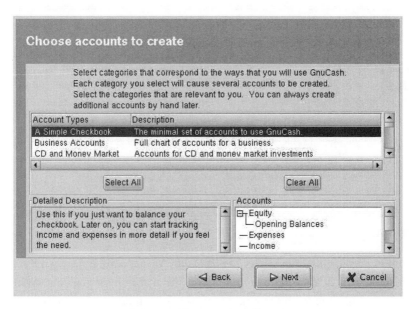

FIGURE 10-3. The account creation page

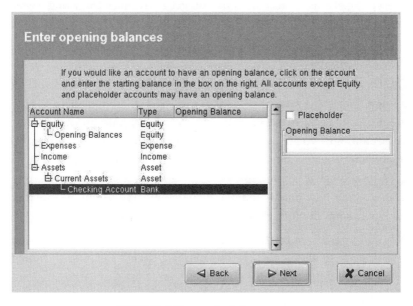

FIGURE 10-4. The opening balances page

Saving your progress

If you are using *Move* with a USB key you will probably want to save your account setup to a file that will contain all your financial records. Click the Save button in the toolbar, enter a filename, and click OK to save the accounts to that file. GnuCash will open this file automatically the next time you run the application. If you don't have a USB key, all of your account information and data will be lost each time you reboot the computer.

The Account

Fundamental to GnuCash is the *account*. An account is just what you think it is: a place where money comes in and money goes out. When most people think of accounts, they think of their bank accounts and credit card accounts. GnuCash treats these as accounts, but it treats everything else as an account too. You get a paycheck from work; where does the money come from? It comes from your Income account. You spend $30 at the grocery store; where does the money go? It goes to your Food account.

GnuCash uses the *double-entry accounting method* to keep track of your money. This is the same method that professional accountants and CPAs use to keep track of billions of dollars in corporate and government assets, and now you're going to use it too. (Don't you feel important?) In double-entry accounting, money always comes from one account and goes to another account. Always. The value of any account at a given time is either how much money is actually in that account or how much money has passed through it.

Not all accounts are treated equally in GnuCash. Five types of accounts will be covered in this introduction: Assets, Liabilities, Income, Expenses, and Equity.

Asset accounts

> Think of asset accounts as keeping track of things you own. Your checking account is an asset. If money is in this account, you own it. A house is also an asset. The value of that account is the current value of your home. In general, you want asset accounts to *increase*.

Liability accounts

You can also think of liability accounts as keeping track of things you own. The only difference is that you don't want to own them! If you have a house, you probably have a mortgage. You "own" this promise to pay your lender a certain amount. The amount you have left to pay is the balance of your mortgage account. Credit card balances, car loans, and IOUs are examples of liabilities. In general, you really want liability accounts to *decrease*.

Income accounts

Unlike asset and liability accounts, income accounts don't represent money you own (at least not directly). Think of an income account as a window into someone else's (usually your employer's) check register. When your boss writes a check to you, it gets recorded on the withdrawals side of his register. If you can imagine those records also showing up in your income account (giving you a glimpse into the portion of his checkbook that concerns you), then you have some idea of how income accounts work. Money doesn't usually stay in these accounts; it immediately goes into one of your asset accounts (usually your checkbook). The value of this account at any time is the total amount you have been paid. It probably goes without saying that you always want these accounts to *increase*.

Expense accounts

Expense accounts also don't represent money you own. You can think of them as a glimpse into the deposit side of the checkbook of whomever you are paying. The value of each expense account is the total amount you have paid to that person, business, or activity so far. While you can't *decrease* the value of expense accounts (except via refunds and rebates), you do want to manage them well.

Equity accounts

Equity accounts are the odd man out in this group. While there is a formal definition of equity in the accounting world, it is beyond the scope of this introduction. The easiest way to think of an equity account is as the place where opening balances come from. Remember that, in GnuCash, money must always come from some account and go to some other account. So where did your opening balance come from? It didn't come from income, since it's not like you got a paycheck for that opening balance. Instead, it came from the equity account.

The GnuCash Accounts Window

The main window of GnuCash, shown in Figure 10-5, is the *accounts window*. This shows all of your accounts in the currently open file. The accounts are listed in tree form because accounts can contain sub-accounts (more on this later). For now, all you need to know is that a plus sign to the left of an account name indicates that is a parent account of one or more sub-accounts, and that clicking on the plus sign expands the listing so you can see all accounts under the parent.

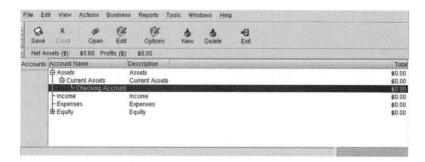

FIGURE 10-5. The GnuCash accounts window

The accounts listing shows the account name, a description, and the current account total by default. If an account is a parent to one or more sub-accounts, the account total is the combined total of all its sub-accounts as well as the parent account itself. Clicking once on an account selects it. Right-clicking an account shows a context menu with options to create a new account, delete an account, edit an account's properties, and perform numerous other tasks. Double-clicking an account brings up the associated account *ledger*, or *register*. You will learn more about ledgers later.

Creating New Accounts

There are several ways to create a new account. The easiest is to simply right-click on an empty area in the accounts window. You can also select New Account under the File menu. Create a new account now by selecting the Income account and right-clicking it. Select New Account from the context menu to begin.

Figure 10-6 shows the New Account screen. The first thing to do is give the account a name. Since you're going to record all the money you get from your job in this account, type **Paycheck** in the Account Name field.

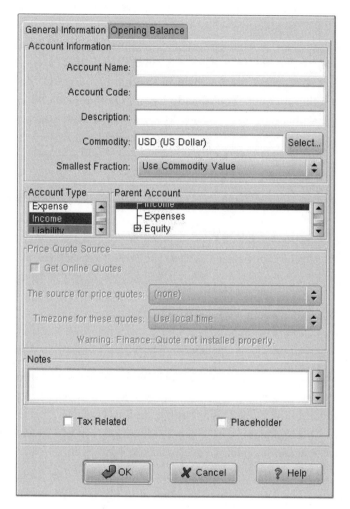

FIGURE 10-6. The New Account screen

The Account Code and Description fields are for your personal use if you need to record an account code (like an account number from your bank) or a description of your account. You can set the commodity of this account just as you did for the main accounts file. By default it uses the commodity (USD, euro, GBP, etc.) and commodity type (Currency) of the main file, but you can change this to use other commodities (for example, if you're a spy and have a numbered bank account in Zurich) or other commodity types. This is useful for tracking stocks, bonds, and other financial instruments. The available commodity types are determined by the account type you select below.

In the Account Type box, you'll find the five account types introduced earlier as well as other types used for special purposes. The point of our Paycheck account is to keep track of income, so scroll down to the Income entry and select it. After Account Type is the Parent Account box. Accounts can be *nested*, which means that one account can exist as part of another account. You already have an account called Income, so click on the plus sign next to New Top Level Account, which expands the tree to show your existing accounts. Scroll down until you see the Income account and select it. This puts your Paycheck account under the Income account.

Missing fields?

If you don't see the Account Type and Parent Account fields, try resizing the window to be taller. If the window is already as tall as your screen allows, you probably need to adjust your resolution as outlined in the Appendix.

If you were using this account for stocks and other special commodities, you could set up a way to get price quotes (say, to check the value of a stock) online in the Price Quote Source section. However, this is beyond the scope of this chapter. The Notes field just lets you add notes to yourself which you can see later if you go back to this screen.

Finally, there are two checkboxes near the bottom: Tax Related and Placeholder. The Tax Related checkbox links this account with tax information so that certain tax values are automatically calculated. Using this property is beyond the scope of this chapter. The Placeholder box is for accounts that serve only as organizers for other accounts. For example, you may have three sources of income: Job, Parents, and your weekend Web Design business. In this case, you would place all three accounts under the Income account. Now the Income account shouldn't have any activity of its own, because all of your income comes from one of these three sources. To enforce this rule, you would check the Placeholder option in the Income account's settings window. This disallows entries in the Income ledger, so you can be sure that income is properly recorded in one of the three sub-accounts. You don't want this option for your Paycheck account, however, so keep the box unchecked.

Now click OK and you are taken back to the main account window page. You can see that the newly created Paycheck account has been highlighted. Also notice that it has been placed under the Income account, just like you wanted.

If you want to edit the properties of an existing account, simply click on that account to select it, then right-click it to bring up the context menu. Select Edit Account under the context menu to bring up the properties screen.

Deleting Accounts

If you create an account erroneously, select that account and right-click it to bring up the context menu. Select the Delete Account menu item to delete that account from your file. Be aware that this affects all records pertaining to this account and may leave your accounts in an unbalanced state.

Don't delete closed accounts

Do *not* delete an account just because you have closed it (for example, you paid off a credit card and cut it up or you closed an account at an old bank). Even though the account is closed, you do not want to lose all records of the transactions contained in that account, and deleting it may unbalance your other accounts.

Unfortunately, there is no real way to hide closed accounts so they no longer appear in your accounts window. There is a cheat, though: simply create a new top-level account called Closed as a placeholder account, and move all closed accounts under that account by setting it as the parent account. Since you can click the minus sign to collapse the closed accounts, all you see is the parent account. This trick isn't particularly elegant, but it works.

Transactions

If the account is the heart of GnuCash, transactions are the blood. Without transactions, you simply have a bunch of accounts listed in a window. This isn't terribly useful—you want to *do something* with all these accounts. Recording transactions is exactly what makes GnuCash useful.

A *transaction* in GnuCash is a record of a specific event. This event is usually money being transferred from one place to another, but it could also be the equivalent value in stocks, bonds, or real estate. For a concrete example of a transaction, look no further than your own checkbook. If you keep a register, the individual entries in that register are records of transactions. When you use GnuCash, you simply record those transactions in the computer instead of in your checkbook. (Of course, a prudent person would do both.)

Entering Transactions

To enter transactions, you must open an account's *register window*, shown in Figure 10-7.

FIGURE 10-7. The account register window

You can access the register window for any account by double-clicking on the account in the accounts window. Let's start by recording a simple income transaction. Say you just mowed the lawn for Aunt Mary and she paid you $25 for your troubles. Here's how to record the transaction in GnuCash:

1. Expand your Assets account, followed by the Current Assets account, and then double-click on Checking Account to bring up the register.

2. Today's date is already in the Date field. Hit the Tab key to move to the next field (Tab moves you forward through fields; Shift-Tab

moves you backward). The Num field lets you enter your check number or any other tracking number you need for this transaction. In this case, we'll say that Aunt Mary gave you check #100, so put 100 in the field.

3. Tab to the Description field and enter something, well, descriptive. `Mowed Aunt Mary's Lawn` would work.

4. Tab to the Transfer field. This is one of the most important fields. Remember that in GnuCash, money always comes from one account and goes to another. In this case, you want money to go from your income account into your checking account. The good thing about this (and every other) field is that it auto-completes for you. Just enter `In`, and GnuCash should display an account list and select the Income account automatically.

5. Since you are receiving money from Aunt Mary, tab to the Deposit field and enter 25.00.

When you press Enter the transaction is recorded. When you close the register window and look at your accounts, you can see that both the income account and the checking account have increased to 25.00. Notice also that the parent accounts of checking account also show 25.00. Parent accounts show the sum of all accounts below them. At a glance, you can see that you have made 25.00 in income so far and that you have 25.00 in your checking account.

Deleting transactions

To delete a transaction, go to the register containing the transaction, right-click on the transaction, and select Delete. Doing this removes the transaction from all affected accounts. In the case of the check from Aunt Mary, the transaction is removed from the income account and the checking account.

Recording Split Transactions

So let's say you have a paycheck in hand, ready to enter into GnuCash. If you're like most people, the amount you get paid is different from the amount you earned. The rest of the money goes to federal, state, and local taxes. You could just enter the amount for which the check was written, but what if you wanted to keep track of *total* income and expenses, including gross income and taxes? You can do this in Gnu-Cash by using the *split transaction*.

Split transactions provide a way to record multiple sources and destinations of money as a single transaction. In this example, one single transaction can record that you earned 500.00, and 100.00 went to federal tax, 50.00 to state tax, and 50.00 to local tax, leaving you with a 300.00 deposit to your checking account. Split transactions work by *balancing* money in versus money out among multiple sources and/or destinations. GnuCash allows you to have an unbalanced split, but it will complain loudly.

To enter a split transaction, follow these steps:

1. Open an account register. Split transactions are usually recorded at the logical source or destination. For a paycheck, it is common to record the transaction inside your checking account.

2. Enter the date and description as you would any transaction.

3. Click the Split button on the account register's toolbar.

4. Press Tab to advance to the first sub-transaction.

5. Enter each part of the transaction as you would a normal transaction. Here's the tricky part: Deposit and Withdrawal apply to the account you're transferring money to/from at the time. For this example transaction, you are *withdrawing* 500.00 from your Income: Paycheck account in the form of wages, and splitting that into several deposits in your Expenses account and your Assests:Current Assests:Checking Account. At first it may seem counterintuitive that taxes are a deposit in an account, but if you go back to the earlier definition of an expense account it should make sense. Use Figure 10-8 as a guide for filling out this transaction. When you finish with a sub-transaction, press Tab to go to the next one. I find it convenient to perform transactions like this by making my first sub-transaction the withdrawal from the Income account. This helps with the balancing that GnuCash automatically performs on the splits that follow.

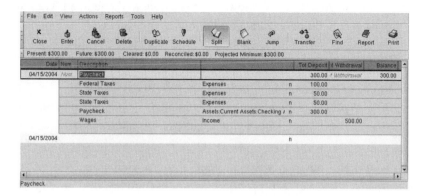

FIGURE 10-8. Example of a split transaction

6. Press Enter to finish the split transaction. If the transaction is not balanced (money in does not equal money out), GnuCash warns you and offers several solutions. GnuCash realizes that you're not as good at math as the computer is, so it displays the amount remaining on the last sub-transaction line. Once everything balances correctly, the split transactions collapse into a single line.

7. To see an already recorded split, select that transaction and click the Split button on the toolbar.

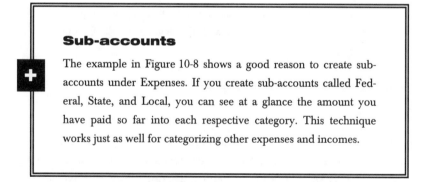

Sub-accounts

The example in Figure 10-8 shows a good reason to create sub-accounts under Expenses. If you create sub-accounts called Federal, State, and Local, you can see at a glance the amount you have paid so far into each respective category. This technique works just as well for categorizing other expenses and incomes.

Scheduling Transactions

You probably pay certain bills at about the same time every month, and entering those transactions every time can become a chore. GnuCash's transaction scheduling feature allows you to create transactions that automatically recur at a certain interval. To schedule a transaction, follow these steps:

1. From the Accounts Window, select Actions → Scheduled Transactions → Scheduled Transaction Editor.

2. Click New.

3. Enter the name of the scheduled transaction (e.g., `Electric Bill`), the start date, the frequency, and the end date (if applicable).

There is a template transaction at the bottom of the window. This is where you tell GnuCash how much money to transfer at the specified intervals. Click in the Description field and create a transaction just like you would any other in your checking account. Remember, when you are paying a bill you are probably depositing money into an expense account and withdrawing money from your checking account. The template transaction needs to reflect both sides of the transaction. At the specified time interval, this transaction will occur in the accounts involved.

Quick scheduling

A quick way to make any transaction a scheduled transaction is by right-clicking on the transaction and selecting Schedule. If you are having trouble figuring out how to manually enter a template transaction, you can cheat by creating one this way, clicking the Advanced button, and seeing how GnuCash automatically fills out the template transaction.

Reports

Once you have spent a few months entering your financial details into GnuCash, you will start to appreciate the power that comes from having detailed records of your money habits. It's one thing to have all this information available, but it's quite another to organize it in a way that can help you spot trends or solve problems. Fortunately, GnuCash has a wide selection of *reports* to give you a firm grasp on almost every aspect of your financial life. The following table shows a list of some of the most common reports and what you can expect each to tell you. You can access any of these reports by navigating through the Reports menu in the accounts window.

Report	Description
Account Summary	Gives you an at-a-glance view of the balances for each account.
Asset Barchart/Piechart	Lets you see how your net worth is divided. For most people, their net worth is primarily in their house, bank accounts, and retirement funds.
Liability Barchart/Piechart	Breaks down your liabilities by percentage. For most people, houses and cars are the greatest liabilities, followed by credit cards and consumer and student loans.
Net Worth Barchart	Net Worth = Assets − Liabilities. This is a graphical representation of that formula. In general, you want the blue and green bars to get higher, and the red bar to get lower.
Expense Barcart/Piechart	Shows you where your money is going. If you spend 80% of your money each month on clothes, this will tell you that (assuming you have structured your expense accounts correctly).
Income Barchart/Piechart	Shows you where your money comes from. You may think that most of your money comes from your job, but this report may surprise you with how much of it comes from other sources, such as mom and dad and contract work (once again, assuming you have set up your accounts correctly).

To be truly informative, most of these reports require you to have an intricate account tree set up. For example, if you have one big Expenses account to which you send all of your money, then the Expense Report will show that 100% of your money goes to Expenses—not very helpful. To get the most out of the reports, you must structure your account tree so that each category of expenses has an account under the main Expenses account, and ditto for Income, Liability, and Assets. In general, the more structured your accounts, the more you will get out of GnuCash.

Changing report dates

By default, GnuCash reports from the start of the current year to the current date. You can change this (e.g., to show expense allocations for April) by clicking the Options button in the toolbar.

When you activate a report, it creates a tab to the far left of the window; above that tab you should also see Accounts. Use this to switch back and forth between the accounts window and your reports. Click the Close button on the toolbar to close a report.

Don't click Exit

Clicking Exit will not just close the report window—it will exit GnuCash entirely!

Real-Life Examples

Learning the basics of GnuCash is one thing; actually using it in day-to-day scenarios is quite another. You have already seen how to enter a paycheck so that total income and tax expenses are recorded. Here are several other real-life examples to get you started on the most common tasks.

Going to the Grocery Store

I've mentioned the importance of setting up a sufficiently detailed account structure before, but what I didn't tell you is how easy it is to do it. First of all, you don't have to set up all those accounts in advance. Knowing that you can create them as you go along gives you the motivation to do it right.

Here's what to do:

1. Open the Checking Account register.
2. Create a new transaction with today's date and **Grocery Store** as the description.
3. In the transfer field, enter **Ex**, and Expenses will be selected automatically. Use the right arrow key to complete the auto entry. Now type **:Food**. The colon tells GnuCash to make Food a sub-account of Expenses.
4. Press Enter to accept your new category and Tab to leave the transfer field. A dialog box will appear, asking you if you would like to create the Expenses:Food account. Click Yes.

5. The New Account window appears. The defaults should be fine, so click OK.

6. Skip the Deposit field, enter **50.00** in the Withdrawal field, and press Enter.

Congratulations! You have not only created a transaction recording your food purchase, but you've also created the expense account for it. Future food transactions can now go into this account, and a quick glance at the accounts window will show you exactly how much you have spent on food.

Auto-completion

GnuCash's auto-complete feature is very helpful. Once you have created sub-accounts, typing a colon after an auto-completed account will jump directly to the end of that account and begin with a listing of its sub-accounts.

Getting a Tax Refund

Most people think of tax refunds as income, but they aren't—they are *rebates*, because money that was taken from you earlier is now being returned. If you keep track of your taxes from each paycheck, recording a tax refund is as simple as creating a rebate from your expense account to your checking account. Here's how it works:

1. Open the Checking Account register.
2. Create a new transaction with today's date and **Tax Refund** as the description.
3. Since you recorded federal taxes from your paycheck as going to the Expenses account, enter **Expenses** in the transfer field.
4. Enter **50.00** in the Deposit field.
5. Press Enter to complete the transaction.

You now have another $50 in your checking account, but if you look at the accounts window, you will notice that your income has not increased. Instead, total assets have increased and expenses have decreased. This is an accurate depiction of what happens when you get a tax refund. No longer can you fool yourself into thinking that a tax refund is extra money you make every year. You already earned it; you're just getting it back!

Buying a Car

An automobile is a big expense. And if you're buying a vehicle on credit, it becomes even more costly. Luckily, GnuCash can keep track of every cent of the purchase, as well as what portion of your monthly payment goes toward principal and what portion is lost as interest. The process of setting up a car purchase is also a good example of how to handle a house purchase or other type of loan.

Here's the scenario: you've just bought a brand-new car for $20,000. You put down $5,000 and will be paying a $400 monthly payment for 60 months. You may have received an amortization table from your lender showing you how much money goes to principal and interest each month. If you didn't get an amortization table, you might want to ask your lender for one or create one yourself using tools available at web sites such as *http://www.bankrate.com*. You will probably be surprised at how much money you spend on interest. To record a car payment transaction:

1. Begin by creating a new account. Call it Car Loan, set its parent account to New top-level account, and its account type to Liability.

2. Create a second new account called Car, set its parent account to Assets:Current Assets, and its account type to Asset.

3. Open the account register for the Car account.

4. Start a new transaction. Enter Buy Car as the description and then click the Split button on the toolbar.

5. The first sub-transaction records the car's value. Enter Car Value as the description, Assets:Current Assets:Car as the account, and 20000.00 as the increase value.

6. That 20 grand has to come from somewhere. The first place is your down payment. Enter Down Payment as the description, Assets:Current Assets:Checking Account as the account, and Decrease the account by 5000.00. (Yes, this makes your bank account negative. Don't try this at home!)

7. Unfortunately, tax, title, and license cost you another $1,500. Enter **TT&L** as the description, Expenses as the account, and Increase the account by **1500.00**.

8. You now have a $16,500 balance for the transaction; this is your loan amount. Enter **Loan Principal** for the description, Car Loan for the account, and Decrease the account by **16500.00**.

9. Complete the transaction. The accounts window should show the results of your hard work.

You've had the car for about a month now and it's time to make the payment. A quick look at the lender's amortization table shows that $300 of your payment goes to interest and $100 goes to principal. Here's how to record that:

1. Open the Checking Account register.

2. Start a new transaction. Use today's date and enter **Car Payment** in the description field. Click the Split button to begin a split transaction.

3. Your payment is $400, so enter **Payment** as the description, Assets: Current Assets:Checking Account as the account, and Withdraw **400.00**.

4. $300 goes to interest, so enter **Interest** as the description, Expenses: Interest as the account (click Yes and OK after tabbing off the field to create the sub-account), and Deposit **300.00** into the account.

5. The rest goes to principal. The $100 balance should already appear in the Deposit field, so just enter **Principal** in the description and Car Loan for the account. Press Enter to complete the transaction.

Looking at the accounts window, you'll see that the Car Loan account has decreased by $100 and the Expenses account has increased by $300, exactly as it should be. No longer will you have to consider all of your car payment as an expense, as some of it goes to decreasing liability (and therefore increasing net worth). And now you can see it happening every month!

This transaction is an excellent example of one that should be scheduled to recur every month, saving you the hassle of typing it in every time. With each payment, be sure to change the interest and principal amounts as the amortization table indicates.

11 +

!

THE
COMMAND
LINE

So far, this book has explored using Linux from the KDE desktop environment and several graphical programs. But these programs represent only one way in which you can interact with a Linux computer. Underneath all of the glitter and eye candy of the graphic layer lurks another user interface—the command line.

The command line is an all-text interface to the operating system. It is the playground and work environment of Linux users everywhere. You are not considered to have truly arrived as a Linux user until you have mastered the command-line interface. And once you've done so, you will know why Linux users swear by it. The command line is simply the easiest, fastest, and most powerful way to get certain types of work done.

Linux users also use the command line to perform routine maintenance on their computer, configure hardware, or tweak the system for performance. It's a lot like being trained in auto repair and being able to perform you own routine maintenance on your car. A skilled home mechanic can fix her car quickly, with minimal cost, and with the assurance of quality work being done.

This chapter is a basic introduction to the Linux command line. It is based around simple tasks that will familiarize you with the interface and are useful for you to know. The content of this chapter is similar to that of Chapter 3, where you learned to manipulate files using Konqueror. In this chapter you'll learn how to copy, move, delete, and rename files and directories, compress files with various zip utilities, and identify runaway programs and stop them. You'll even learn how the command line itself can teach you how to use it better. Though this is just the beginning of what you can do on the command line, it should be enough to make you feel comfortable with this interface as you continue your exploration of Linux.

Understanding the Command Line

Linux users interact with Linux on the command line through a *terminal* program, also called a terminal emulator, xterm, shell, or console. KDE comes with a very useful terminal emulator called Konsole (Figure 11-1). To launch Konsole, click K Menu → Administer your system → Use a terminal emulator.

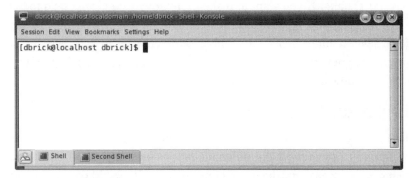

FIGURE 11-1. Konsole is the terminal emulator in KDE

The text already visible inside the program window is called a prompt. By typing various commands at the prompt, you can control the operating system. Most commands accept options and arguments. An *option*, sometimes called a *switch*, modifies the way a command works. It usually consists of a single character prefixed with a dash. An *argument* tells the command which files, directories, or other targets a command should operate on. You can use the arrow keys and delete keys to correct typing mistakes. Press Enter to execute your command.

Konsole is just one of many terminal programs available on Linux, and it provides several nice features. Keep in mind that these features are properties of Konsole, not terminals in general, so don't expect to find all or even most of them in other terminal programs.

Just like Konqueror, Konsole has tabs that can represent different command lines within the same window. Create a new tab by pressing Ctrl-Shift-N. You can move between tabs by clicking the tab with your mouse or pressing Shift-Left Arrow or Shift-Right Arrow, and reorder the tabs by using Ctrl-Shift-Left Arrow and Ctrl-Shift-Right Arrow. For easy reference, give the tabs names by double-clicking on them and entering a name in the window that appears. If you need to separate a tab from the main window, just right-click the tab and choose Detach Session. When you are done with a Konsole tab or session, simply type **exit** and press Enter to close it.

Konsole's appearance is customizable to some degree. You can make several quick adjustments from the Settings menu, and especially from the Fonts and Schema submenus. (My personal favorite is the Green on Black Schema.) To make these quick changes stick, choose Settings →

Save as Default. If you want to make more advanced changes, go to Settings → Configure Konsole. In this configuration window you can perform several adjustments, including making changes to existing schemas or creating new ones. When you are finished making changes, give your schema a new name and save it.

Important Commands

In Linux you can run hundreds of commands on the command line. When you consider all the different options and arguments each command can accept, you have millions of possibilities. Many commands are used primarily by programmers and system administrators, but there are many others that are very useful for regular desktop users.

Learning these basic commands is a great way to become comfortable with the command line. Once you are familiar with some commands, you'll see that they are often easier and faster to use than clicking around on menus and icons. As you get more experienced with Linux, you will probably find yourself using the command line more and more often.

The following examples use a test user account named jharris. Be sure to perform all the steps in order—if you don't, you might end up with different results than what's described here.

Commands are case sensitive

In Linux, everything you type at the command line is case sensitive. A file named *README* is a different file than one called *Readme*. A command of ls is different than a command of LS.

Getting There from Here

When you begin a car trip, knowing where you're going is only slightly more important than knowing where you are. Directions to the airport are useful only if they start from the place you're at or that you know how to get to. On the command line, it's easy to lose track of where you are. Luckily, the command-line prompt on *Move* is configured to give you some information. Your command prompt in your Konsole window should look something like this:

    [jharris@localhost jharris]$

Let's go through this from left to right to understand its meaning: a user named jharris is on a machine called localhost and is inside a directory called *jharris*. (As mentioned in Chapter 3, directories are the same as folders.) The $ indicates that jharris is a regular user.

While a prompt that tells you who you are and where you are is useful, it doesn't tell you the whole story. Imagine there are five directories on your machine called *jharris*. How do you know which one you're in? It's like giving a friend directions to your house by telling them to start at McDonald's, but not telling them which one. Happily, there is a command that can tell you this information. Type the following at the prompt:

```
[jharris@localhost jharris]$ pwd
/home/jharris
```

The pwd command displays your present working directory; that is, it tells you where you are. In this case, I am in my home directory, */home/jharris*.

About command names

You'll notice that a lot of Linux commands are "shorthand" for the words they represent. In this case, pwd stands for print working directory. Knowing the "shorthand" makes it much easier to remember the commands.

Listing files and directories

Besides knowing where you are, it's also nice to know what that place looks like. You can use the ls (list) command to list the files in your current directory:

```
[jharris@localhost jharris]$ ls
Desktop/tmp/
```

If you haven't been saving items to a USB key, your home directory listing probably looks a lot like this one. There are several ways you can modify your listing to control how it is displayed and how much information it shows. For instance, to display your directories and files as a single column, specify the -1 (the number) option:

```
[jharris@localhost jharris]$ ls -1
Desktop/
tmp/
```

Type it right

Note that in all commands, the option is separated from the command with a space.

If you want to see more information about your files, like who owns them, when they were last changed, and how big they are, use the -l (the letter) option:

```
[jharris@localhost jharris]$ ls -l
total 0
drwx------3 jharris  jharris  140 Dec  Chapter 9 02:00 Desktop/
drwx------3 jharris  jharris   40 Dec  Chapter 8 20:59 tmp/
```

You may recall from Chapter 3 that there are a lot of configuration files in your home directory that are normally hidden from view. All these files begin with a period (.), which is the way that Linux hides files and directories that do not need to be seen in normal circumstances. To see these hidden files, add the -a option to the previous command:

```
[jharris@localhost jharris]$  ls -al
total 29
drwx------ 22 jharris jharris 2560 Jan 14 02:27 ./
drwx------ Chapter 4 jharris jharris  512 Jan 13 20:12 ../
-rwx------ Chapter 1 jharris jharris  302 Jan 14 02:19 .bash_history*
-rwx------ Chapter 1 jharris jharris   24 Jan 10 23:21 .bash_logout*
-rwx------ Chapter 1 jharris jharris  191 Jan 10 23:21 .bash_profile*
-rwx------ Chapter 1 jharris jharris  124 Jan 10 23:21 .bashrc*
-rwx------ Chapter 1 jharris jharris   66 Jan 14 01:12 .DCOPserver_
localhost.localdomain__0*
drwx------ Chapter 3 jharris jharris 1024 Jan 13 02:49 Desktop/
drwx------ Chapter 2 jharris jharris 1536 Jan 13 03:40 .figures/
drwx------ Chapter 2 jharris jharris  512 Jan 14 01:12 .gconf/
drwx------ Chapter 2 jharris jharris  512 Jan 14 01:14 .gconfd/
drwx------ Chapter 2 jharris jharris  512 Jan 11 04:21 .gnome/
drwx------ Chapter 3 jharris jharris  512 Jan 11 04:21 .gnome2/
drwx------ Chapter 2 jharris jharris  512 Jan 11 04:21 .gnome2_private/
drwx------ Chapter 4 jharris jharris 1024 Jan 11 04:21 .kde/
drwx------ Chapter 4 jharris jharris  512 Jan 13 03:40 .lgames/
-rwx------ Chapter 1 jharris jharris 1660 Jan 13 02:48 .mailcap*
drwx------ Chapter 3 jharris jharris  512 Jan 11 04:21 .mcop/
-rwx------ Chapter 1 jharris jharris   31 Jan 14 01:12 .mcoprc*
drwxr-xr-x Chapter 4 jharris jharris 1024 Jan 14 01:12 .mdkmove-truefs/
-rwx------ Chapter 1 jharris jharris  635 Jan 13 02:48 .mime.types*
drwx------ Chapter 3 jharris jharris  512 Jan 13 02:47 .netscape/
drwx------ Chapter 3 jharris jharris  512 Jan 13 02:47 .netscape6/
drwxr-xr-x Chapter 5 jharris jharris 1024 Jan 13 02:49 .openoffice/
drwx------ Chapter 2 jharris jharris  512 Jan 14 01:12 .qt/
```

```
-rwx------  Chapter 1 jharris jharris 3729 Jan 10 23:21 .screenrc*
drwx------  Chapter 2 jharris jharris  512 Jan 11 05:01 .ssh/
-rwx------  Chapter 1 jharris jharris   65 Jan 13 02:48 .sversionrc*
drwx------  Chapter 3 jharris jharris  512 Jan 11 04:48 .thumbnails/
drwx------  Chapter 2 jharris jharris  512 Jan 10 23:21 tmp/
```

This is an example of how you can often *combine* options after a single hyphen to manipulate your results in more than one way.

Moving to different directories

Now that you know where you are and what's around you, you need to know how to get somewhere. Let's go someplace interesting–the *.kde* directory of your home directory. The *.kde* directory holds all the configuration files that control how KDE is set up. To move to a different directory, you use the cd (change directory) command, followed by the path to the directory. (A *path* is like a set of directions starting with where you are and ending with where you want to go.) So to change to the *.kde* directory, use this command:

```
[jharris@localhost jharris]$  cd .kde/share/config
[jharris@localhost config]$
```

Notice that the prompt now shows the *config* directory instead of *jharris*. If you now do an ls command in this directory you will see dozens of configuration files for KDE.

To change back to your home directory, just run cd by itself. Its default action is to take you back to your home directory. If you want to go back only one directory, cd provides a special argument just for that, as shown below (the use of pwd is just to show where you are):

```
[jharris@localhost config]$  pwd
/home/jharris/.kde/share/config
[jharris@localhost config]$ cd ../
[jharris@localhost share]$  pwd
/home/jharris/.kde/share
```

As you can see, the ../ argument moved you back exactly one directory. You can repeat this option twice to go back two directories (cd ../../), three times to go back three directories, and so on. You can also use ../ when you want to go back one directory and go forward into another one, like this:

```
[jharris@localhost share]$ cd config
[jharris@localhost config]$ cd ../applnk-mdk-simplified
[jharris@localhost applnk]$ pwd
/home/jharris/.kde/share/applnk-mdk-simplified
```

As you can see, you are now in */home/jharris/.kde/share/applnk-mdk-simplified.* If you had made customizations to your K Menu (which you can't do with *Move*), this is where the configuration files would be. In most versions of Linux, you would find these custom menu files in *.kde/share/applnk/.*

Controlling Files and Directories

Now that you know how to move around on the command line at will, you're ready to start managing your files and directories. There are several commands that you need to know to create, delete, and move files and directories.

Go Home

Remember, if you get lost while you're on the command line, just type **cd** to go back to your home directory.

Making directories

One thing you'll often need to do is create new directories to store your files. Linux provides the command mkdir (make directory) to create new directories. Here, you'll use this command to create a test directory, so that you can then practice your commands without messing anything else up. Change to your home directory (**cd**) and then run the following commands:

```
[jharris@localhost jharris]$ mkdir testing
[jharris@localhost jharris]$ ls
Desktop/testing/tmp/
[jharris@localhost jharris]$ cd testing
[jharris@localhost testing]$ pwd
/home/jharris/testing
```

These commands create a directory called *testing*, show you that it was created, take you into it, and then show you that you are in it. (Of course, you don't have to go through all this every time you create a directory; you're just practicing what you've learned in this chapter.)

Removing directories

You can delete directories with the rmdir (remove directory) command. To practice this, back out of the current directory and delete the *testing* directory:

```
[jharris@localhost testing]$ cd ../
[jharris@localhost jharris]$ rmdir testing
[jharris@localhost jharris]$ ls
Desktop/tmp/
```

The *testing* directory is now gone, as you can confirm by running ls. Now, re-create the *testing* directory and cd to it, because you need a place to practice a few more commands.

Copying files and directories

To practice file management, first you need some files to work with. Since you've already visited the *.kde/share/config* directory, you know there are a lot of files in there you can use. First, though, you need to copy (cp) them to your test directory with the following command:

```
[jharris@localhost testing]$ cp ~/.kde/share/config/* ~/testing/
cp: omitting directory `/home/jharris/.kde/config/kresources'
```

This command copies all the files in the *.kde/share/config* directory and places them in your *testing* directory. The tildes (~) in the command are just a shorthand way to specify your home directory, and the asterisk (*) is known as a wildcard, and it tells the program to select everything in the *config* directory. Now, if you run an ls in the *testing* directory, you will see that all of the files have copied over.

You probably also noticed that the command reported that it was omitting the directory *kresources* from the copy (if the directories *colors* and *session* exist, they are also ommitted). As you can tell from the path in the error, this directory is actually inside the *config* directory. The regular cp command doesn't copy directories, just files. To copy this directory along with the files, you must use the -R option to tell the cp command to descend into directories and copy the files found there:

```
[jharris@localhost testing]$ cp -R ~/.kde/share/config/* ~/testing/
cp: overwrite `/home/jharris/testing/dummy'?
```

This time, instead of just copying the files, the cp command raises a question: is it okay to copy over the file called *dummy* that is already in the *testing* directory? This occurs because you already copied *dummy* to the *testing* directory with your first copy command, and now you are trying to do it again. You could answer the question by pressing y and then Enter, but there are a lot of files, and you'll have to provide an answer for each one. So in this case it's better to cancel the copy, and then rerun it to automatically answer yes to all questions. To cancel the copy, use the standard keyboard command to "break" a process:

```
cp: overwrite `/home/jharris/testing/dummy'? Ctrl-C
[jharris@localhost testing]$
```

Ctrl-C can be used to cancel pretty much any command-line process. Now, to tell the copy command to ignore any filename conflicts, use the -f (force) option:

```
[jharris@localhost testing]$ cp -Rf ~/.kde/share/config/* ~/testing/
```

You will see no indication that the copy happened; you are simply returned to the prompt when it finishes. You can run an ls command to confirm that the files and directories were copied.

Moving and renaming files and directories

It's very easy to move files from one directory to another in Linux using the mv (move) command. The following command, run from the *testing* directory, moves the *kmailrc* file from the *testing* directory into your home directory:

```
[jharris@localhost testing]$ mv kmailrc ~
[jharris@localhost testing]$ ls ~
Desktop/kmailrctesting/tmp/
```

It's that simple to use the mv command—just specify the file or directory you want to move and the location you want to move it to. The mv command does not require the -R option to move directories or their contents.

You can also use mv to rename files and directories. This may seem a little odd at first, but from the standpoint of the way an operating system handles files on a disk it makes perfect sense. Here is an example of how to use the command in this way (after creating a work directory for your moves):

```
[jharris@localhost testing]$ mkdir moved
[jharris@localhost testing]$ mv konquerorrc moved/
[jharris@localhost testing]$ ls moved/
konqrc
```

This command moves the configuration file for *konquerorrc* to the *moved* directory and renames it to *konqrc*. As you can see, it is very similar to moving a file, except that the second path ends with a new filename instead of ending with a directory. If that file already exists, then this command replaces it with the one you are moving.

Here's how to use mv to rename a directory:

```
[jharris@localhost testing]$ mv moved/ renamed
```

This is just like renaming a file, except that you are ending with a directory name that doesn't already exist (in this case, *renamed*). If the directory *had* already existed, you would have ended up moving the first directory into the second one.

Deleting files

If you keep up with your file management, you'll often need to delete files. The command to do this is rm (remove). It is used just like rmdir is used to delete directories. For example:

```
jharris@localhost testing$: rm renamed/konqrc
rm:  remove regular file `renamed/konqrc'? y
```

One you type y and press Enter, this command removes the *konqrc* file you created a few steps ago. You can specify multiple files by placing a space between them. Linux requires you to confirm that you want to remove the file for your own protection—unlike using Konqueror to move a file to the Trash, once you remove a file from the command line it is gone for good. Like most things in Linux, this is a configurable option, but it's beyond the scope of this chapter to tell you how to change this setting.

Linux Helps Those Who Help Themselves

So now you know some commands that will help you manage your files. As you've probably noticed, many commands, such as ls and cp, have multiple options. As you get used to using Linux, you'll quickly memorize the most useful options to common commands. But sometimes you'll forget exactly how to use an option, or you may need to use an obscure option. Linux kindly provides self-help files that tell you exactly how to use all the options of these commands. These help files are called *man* (manual) pages.

To bring up the man page for a command, just run man, followed by the name of the command, like this:

```
[jharris@localhost jharris]$ man ls
```

To move around in a man page, use the up and down arrows to scroll a line at a time, and the Page Up and Page Down buttons to scroll a page at a time. Press Q to quit the program.

Help files in Linux follow a standard format. Once you learn it, you can usually understand most man pages. First off is the NAME section:

```
NAME
        ls - list directory contents
```

This section simply lists the various names by which this command is called. In this example, you can see that it is just called ls.

Next is the SYNOPSIS section:

```
SYNOPSIS
        ls [OPTION]... [FILE]...
```

The SYNOPSIS listing tells you how you should format the command. For example, ls may be followed by one or more options and by a filename. Because [OPTION] and [FILE] are in brackets, it means that they are not required, and that the ls command will do *something* even if no options are specified. If they were not in brackets, it would mean they *were* required in order for the command to work. (Look at the man page for cp for an example; SOURCE and DEST are required elements to use the cp command.)

Next up is the DESCRIPTION section. This is simply a description of the command, frequently accompanied by examples of it in actual use. These descriptions are sometimes very clear and simple to follow, and other times are extremely complex with a lot of technical jargon. The DESCRIPTION also lists the alphabetic and numeric options that can be passed to the command. You'll want to read this section carefully, because it's where you learn to manipulate the command to make it even more useful.

Konquering man pages

Here's a neat trick. Open Konqueror and type `man:/ls` in the URL box. Konqueror will find the man page and display it in an easy-to-read format. This is a convenient way to print out man page documentation. If you just type `man:/`, you'll get a listing of all the man pages divided into sections.

Useful Navigation Tips

So far in this chapter, I've covered just the basic commands and some simple command-line interaction. This section presents a few easy-to-understand tips to help you get around the command line.

The command-line interface on *Move* is configured to remember everything you type in. To bring up the command-line history, just press the up arrow on your keyboard. This shows you the most recent command you typed in. Each additional press of the up arrow shows you the next oldest command in your history, and each press of the down arrow displays the next most recent command. The *bash* history is usually configured to store the 500 most recently used commands.

One obvious use of this history is to correct a command that you typed incorrectly. For example, suppose you wanted to run the date command, which displays the current date and time on the system. But instead of typing date, you typed dat instead:

```
[jharris@localhost jharris]$ dat
bash: dat: command not found
```

As you can see, the dat command doesn't exist (or it can't be found). Now, press the up arrow to bring up the command you just typed and add the missing **e**:

```
[jharris@localhost jharris]$ date
Thu Dec 9 18:29:26 EDT 2004
```

Another useful feature in Linux is called *command-line completion*. When you type the first few letters of a command and then press Tab, the computer attempts to display any single command that matches what you type. Try this out by typing **dat** at the command prompt and then pressing Tab. Linux completes the command for you by entering the final **e**. Of course, the computer didn't actually "guess" what command you want to enter–it simply compares what you typed against all the commands it knows about. Then, by process of elimination, it showed you the only command that starts with the letters you typed; there simply are no other commands that start with "dat".

You can also use tab completion to find commands you don't quite remember. For example, let's say you want to delete a directory. You may remember that the rm command removes *files*, but you can't remember how to remove *directories*. Try using Tab completion to find out which commands are available:

```
[jharris@localhost jharris]$ rm <press Tab>
rm    rmdir rmiregistry rmmod-24  rmmod.old  rmt
rman rmid   rmmod rmmod-25 rmold
```

Now you'll see all the commands that start with rm, and can probably figure out that the one you're looking for is rmdir.

Tab 2x

Move is configured to require just a single Tab to display available options, but most command lines require you to press Tab twice to get the same results.

You can use tab completion on more than just commands; it can be used to complete filenames and paths as well. For example, to change from your home directory to the *testing/renamed* directory you created earlier, type **cd test** → **Tab** → **ren** → **Tab** → **Enter**. Just as with command completion, if there is more than one match for what you typed, the system may beep and display the matches so far, and you'll have to enter more information before Tab completion can work.

There are many more command-line editing tricks that can come in handy. But be warned–once you start using these shortcuts, you may find it impossible to function without them. Table 11-1 summarizes some of the most useful tricks.

TABLE 11-1. Useful editing keystrokes

Keystroke	Function
Up arrow	Move back one entry in the history list.
Down arrow	Move forward one entry in the history list.
Left arrow	Move back one character.
Right arrow	Move forward one character.
Backspace	Delete previous character.
Tab	Attempt to complete the current filename command.
Alt-B	Move back one word.
Alt-D	Delete current word.
Alt-F	Move forward one word.
Ctrl-A	Move to beginning of line.
Ctrl-D	Delete current character.
Ctrl-E	Move to end of line.
Ctrl-K	Delete to end of line.
Ctrl-L	Clear the screen, placing the current line at the top of the screen.
Ctrl-U	Delete from beginning of line.
Ctrl-Y	Retrieve last item deleted.
Esc.	Insert last word from the previous command. (Esc is pressed before the dot, not at the same time.)
Esc ?	List the possible completions. (Esc is pressed before the question mark, not at the same time.)

Finding and Stopping Runaway Programs

At any moment, there's a lot going on with your computer. Programs and processes are controlling hard drive access, determining what you see on the screen, managing what is written to event logs, and watching for input from you. If you've ever looked at the Task Manager on Windows 2000 or XP (press Ctrl-Alt-Del and click Task Manager to bring it up), you've seen a lot of programs running that you probably couldn't identify.

Sometimes programs crash or become unresponsive. I wish I could say that Linux was immune to problems like this, but it isn't. When a problem occurs, the affected program process may get hung up, and hang around, using up a lot of your computer's time and memory and slowing other programs down. You need to know how to find runaway program processes like this and force them to stop.

There are several ways to view running processes in Linux. One of the most popular is the top program. Here is the output from my laptop:

```
dbrick@rivendell $: top
top - 19:46:56 up 1 day, Chapter 8:18, Chapter 1 user,  load average: 0.02,
0.06, 0.05
Tasks:  48 total,  Chapter 1 running,  47 sleeping,   0 stopped,   0 zombie
Cpu(s):  Chapter 2.5% user,  Chapter 1.1% system,   0.9% nice,  95.5% idle
Mem:    514756k total,   491716k used,    23040k free,   101568k buffers
Swap:   521632k total,      196k used,   521436k free,   178524k cached

  PID USER      PR  NI  VIRT  RES  SHR S %CPU %MEM    TIME+  COMMAND
 2013 root      14   0 70524  24m 2296 S  2.0  4.8  14:21.21 X
25020 dbrick    11   0   924  924  736 R  2.0  0.2   0:00.03 top
  154 root       9   0   924  900  628 S  0.0  0.2   0:00.04 devfsd
 1296 root       9   0   680  672  532 S  0.0  0.1   0:00.00 syslog-ng
 1350 root       9   0   528  524  476 S  0.0  0.1   0:00.00 apmd
 1641 root       9   0   652  528  488 S  0.0  0.1   0:00.00 cardmgr
 1670 root       9   0   456  444  408 S  0.0  0.1   0:00.00 dhcpcd
 1787 root       8   0  1188 1164 1024 S  0.0  0.2   0:00.00 sshd
 1841 root       8   0   652  652  568 S  0.0  0.1   0:00.03 cron
21215 dbrick     9   0   876  872  776 S  0.0  0.2   0:00.01 kde-3.3.0
21221 dbrick     9   0   984  980  856 S  0.0  0.2   0:00.03 startkde
```

You may be thinking, "What *is* all this stuff?" Well, to start, the output is divided into two sections. The first five lines contain a lot of condensed information. You may be able to guess what some of it means—check the man page for top to see if you are right.

For now, concern yourself with the second portion of the top output, which is a listing of currently running processes. By default, the processes are sorted by how much processing power they use. In this case, the X program that controls the drawing of images on the screen is using 2 percent of my processing power and 4.8 percent of my memory.

When you have a misbehaving program, the information you need is in the first column, PID, which stands for process ID. Every running program on Linux has one or more processes, and every process has a PID; think of it as a name for your process that your computer can understand.

You can use the PID from top to identify and stop runaway programs. For instance, if you are running KWrite and it has stopped responding, you can't close it by clicking the close button on the title bar or by using a menu command or keyboard shortcut. You'll have to close it from the command line instead. To do this, you first have to identify KWrite's current PID. A runaway program is usually consuming a lot of processing power, so when you run top, the troublesome program should be right at the top. Once you know the PID (let's pretend it's 1000), you can stop the process by issuing a `kill` command. (Don't actually do this unless you have a real runaway process.)

```
[jharris@localhost jharris]$ kill 1000
```

If the command is successful, the program window will close. However, it's possible for a program to be so badly hung up that it doesn't respond to this command. That means you need to pass `kill` the `-9` option, which basically means to kill with a vengeance.

Use the `man` command to read more about `top` and `kill`. You can quit the `top` program by pressing Q.

Graphical process viewer

From the KDE desktop, Press Ctrl-Esc for a graphical way to view processes. This window will take several seconds to come up. It lists all processes by default, but you can use the drop-down list at the bottom to view only your processes (User Processes). To stop a process, highlight it in the list and click the Kill button.

Zipping and Unzipping Files

One of Windows' most popular utilities is the compression program WinZip. This handy program lets you group a bunch of files together and compress them into one smaller file. This smaller file size means little when you consider the large hard drive capacities most computers have today, but it can be a real blessing when you want to send a lot of files, like all the pictures of your wedding, to friends and family via email. Also, you often need to unzip programs you download from the Internet before you can install them. This is true for both Windows and Linux.

Linux has long had the ability to zip and unzip files. In fact, it has several programs, both command-line and GUI, to perform these tasks. Some of them use the same compression algorithm used by WinZip, while others use a free variant. I'll explain how to use both types of programs.

Let's pretend that you've received an email from your sister, with a zipped attachment containing pictures of your nephew's first birthday party. Though you could open this attachment and view the files using Konqueror (covered in Chapter 3), let's use the command line instead. Save the file attachment to your home directory and open a Konsole window. The command to open a zipped file archive is simply unzip:

```
[jharris@localhost jharris]$ unzip nephew.zip
Archive:  nephew.zip
 extracting: nephew1.jpg
 extracting: nephew2.jpg
 extracting: nephew3.gif
```

As you can see, the unzip program extracted three files from the zip archive and placed them in your current directory. You can run ls to confirm their location. To put the files into a new directory called *birthday* instead of in the current directory, modify the command by adding the -d option (destination) with an argument naming the directory you want to create:

```
[jharris@localhost jharris]$ unzip nephew.zip -d birthday
Archive:  nephew.zip
 extracting: nephew1.jpg
 extracting: nephew2.jpg
 extracting: nephew3.gif
```

Again, run ls to confirm that a directory called *birthday* has been created and that copies of the files are now in that directory.

If the situation were reversed and you wanted to send several photos to your sister, you would need to create a zip archive yourself. Let's pretend that you are in your home directory and want to send your sister only the *.jpg* images, not the *.gif* image. Here's the command you would use to do this:

```
[jharris@localhost jharris]$ zip nephew *.jpg
  adding: nephew1.jpg (stored 23%)
  adding: nephew2.jpg (stored 50%)
```

Let's walk through this command. First, type in the command **zip**. (Pretty intuitive, right?) Next, type in the name of the zip file you want to create. (The zip command automatically adds the *.zip* file extension when the file is created.) Finally, type in the files you want to put in the zip. In this case, using the * wildcard, you specified that you want to zip all the files in the current directory that end with *.jpg*. (Even if you had a directory with 50 *.jpg* images and 50 *.gif* images mixed up together, this simple command could accomplish the task in seconds. Imagine how long it would take with a GUI tool—you would have to select each JPEG file by hand!) Read the man pages for zip and unzip to find out about more options, like how to add a file to a zip archive you've already created.

As you use Linux, you'll frequently come across files that have been compressed using the gzip program, which is like an open source variant of WinZip. When sending files to Windows users, you should probably zip your files. But when sharing with Linux users, it is polite to gzip them, as gzip works better with standard Linux tools.

Files on the Internet that have been gzipped include program installers, source code, images, text files, music files, and anything else that Linux users want to share with each other. These files usually end with the file extension *.tar.gz*, which hints at one of the differences between a gzipped and a zipped file.

Zip programs group and compress files at the same time. Gzip programs simply compress files—they do *not* group them together. To group your files, you need to use an additional program called tar. This results in what is commonly referred to as a *tarball* of your files (cool name, huh?), which you can then compress with the gzip program.

For example, say you have downloaded a gzipped file called *crystal.tar.gz* from a web site. You need to first unzip this file using the gzip uncompressing program gunzip, and then unpackage the tarball using the tar program. Here's how you would do that:

```
[jharris@localhost jharris]$ gunzip crystal.tar.gz
[jharris@localhost jharris]$ tar -xvf crystal.tar
README.txt
crystal1.tif
crystal2.txt
```

The gunzip command in basic use is pretty simple. Just type in the command, and then specify the file you want to uncompress. Besides uncompressing the gzipped file, it also removes the gzipped file, leaving behind just a *.tar* version. You can confirm this by running ls before you use tar. The tar command requires a few options to be passed to it. The -x option means expand; the -v option means show the output (verbose); and the -f option means perform this action on the file specified. And since gunzip and tar are so often combined, tar provides a one-command way to both uncompress and untar a file by using the -z option:

```
bash-2.05b$ tar -xvzf crystal.tar.gz
README.txt
crystal1.tif
crystal2.txt
```

To reverse the situation, you can use tar and gzip to group these files together and compress them. This is how to do it with two separate commands:

```
bash$: tar -cvf crystal.tar README.txt crystal1.tif crystal2.txt
README.txt
crystal1.tif
crystal2.txt
bash$: gzip crystal.tar
```

The -c option for tar creates a new tarball with the filename you specify. Unlike with the zip command, you need to add the *.tar* extension yourself. The tarball name is followed by arguments for which files you want to include. Tab completion can be a handy way to add a lot of individual files. Finally, you compress the file with the gzip command, which takes the name of the *.tar* file as its argument.

Once again, the -z command can do double duty by creating the gzip file automatically when the tar file is made, so you only need to use one command:

```
bash$: tar -cvzf crystal.tar.gz README.txt crystal1.tif crystal2.txt
README.txt
crystal1.tif
crystal2.txt
```

And again, unlike zip, if you want the final filename to end with *.tar.gz*, you need to specify that in the command. To find out more about gzip, gunzip, and tar, check out their man pages.

Konquer the Command Line

So far, this book has explored Konqueror's abilities as a file manager, web browser, and all-purpose network filesystem access program. And as if all that weren't enough, Konqueror also includes an embedded command line. Open this from within Konqueror by clicking Window → Show Terminal Emulator. This opens a small terminal program (like Konsole) at the bottom of the current Konqueror window. Inside this window, you can use all of the tips and tricks taught in this chapter. Combining GUI and command-line file management in this way allows you to utilize the strengths of both.

This chapter just scratches the surface of the Linux command line. To continue our mechanics metaphor, it's the equivalent of high school shop class, not ASE certified mechanics certification. I've focused on file and directory management, not because that's all you can do on the command line (far from it!), but because it lays a firm foundation from which to build your knowledge. Although it's possible to use Linux without using the command line, you'd really be missing out on part of what makes Linux such a powerful operating system. To explore the command line further, pick up the *Linux Pocket Guide* or *Linux in a Nutshell,* both from O'Reilly.

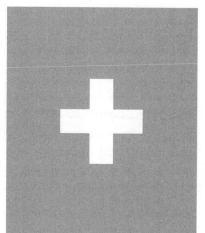

12

GREAT PROGRAMS THAT AREN'T ON THE CD

When you test-drive a car, your only option is to drive one on the dealer's lot. This car may not have the leather seats you want or may be the wrong color, but that's okay. You just want to see how the car feels and how it drives, and to make sure it's comfortable for you.

Test-driving Linux with the *Move* CD is the same thing. This CD doesn't include every available Linux program—there wouldn't be enough space for it. But it's still a good way to test-drive Linux because it gives you 90 percent of the features that you will have once you install a Linux distribution to your hard drive.

Still, there are a few programs of note that *Move* is missing, so I'll cover them here. These are by no means all of the programs Linux has to offer; they are just a few popular alternatives to the software covered earlier, as well as some useful programs that have no counterparts on the *Move* CD. My intent here is simply to inform you of other good open source programs, not to tell you how to use them.

Finding more programs

There are thousands of open source programs you can try. Some distributions include multiple CDs or even DVDs to give you a convenient way to install these programs. Many more can be searched for at web sites such as *http://freshmeat.net.*

In a couple of instances I make note of alternative live CDs that will let you try out the feature described. You can also test-drive programs such as Firefox, Thunderbird, Nvu, and Gaim on your Windows computer. The more open source programs you are comfortable using in Windows, the easier your transition to Linux will be.

GNOME: An Alternative to KDE

KDE isn't the only desktop environment available on Linux. In fact, there are dozens, but the most well known after KDE is GNOME (pronounced Guh-nome, but people forget to say it that way all the time).

Switching desktop environments from KDE to GNOME completely transforms the look and feel of your computer. You will not use more than one desktop environment at a time, but you can freely switch between them when you log into your computer.

The GNOME project started in 1997 as an alternative to the KDE environment, because some people didn't like that KDE was using a non-open source tool in its programs. Even though this sore point has since been addressed to most people's satisfaction, the GNOME project had a lot of talented coders working on it and has continued to be developed. It's debatable as to which is the best or most popular, but you would be doing yourself a disservice if you did not try out GNOME at some point.

GNOME takes a different approach to the desktop than KDE does. Rather than making every element tweakable, as KDE tends to do, GNOME prefers to hide its complexity behind a set of sensible defaults. There is still a lot of tweaking that can be done, but in GNOME it is just hidden under the hood, where its presence won't confuse new users.

The GNOME desktop as it appears in the Ubuntu distribution is shown in Figure 12-1. Note the presence of the bars at the top and bottom of the screen. The topmost bar contains the GNOME menu, which is similar to the K Menu and the Windows Start button. It is usually represented by a footprint icon, and in this screenshot has the word Applications attached to it. Next to the GNOME menu there may be more menus containing more program launchers or settings to control the computer. This may be followed by a few single-click icons to run some common programs, a bunch of empty space, and then a system tray that tells you useful things about your computer. The contents of the system tray vary depending on what you are doing on your computer; it always contains a clock, and sometimes items like a wireless signal strength indicator and a battery life monitor.

The bottom bar is dominated by the taskbar, which is where icons representing your running programs will appear. At the far left is a small icon that minimizes all your windows when clicked. Clicking it again raises all the windows. At the far right is a pager that lets you switch virtual desktops, and a small wastebasket where your deleted files will be put until you empty it.

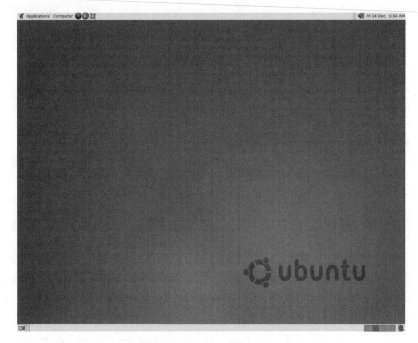

FIGURE 12-1. A typical GNOME desktop

The exact look of GNOME varies depending upon the distribution, but what you see here is pretty common to most setups. A few distributions don't use the top bar and move most of its functions to the bottom one, which makes it more like Windows. Users can customize their system either way.

The email client most often associated with GNOME is Evolution, which is described in the next section. GNOME is in the process of changing default web browsers to Firefox, described in the section after that.

Ubuntu live CD

A great way to try out the GNOME desktop, Evolution, and Firefox is to download the live CD for Ubuntu from *http://www.ubuntulinux.org*. This live CD also comes with several Windows installers that allow you to install Windows versions of many of the programs you see here. Just stick the CD in your drive while running Windows to see these installers.

The GNOME file manager is known as Nautilus. This simple-looking program has a lot of features that aren't immediately obvious, like the ability to burn CDs. What is obvious is that as you click through folders, each one opens in a new window. This is annoying to a lot of people because it clutters the screen, but familiar to classic Macintosh users and people who never changed the defaults in Windows 95 and 98. This is actually a recently introduced feature known as *spatial views*, and it is an improvement upon similar concepts that were implemented in earlier operating systems.

The idea behind spatial views is that each window will open in exactly the same place, with exactly the same size, using exactly the same view (list, large icons, small icons, etc.) as the last time you opened it (Figure 12-2). The GNOME programmers think this will make managing files easier because users will associate files with the appearance, location, and size of the directory window on the screen. This is different from users thinking of files as being located somewhere within a nest of directories and as something they have to "drill down" to get to. Personally, I don't like spatial views, but many people who have spent time with Nautilus love it. It can, of course, be turned off.

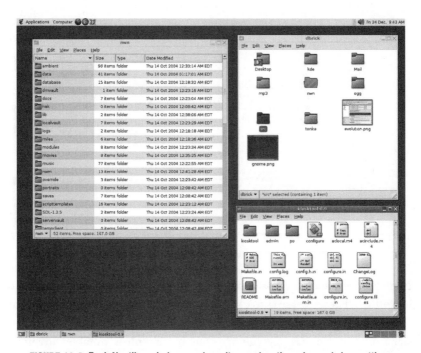

FIGURE 12-2. Each Nautilus window can have its own location, size and view settings

Evolution: An Outlook Work-Alike

Kontact is KDE's version of Microsoft's Outlook personal information manager, and Evolution is GNOME's. Though Evolution does bear a strong resemblance to Outlook in appearance (Figure 12-3), it has many advanced features that make it a very useful program in its own right. One such feature is called the Novell Connector, which allows a user to connect Evolution to a Microsoft Exchange Server so that calendars and contacts can be shared with Outlook users. Unlike Kontact, which is a parent program designed to hold several child programs like KMail and KOrganizer, Evolution was designed from the beginning to be a single application with calendar and contact features. As a result, it feels a little more polished, and you won't encounter any odd behavior when you switch between components.

FIGURE 12-3. The main Evolution window in email mode

Evolution provides the basic functions of email, contacts, calendars, and to-do lists. These features work, and they work well. If you are familiar with Outlook or Outlook Express you won't have any difficulty understanding how to use Evolution. One of the most notable advances

Evolution makes over Outlook and other email clients is the notion of *virtual folders*. These folders are a lot like the saved searches for KMail described in Chapter 6, and the same advantages described for KMail's saved searches apply to virtual folders. My personal experience is that virtual folders work better.

Evolution is most often associated with the GNOME desktop. However, there is no reason you can't run it on a KDE desktop, and many people do just that. However, since it was programmed with different tools than KDE, there will be some slight differences in the look of the program. For instance, in a typical window the Cancel button is on the left and the OK button is on the right. But I think you'll be able to handle it.

Firefox: A Powerful Web Browser

Microsoft's Internet Explorer web browser has been the dominant browser since about 1997. It is so pervasive that Microsoft has not felt the need to correct many of its flaws or security holes, a situation that has left Windows computers vulnerable to exploit by malicious code downloaded from web sites.

Firefox, shown in Figure 12-4, was originally called Phoenix because it rose from the ashes of the formerly dominant and now dying Netscape Navigator. However, that name was already taken by another software program, so the project went through a few name changes before settling on Firefox. Based upon the Gecko HTML rendering engine (the part of the program that determines how web pages look) that is at the heart of the Mozilla web browser, Firefox is a lean, fast web browser with a lot of built-in functions such as tabbed web browsing and pop-up ad blocking. It also supports all of the major plug-ins that run on Linux, such as Java, JavaScript, and Flash.

Firefox runs on 10 different operating systems, including Linux, Mac OS X, and Windows. That means you can take it for a test drive on your current Windows machine by visiting *http://www.mozilla.org* and downloading the Windows installer.

Firefox can be improved through the addition of small programs called *extensions*. Anybody can program these and upload them for others to enjoy. There are currently dozens of extensions to Firefox that add such diverse functions as quick access to multiple search engines, a weather report in the status bar of the browser, and even automatic usernames

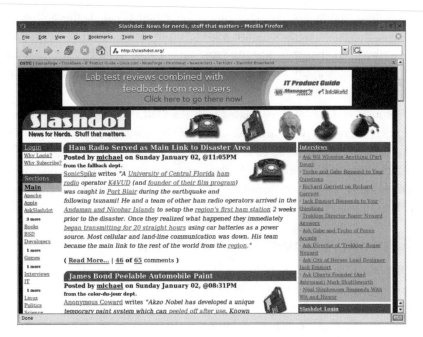

FIGURE 12-4. Firefox displaying the main page of the geek web site Slashdot

and passwords for news sites such as the New York Times. Extensions are easy to find; just go to Tools → Extensions and click Get More Extensions in the window that appears (Figure 12-5). All extensions can be updated with a single click of the Update button in the same window.

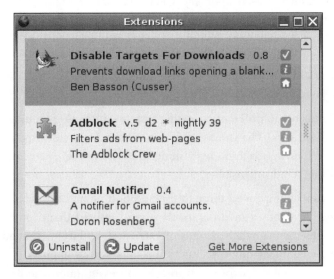

FIGURE 12-5. The Firefox Extensions window

Recent evidence suggests that IE is starting to lose its long-held dominance on the Web, as Firefox and other browsers begin to erode its market share. It's hard to gauge exactly how much certain browsers are used, but there appears to be a consensus that IE has lost about 6 percent of its market share in the past eight months. Not bad, considering Firefox only reached Version 1.0 in November 2004. Though IE still has 89 percent of the market, further evidence suggests that computer power-users are switching from it in droves as webmasters at technical web sites report Firefox or Mozilla usage as high as 50 percent.

Make Windows safer

If you're running a version of Windows prior to Windows XP I strongly encourage you to switch to Firefox right away. Microsoft is providing patches and updates only to the version of IE on Windows XP, which means that your machine is becoming increasingly vulnerable to malicious code on the Internet. Firefox is largely immune to these security problems, and when problems do arise they are typically fixed very quickly.

Thunderbird: A Feature-Rich Email Client

While Firefox is based upon the Gecko HTML rendering from the Mozilla project, Thunderbird is based upon Mozilla's email client code. Think of it more as an alternative to Outlook Express than as a replacement for Outlook. Thunderbird supports POP3 and IMAP clients, and beyond the typical email features it also provides a highly accurate statistical spam filter and a newsgroup reader. A statistical spam filter determines the likelihood of a particular message being spam, based upon you teaching it what you consider spam. After a few days of training, it should achieve an accuracy rate as high as 99 percent. Figure 12-6 shows the main configuration screen for Thunderbird's spam filter.

Thunderbird also runs on Windows and Mac OS X, so you can try it out without switching to Linux. And you might consider doing so, because Thunderbird is more secure than Outlook Express, and also provides superior features such as the spam filter and an RSS news aggregator.

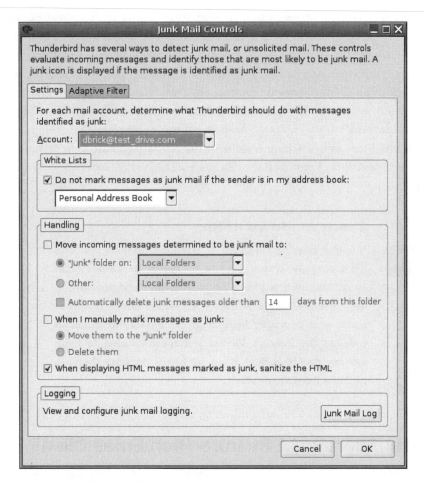

FIGURE 12-6. Thunderbird's main junk mail configuration screen

Make the Web come to you

RSS stands for Really Simple Syndication. It is just a method to
have web sites tell you when they have been changed. When you
subscribe to an RSS feed for a web site such as *cnn.com*, it will tell
you when it has new stories without you having to visit. This can
save a lot of time if you normally browse many web sites looking
for one that has a new story to read.

Like Firefox, Thunderbird can be enhanced with the use of extensions. There aren't as many extensions as for Firefox, but that situation will change as Thunderbird becomes more widely accepted.

You can find more information about Thunderbird at its web site, *http://www.mozilla.org/products/thunderbird/*.

MythTV: TiVo for Your Linux Computer

If you're reading this book, you're probably tech-savvy enough to have heard of TiVo, the handy appliance that records television for you. Yes, that is what a VCR does, but the difference is that TiVo can hold 40 or more hours of high-quality video, provides a graphical and easy way to program shows to record, lets you jump around almost instantly in a recorded show, and even gives you the ability to pause the Superbowl while you go to the bathroom. TiVo is part of a new category of appliances known as Personal Video Recorders (PVRs) and sometimes called Digital Video Recorders (DVRs). TiVo has become so popular that *TiVoed* has become a verb. What few people know is that TiVos run on Linux. This makes it a lot like Google, which also runs on Linux and has its own verb—*Googled*.

Unfortunately, the TiVo program code is not available for download, which means you can't make your own. But about three years ago, someone decided to create his own alternative. Isaac Richards started the MythTV project in 2002 to create a PVR for himself. He opened up his code and made it available for others to contribute. The result is a very successful project used by many Linux users to create their own multimedia center for their home. You can find out more at the project's homepage, *http://www.mythtv.org*.

I say that MythTV is a multimedia center because it has moved beyond the basic recording abilities of TiVo. It can also play music files, display digital images, play random video files you create yourself or download from the Internet, play DVDs, check the weather, and even make long-distance phone calls over the Internet. And if you think the XMame program covered in Chapter 5 sounded like fun, you'll be happy to know that you can run classic arcade games on your TV using XMame and MythTV.

MythTV got its name because it is the mythical convergence box that tries to meet all your multimedia needs in one place. Microsoft makes a version of Windows called Windows Media Center 2005 that comes close, but doesn't quite reach the functionality of MythTV.

To create a MythTV box you need a computer with at least a 1 Ghz processor, a lot of hard drive space, a video capture card, and limitless patience. It seems like most people prefer the Win-PVR video capture cards from Hauppauge. Where you get your patience from is up to you.

MythTV downloads television programming information from a web site called ZAP2it. To get this information into your MythTV system so you can program shows to record, you need to register a free account with ZAP2it and answer a very short survey every three months. Figure 12-7 shows TV schedule information in MythTV. This screen is just one of the places where you can set your programs to record.

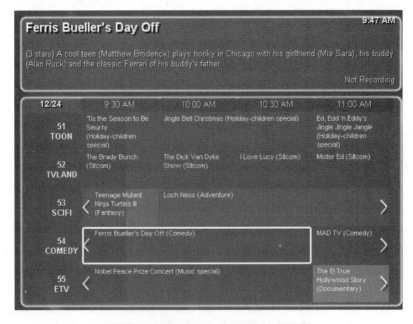

FIGURE 12-7. The recording scheduler in MythTV

The Media Library screen, shown in Figure 12-8, is where you choose which of your recorded shows to watch. This screen conveniently groups your shows together, displays a description of each show, and lets you delete shows when you are finished viewing.

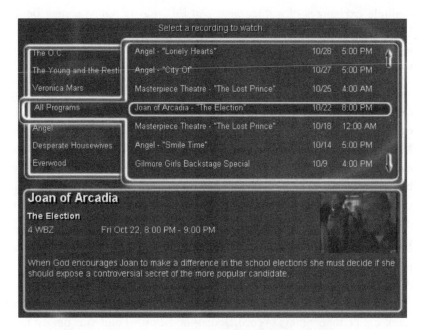

FIGURE 12-8. The Media Library screen lets you select shows for viewing

MythTV is in a constant state of development. If you choose to create a MythTV box, be sure to search the Web for the latest documentation on how to do it. A good place to start is *http://www.mythtv.org/modules. php?name=MythInstall.*

The MythTV live CD

There is a live CD called KnoppMyth that helps you set up a MythTV system. You can download it from *http://www. mysettopbox.tv/knoppmyth.html.* You can't run MythTV from the CD; it simply helps you set it up quickly.

Running Microsoft Office on Linux

You may be one of those people who really need to use Microsoft Office. If you're like me, you use Microsoft Word because you collaborate with others who use Word, and fixing formatting problems across multiple exchanges of a document can be a hassle. Or you may be an Excel power-user with a lot of macros that you just don't have time to rewrite for OpenOffice.org Calc. Regardless of your reason, you just know that you can't use Linux until it runs Microsoft Office.

Well, the good news is that Linux can run Microsoft Office. A company called CodeWeavers (*http://www.codeweavers.com*) has created a product called CrossOver Office that enables you to run your Windows copy of Microsoft Office (not a Mac copy) under Linux. This book was written using this product to run Word on Linux. CrossOver Office isn't free, but it's only $39.95 for a single user. Obviously, you need to provide your own copy of Microsoft Office. CrossOver Office also supports other programs like Photoshop, Quicken, and QuickTime.

I can't say that it's flawless, but most issues are more quirks than real problems. For example, when I first open a long document, sometimes there isn't a scrollbar along the right-hand side. If I minimize the window and bring it back up, the scrollbar is back. Also, some programs work better than others. Word, Excel, and PowerPoint run nearly perfectly, but Outlook and Internet Explorer have more glaring bugs.

Is CrossOver TOO good?

Rumor has it that CrossOver replicates the Windows environment so well it can run Windows viruses! Don't worry, though— even if it could, it can't infect your Linux system.

CrossOver Office is very simple to use. You install it through a graphical installer that asks only a few questions. To install Office itself, you have to launch the CodeWeavers Office Setup tool (Figure 12-9). From inside this program you can launch the installer for Microsoft Office. When Office is installed, it places icons for the components in your KDE or GNOME menu, which you can then use to launch the programs.

From this point on, using Office is just like using it on Windows. If you click an Office document it opens in the proper program, and all menus, options, and commands work as usual (Figure 12-10).

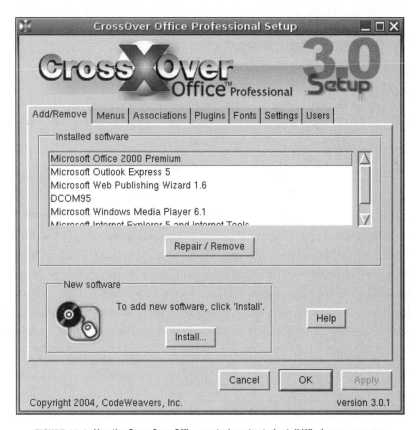

FIGURE 12-9. Use the CrossOver Office control center to install Windows programs

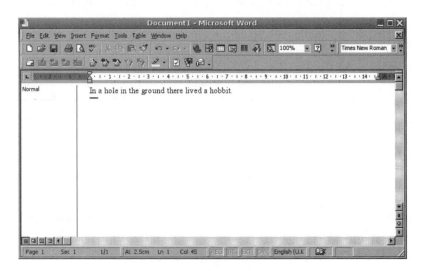

FIGURE 12-10. Microsoft Word running on Linux

Supported programs

CrossOver Office can be used to install other Windows programs as well. You can see the supported programs on the product page for CrossOver, *http://www.codeweavers.com/site/products/cxoffice/*. It's possible that dozens or even hundreds of other programs also work; they just haven't been tested yet. Once you are running Linux you can download a trial version of CrossOver Office and try out any other Windows programs that are important to you.

CodeWeavers bases their program on the open source project known as WINE. This project has the big, hairy, audacious goal of allowing all Windows programs to run under Linux. CodeWeavers employs several of the main WINE programmers and contributes their improvements back to the project, with the exception of their easy-to-use installer. If you don't want to pay for a copy of CodeWeavers or are willing to invest some time installing Windows programs, try out WINE. The homepage for the project is at *http://www.winehq.com*.

Creating Web Pages

An operating system developed by people communicating over the Internet should have a program to develop web pages. Microsoft devotees use Frontpage, professional designers like Dreamweaver, and Linux purists use text editors. The somewhat less pure use Quanta Plus.

Quanta is a complete web development environment (Figure 12-11). It provides for easy management of multiple web projects, FTP upload of your files to your web server, a text editor view that color-codes your tagging, and even a WYSIWIG view that lets you see how your web pages will look as you are creating them.

Quanta includes a built-in syntax checker that checks not only HTML, but other languages like PHP, Perl, and SQL. This feature helps ensure that all of your web pages are standards-compliant and will display correctly in the widest range of web browsers. More information can be found at *http://quanta.sourceforge.net*.

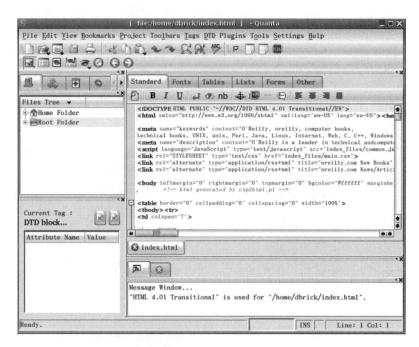

FIGURE 12-11. The main Quanta Plus window with a web page loaded

Quanta isn't the only HTML editor for Linux. The *Move* CD includes a very basic one called Mozilla Composer. You can launch it from K Menu → All Applications → Internet → Web editors → Mozilla Composer.

Recently the Composer code has been improved upon, creating a product called Nvu (Figure 12-12). Nvu is related to Mozilla Composer in the same way that Firefox is related to Mozilla. You can find out more about it at *http://www.nvu.com.* Nvu runs on Windows as well as Linux, so you can try it out without installing Linux.

Quanta is a more mature and more powerful program than Nvu, but Nvu is much easier to use when you just want to create simple web pages or web sites. Beyond that, the program you use will probably depend upon your skills as a web designer.

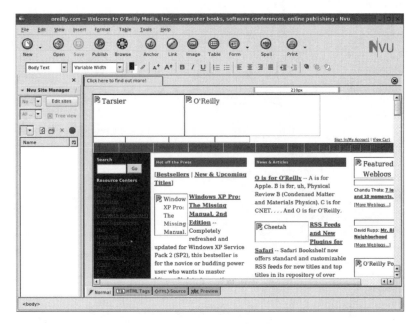

FIGURE 12-12. The main Nvu window with the oreilly.com web page loaded

KDevelop: A Complete Programming Environment

All the code that makes up KDE didn't write itself. It took—and takes—a lot of dedicated people working on the job and in their free time to develop all of these wonderful programs. One of the most important programs these people created was the programming tool they use to write more programs.

KDevelop is the KDE Integrated Programming Environment (Figure 12-13); that is, it's a one-stop program for all of your development needs. It allows you to work with several programming languages, such as Perl, Python, C, C++, and Java, and doesn't limit you to creating just KDE applications. A complete description and feature list for KDevelop can be found at *http://kdevelop.kde.org*.

I think the results that KDevelop produces, namely KDE, are a testament to its usefulness and to the ability of the KDE programmers. What's interesting and great about KDevelop is that it is completely free. Programming environments like this normally cost hundreds of dollars,

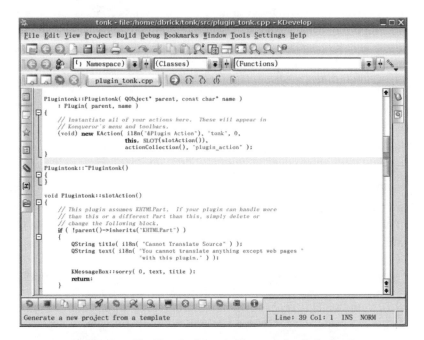

FIGURE 12-13. The KDevelop Integrated Programming Environment

if not more, and have to be licensed per individual programmer. This is cost-prohibitive for almost anyone interested in becoming a programmer, particularly young people.

But Linux, combined with free software compilers, debuggers, languages, and development tools like KDevelop, is a zero-cost environment in which anyone can learn how to program. Combine this with the availability of all the source code that makes up the open source world, the breadth of software projects eager to have someone help out, and the general friendliness of the open source community to people willing to learn, and you have a recipe for many people to find a lifelong hobby, or possibly an illustrious career as a programmer.

Scribus: Designing Magazine and Advertisement Layouts

The professional publishing world is dominated by just a few programs, most of them from Adobe. Chapter 7 already described the GIMP, an image editing tool that seeks to challenge Adobe Photoshop. This section introduces Scribus, an open source desktop publishing tool that seeks to rival Adobe InDesign and Quark XPress. Scribus is a long way from replacing either of these programs in all situations—even the commercial programs aren't adequate to all tasks—but still, Scribus has a few "wins." It is already being used by a small commercial newspaper, and recently the first professional book designed entirely in Scribus was published. Small victories to be sure, but all great things must start somewhere.

You might be interested in Scribus if you want to create a greeting card, design a flyer, or lay out a report for school. If you are a professional, you might have more ambitious needs, such as creating a marketing report, laying out an advertisement for a magazine, or designing a catalog to sell your products. Figure 12-14 shows the main Scribus window with a page spread loaded.

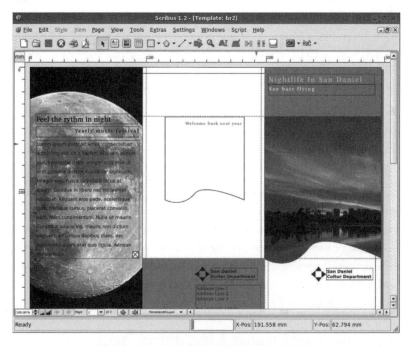

FIGURE 12-14. A page spread displayed in Scribus

Visit the main web site for Scribus at *http://www.scribus.org.uk/index.php* to find out more about the program and see some screenshots that show off some of its features.

Instant Messaging with Gaim

Chapter 6 covered the multi-network IM program Kopete because it is a KDE application and comes on the *Move* CD. But Gaim, another IM alternative, is actually the grand-daddy of all open source IM programs and the one I still prefer. Gaim runs the protocols for all the major networks, such as AIM, MSN, Yahoo, Jabber, IRC, and so on. Just as with Kopete, you can be logged onto different networks at the same time. And it runs on Windows, making it a great, free alternative to other multi-network IM clients you might have to pay for. And when you're finally ready to switch over to Linux entirely, Gaim will be just one more application you're already familiar with.

Gaim's web site is *http://gaim.sourceforge.net*, and information on the Windows version can be found at *http://gaim.sourceforge.net/win32/index.php*. There are links on this page to download a Windows version with or without GTK. GTK is a requirement to run the program, so unless you already have GTK installed on Windows (which is unlikely unless you installed the Windows version of the GIMP), you should probably choose the download with GTK.

Gaim supports file transfer, away messages, typing notification, and those little smiley faces everyone thinks are so cute. My favorite features are the tabbed chat windows, which help me keep all my chats in one easy-to-minimize window, and the spellchecking. I lost my ability to spell when I started using IM almost 10 years ago, and Gaim is helping me to get it back. Figure 12-15 shows the Gaim buddy list and a typical chat window.

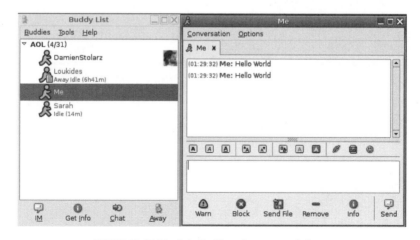

FIGURE 12-15. The Gaim buddy and message windows

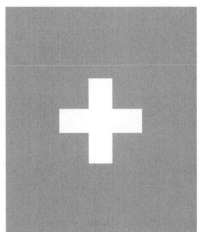

PRE-
SWITCHING
INFORMATION

Years ago, many Windows users had a hard time understanding that Windows Me was an upgrade to Windows 98, and that Windows 2000 upgraded Windows NT. Today, many users are confused about the differences between Windows XP Home and XP Professional. Imagine walking into a computer store and finding 300 different versions of Windows for sale, each created by a different company, and none of them from Microsoft. You would probably feel overwhelmed and confused about which version to buy. Well, I've got news for you: there are over 300 distributions of Linux available. Choice is good, but it can definitely be overwhelming.

A Linux *distribution* is a compilation of the Linux kernel and hundreds of other open source programs and utilities. Remember, by itself the Linux kernel is not a complete operating system. It is only when it is combined with other programs that it becomes a capable alternative to Microsoft Windows. Distributions are created and sold, or provided for free, by a company, group, or individual. It is up to the distribution creators to choose which programs to bundle together to make a complete OS. The distributors also create installers, hardware detection programs, and special configuration programs to aid in the installation, configuration, and maintenance of a Linux system. The choices made by these distributors are what gives each distribution its unique flavor and focus.

The diversity of Linux distributions is possible because they are all based upon free and open source software. That means anyone who wants to can take that software, customize it in whatever way they please, and create a new distribution. That is exactly what hundreds of people have done. You can find the results of their work at the distribution tracking web site *http://www.distrowatch.com*.

However, there's no need to let the diversity in distributions overwhelm you. Though all distributions have their merits and reasons for existence, there are really only about a dozen or so that are of interest to most people. A dozen isn't so bad. It's kind of like buying a car. If you can recognize the difference between a Ford and a Honda, and are capable of deciding between purchasing a Focus or a Civic, you can find a Linux distribution that suits your needs.

To extend the metaphor, a Focus and a Civic are different cars with different features and price points, but in the end, they're still just cars. They have steering wheels, speedometers, and radios, and you drive them using the same skills you learned in drivers education (or, if you're like me, on a dark road at five in the morning). By the same token, Mandrake and Debian are different distributions with different features, but in the end, they are both operating systems. They are controlled by a mouse and keyboard, offer features to listen to music and watch videos, and allow you to surf the Internet using the same skills you learned on Windows, a Macintosh, or from this book.

The Linux distribution on this book's CD is known as *Move*, from the company Mandrakesoft. Though this provides a great test drive of Linux, it shouldn't be your only Linux. Just as you can't use a test-drive vehicle from a dealership as your daily transportation, you shouldn't make *Move* your daily Linux desktop. This chapter is an overview of the most popular Linux distributions, and will help you make a decision as to which one you should try next. The end of the chapter lists some resources you can turn to for more information about Linux and the open source community.

Choose Your Linux

There are several ways to categorize the different versions of Linux. Most methods organize distributions by technical merits that have very little to do with the interests of the beginning Linux user. I've chosen to categorize the distributions by those that are most Windows-like and those that are most Linux-like.

Windows-like distributions are intended for people who want to switch from Windows but don't want to learn Linux itself. These users are usually looking for an operating system that is cheaper, more stable, and more secure than the Windows environment they are using now. They want a distribution that hides the complexities and uniqueness of Linux behind a veneer of simplicity and ease of use. To achieve this near-Windows experience, these distributions often heavily customize the open source software they use and limit the programs available to users.

Linux-like distributions are also easy to use and simple for Windows users to figure out, but they don't try to duplicate the Windows experience. These distributions provide easy access to the command line, use artwork and desktop metaphors that are very different from Windows, and provide configuration tools and utilities that allow the user to manipulate practically everything about the environment. These distributions provide the most flexibility and do very little to limit the user's choice of software.

Which distribution is right for you is really a matter of personal taste and can often only be determined by experimentation. Most Linux users try out several distributions before finding one that they really like. Many distributions provide live CDs like the one in this book; others make their software available as a free download. The commercial vendors may not provide their software for free, but there are some web sites, such as *http://www.cheapbytes.com*, that sell you legal CDs of these distributions for just a few dollars. You won't get support with these cheap CDs, but if you decide that you want that after trying the distribution out, you can always just purchase a boxed set later.

Windows-Like Linux

Most Windows-like distributions use a customized form of the KDE desktop environment, which means that nearly everything in this book is directly applicable to using one of these distributions. Windows-like distributions make great desktops, and can be particularly good for limited-use machines, like a second computer for your kids or spouse. They are fast, secure, and stable, they install easily on modern computers, and they provide a great set of applications for typical desktop activities such as surfing the Internet, sending email, writing letters and reports, and chatting with friends.

As mentioned earlier, I call these distributions Windows-like not because they are easier to use than other distributions, but because they attempt to hide the complexities, flexibility, and power of the Linux operating system behind a user interface that is as much like Windows as possible. You don't have to learn any complex Linux commands or features in order to get enjoyment out of your system. Though this means that the software is very easy for Windows users to learn, it also means that some of what makes Linux unique and powerful gets lost in translation. It's a bit like owning a Porsche 911 with an automatic transmission. It's still a Porsche with a powerful engine, great handling, and head-turning looks, but a driver who really wants to get in touch with his car would want a manual transmission.

You will not find as much community support for the three distributions below as you will find for the Linux-like distributions in the next section. In most cases you should start your support search by visiting the company's web site and reading the FAQ or forums you find there.

Linspire

The Linspire distribution was originally marketed as Lindows, an obvious play on a certain operating system name. Microsoft sued the company for trademark infringement in several countries, and the whole matter was eventually settled out of court with the Linspire company getting $20 million from Microsoft to stop using the name. When this distribution first came on the scene in late 2001, it was almost considered a joke by the Linux community. Though it originally promised to run many Windows applications, it never did, and the name Lindows just wasn't taken seriously. The fact that it jumped from a pre-release version to 3.0 in about a year didn't help matters. The open source community takes version numbering quite seriously, and doesn't like it when a distribution tries to make itself seem better than it is by giving itself a high version number.

However, something changed around Version 3.0, and the distribution and company started to get some respect. It might have been CEO Michael Robertson's tireless evangelism efforts, the lawsuit with Microsoft, the company's support of community projects like *http://www.kde-look.org* and *http://www.kde-apps.org*, or just plain technological improvements. Today, at Version 5.0, Linspire is one of the more popular Windows-like distributions available. In fact, because of an aggressive OEM program, you can purchase new computers with Linspire preinstalled from dozens of computer vendors. (No, not Dell or HP, but you can get these machines from *http://www.walmart.com/* and *http://www.idotpc.com/*.)

The distribution itself uses a KDE desktop environment that has been cleaned up, simplified, and modified to appear as much like Windows as possible. Most of the changes are cosmetic, so in the end, KDE behaves almost exactly as it is described in this book. However, you'll need to choose something else if you want to use GNOME as your desktop environment, as it is not provided on Linspire.

The real selling feature of Linspire is its CNR program (formerly called Click-n-Run), which allows you to easily install Linspire-approved applications, patch security holes, and update existing programs. This program is very simple to use, works quite well, and solves one of the most troublesome problems that new Linux users have: installing software.

Linspire provides a free live CD version of their software. Unlike the CD you have been using with this book, the Linspire live CD does not allow you to save changes to a USB key. In fact, it is more like a demo CD; it allows you to touch and use, but not modify and save. Still, it is a great way to try out Linspire for free before deciding whether to buy it. More information about Linspire is available at the company web site *http://www.linspire.com*.

Lycoris

This distribution is developed just down the road from Microsoft's Redmond campus. In fact, it was originally named Redmond Linux.

Like Linspire, Lycoris does not include the GNOME desktop environment and provides no means to install it. (This is part of the tradeoff for getting a polished, Windows-like KDE.) Lycoris is probably the most Windows-themed of the distributions, as it makes use of Windows desktop metaphors similar to My Computer, My Network Places, and My Documents. Even the file browsing experience and device managers feel a lot like Windows XP.

IRIS is the name of the Lycoris software installation tool. This program connects over the Internet to the Lycoris software repository, where you can search for software or choose programs from a convenient category menu.

Lycoris contains some licensed software, most notably Bitstream fonts. Though using these fonts can enhance your computer experience, it also means you can't install Lycoris on multiple machines without purchasing a separate license for each installation. Lycoris also comes with a partition-resizing tool, and it can resize the NTFS partitions that Windows 2000/XP machines are often configured with. Using this tool, you can set up your computer to dual-boot Windows and Lycoris. There is no Lycoris live CD, so you can't try out this distribution without installing it.

Xandros

I can't think of a single Linux vendor that has done a better job than Xandros at identifying and addressing the most pressing problems a desktop user typically faces when using Linux, particularly on a Windows network.

The Xandros Desktop Business edition is well designed to be a drop-in replacement for a Windows computer in a business environment. It can be easily configured to authenticate off of a Windows server, just like a Windows machine. It comes with CodeWeaver's CrossOver Office, which means you can run Microsoft Office 2000 and higher on your Linux desktop. And it has a custom file manager that discovers and mounts file shares provided by Windows servers and desktops. Based upon KDE, Xandros has been modified to hide some of the complexities of that desktop environment, and provides a smaller set of default programs. Like Linspire, the GNOME desktop environment is not available on Xandros.

Xandros also has Deluxe and Standard editions. The Deluxe version is similar to the Business edition, except that it does not provide the ability to authenticate against Windows servers. The Standard edition lacks this ability as well, and does not include CrossOver Office. Because of the inclusion of proprietary, licensed software like CrossOver Office, Xandros Deluxe and Business edition can only be installed on one machine per purchased license; the Standard edition can be installed on as many machines as you wish. The Deluxe and Business edition boxed sets come with a pretty good users guide.

The Xandros Networks feature makes it easy to install new software, upgrade existing software, and integrate security patches. Only a limited set of programs is available through Xandros Networks, but because it is based upon the Debian distribution, it is a simple matter (for a knowledgeable Linux user, that is) to connect to Debian software repositories and download additional software. This is usually a very smooth process, but it should not be used to modify software that has been customized by Xandros—most notably, KDE itself.

Xandros is easy to install, has excellent hardware detection abilities, and is a great first distribution for users coming from Windows. There isn't a live CD to allow you to give it a test drive, but there is a free download edition, called the Xandros Open Circulation edition, that can be freely used and distributed for noncommercial use. That means you can't use it for your business, but you can use it at home on as many machines as you want.

All versions of Xandros have an easy, four-step install routine that automatically partitions your hard drive for you. Since Xandros includes software to repartition NTFS-formatted hard drives (common on Windows 2000 and XP computers), it is usually a simple process to create a dual-boot system.

Linux-Like Linux

Linux-like distributions have long been the mainstay of the Linux world, and remain the most popular choices for both existing users and new users. These are the distributions to turn to if you are after a Unix-like work environment, if you enjoy tinkering with and customizing your OS, and if you are really interested in learning a new way to use the power of your computer, and not merely duplicating the functions of Windows on a different OS.

Debian

Debian is possibly the most respected Linux distribution. Started in 1993 by Ian Murdock, the name is a combination of his name and that of his wife, Debra. Debian is known for its community, openness, and adherence to free software principles. So strong is this philosophy that Debian has created a Social Contract, which you can view at *http://www.debian. org/social_contract*. Debian has an international community of developers, which means it comes in many languages, and that many support resources on the Web will have users who speak your language.

This distribution has long had the conflicting reputation of being difficult to install, but very easy to update, upgrade, and maintain. Debian Versions 3.1 and higher will include a new installer to make it easier to get this distribution on your computer.

Debian is a minimalist distribution. A Debian release defines a base set of programs that are necessary to have a working system, but after that, it is entirely up to the user which programs get installed. This philosophy, combined with Debian's reputation for security and stability, make it a popular choice for server installs. But these same features also make it attractive for desktop use. Because Debian doesn't have a default desktop environment, you will find that it supports both GNOME and KDE equally well.

According to the Distrowatch web site, over 90 distributions are descended from Debian, including two of the Windows-like distributions covered earlier. One of the newcomers, Ubuntu, has the backing of many core Debian developers and has a desktop focus. The developers are currently focusing upon GNOME integration, but plan to provide better KDE support in the future. If you are interested in trying both Debian and GNOME, I highly recommend Ubuntu. You can download a live CD from *http://www.ubuntulinux.org*, which is a great way to test-drive this distribution. There are several other live CDs that are based upon Debian. The most popular of these, Knoppix, is described in detail in a later section.

Debian is not sold in retail stores, but it is freely downloadable from the Internet. It contains no proprietary software, which means you are free to install it on as many systems as you want. However, the installer does not have the ability to resize NTFS partitions, which means you will need to make other provisions if you want to set up Debian to dual-boot with Windows on an NTFS-formatted hard drive.

Information and support for Debian can be found in dozens of places on the Internet. Here are just a few resources available to you:

http://www.debian.org
#debian channel on IRC freenode
Several newsgroups, including linux.debian.user

Fedora

Fedora is a new community project started by Red Hat in late 2003. When Fedora was first released it was pretty much the same distribution as Red Hat Linux 9. Red Hat plans to use Fedora as a testing ground for new technologies and to periodically roll improvements in Fedora into their flagship product Red Hat Enterprise Linux. Think of it as Red Hat making their product development cycle completely open.

Fedora calls their releases "Fedora Core" with an incrementing number. Currently at Fedora Core 4, this distribution has been advancing rapidly and includes the latest versions of GNOME, KDE, and the 2.6 series of the Linux kernel, which has improved performance, particularly for desktop users. Fedora is also breaking new ground with the inclusion of Security Enhanced Linux (SELinux), a special feature set developed by the National Security Agency to make Linux extremely secure.

Like Red Hat Linux, Fedora concentrates upon GNOME as a desktop environment. Though it includes KDE, it has been modified to look more like GNOME, and most KDE users do not like the Fedora implementation. However, if you do want to try out GNOME, Fedora is one of the best ways to use this excellent desktop environment.

Though Fedora is a community-based project, it is sponsored by Red Hat as the development branch for the flagship product Red Hat Enterprise Linux. That means it is supported and advanced by people who are both passionate about Linux, and are also paid to work on it.

Unfortunately, continuing a policy started by Red Hat Linux, Fedora does not include support for MP3 playing or NTFS partition resizing out of the box. For legal reasons that don't seem to bother other distribution providers, Red Hat decided not to put these features in. The inability to play MP3 files is easily fixed with a simple download once you've installed Fedora, but the inability to resize NTFS partitions means that the Fedora installer won't be of any help if you need to make room for Linux on your Windows XP machine. There are some third-party and downloadable tools that can do the resizing for you, but it would be nice to have it included in the installer.

Fedora is not available in retail stores, but is a freely available ISO download. It contains no proprietary software so you can install it on as machines as you like.

The Fedora community is not yet as strong as that of other distributions, but there are still several useful resources, like:

> *http://fedora.redhat.com*
> #fedora channel on IRC freenode
> Several newsgroups, including linux.redhat

Gentoo

Gentoo users are the true fanboys of the Linux world. They lurk on online forums and tell everyone how great their distribution is, boast about how much faster Gentoo is than other distributions, and extol the virtues of portage, their program installer. For all of their enthusiasm, these users are greeted with ridicule and scorn. There is even a web site, *http://www.funroll-loops.org*, that pokes good-humored fun at Gentoo users. And yet, these days there are more new Gentoo users than you can shake a herring at. I became a Gentoo user about two years ago, and I've stuck with it longer than any other distribution.

Gentoo is a lot like Debian, with the exception that instead of having an easy-to-use system for installing program binaries, it has an easy-to-use system for compiling and installing programs from source. Installing and configuring a Gentoo system is a great way to learn more about how Linux works, and the Gentoo web site provides a complete instruction manual. Despite this, installation can be a frustrating and time-consuming experience with a high potential for error. I wouldn't recommend Gentoo as a beginner distribution, but do give it a try after you have been using Linux for about a year. You might find something you really like.

Gentoo is known for having a vociferous but helpful community. You can find evidence of this in discussion forums at popular web sites like *http://www.slashdot.org*, on the #gentoo IRC channel, and on the Gentoo forums at *http://forums.gentoo.org*. In fact, this friendly community is what keeps many users around despite the initial difficulty in getting the distribution installed.

Online resources for Gentoo are available at:

http://www.gentoo.org
http://forums.gentoo.org
#gentoo channel on IRC freenode

Knoppix

Knoppix is a live CD distribution similar to the one you have been using with this book. It has more features and more software than *Move*, but these additions make it slightly more cumbersome to use. If you want to continue testing Linux by using a live CD, Knoppix is a good choice to continue your exploration.

One of the best features of Knoppix is its hardware detection capabilities. If you are purchasing a computer at a retail store and plan to run Linux on it, bring a Knoppix CD and try to convince the clerk to let you boot the machine with Knoppix. Doing so will let you see how well Linux supports the computer's hardware.

Knoppix is based upon Debian. In fact, you can use Knoppix to install Debian on your system. This is particularly convenient because the installer is simpler to use than the one provided with Debian, and it uses the hardware configuration created when Knoppix booted to set up all of your hardware. O'Reilly has provided instructions on how to use this installer at *http://www.oreilly.com/catalog/knoppixhks/*. (This is just one of the 100 hacks in the O'Reilly book *Knoppix Hacks*.)

For more information about Knoppix, or to download it, visit:

> *http://www.knoppix.net*
> *http://www.knoppix.com*

Mandrake

By this point in the book, you should be quite familiar with the Mandrake distribution because the *Move* CD is based upon it. Mandrake is produced by the French company Mandrakesoft, and is considered by many to be the best Linux distribution for new Linux users. This is because Mandrake does an excellent job of providing a simple installation program, a great selection of default applications that work well together, an improved menu structure, and an easy-to-use application installation program called *urmpi*. If you talk to a lot of Linux users, you will find that many of them tried Mandrake first and have since moved on to other distributions, but over four million of them have stuck with Mandrake. And, although many people think of Mandrake as being a distribution for the desktop, it is also a very capable server OS. Mandrakesoft estimates that about 40 percent of Mandrake installs are on servers.

The default desktop environment for Mandrake is KDE. Though Mandrake features the applications I've covered in this book, it also provides all of the applications mentioned in Chapter 12. You shouldn't expect any surprises with Mandrake; it's just a hard drive install of the live CD you have already been using. The difference is that it boots faster, runs quicker, has a greater selection of applications out of the box, and lets you install even more applications.

At the time of this writing, the current version of Mandrake is Version 10.1. It is sold via the Web from Mandrakesoft and on Amazon, and you may see it at Borders bookstores. Once you purchase or download

Mandrake, you are allowed to install it on as many machines as you want. That means that if you have 10 computers in your business, you can put Mandrake on all 10, but only have to pay for it once—*that's* something you can't do with Windows! (At least, not legally, and without threat of Federal Marshals storming your business.) However, note that any support included in the purchase price is applicable only to one machine.

Mandrake comes in several different versions, which can be distinguished by the amount of software on the CDs they include and how much support you get from Mandrakesoft. In the U.S., Mandrake Linux is sold in two book and CD sets under the names *Discovery 10.1: Your First Linux Desktop* and *PowerPack 10.1: The Full Power of Desktop Linux.* The books are written by Mandrakesoft and provide a nice complement to this book, since they cover how to install Linux on your computer, add new programs, and configure hardware.

Mandrake Linux also comes as a free download edition. You can get this from numerous places, but the most popular way is through the peer-to-peer distribution method known as BitTorrent. Just do a web search for the terms *Mandrake* and *torrent* to find a site you can download from. (This is perfectly legal, by the way.) The limitation of the download edition is that it does not come with some of the proprietary applications that are in the other versions. This includes Adobe Acrobat Reader, RealPlayer, and FlashPlayer, as well as some accelerated video card drivers for the latest graphics cards from ATI and NVIDIA. It also does not come with any support or documentation.

The Mandrake installation program can resize partitions, including NTFS-formatted ones. This means you can easily install it alongside Windows and create a system that can boot either Windows or Linux.

More information about Mandrake, Mandrakesoft, and the Mandrake-Club is available at:

http://www.mandrake.com
http://www.mandrakesoft.com
http://www.mandrakeclub.com
#mandrake channel on IRC freenode
The newsgroup alt.os.mandrake

Red Hat

Red Hat is the largest Linux vendor. This distribution has been around since 1994, and it used to be one of the primary distributions for hobbyists. However, when Red Hat released the community distribution Fedora in late 2003, they stopped providing the freely downloadable version that made them so popular. If you are interested in Linux for your desktop and you want the product that is most like commercial Red Hat, take a look at Fedora. On the other hand, many previous users of Red Hat find this recent change a stimulus to try out other distributions.

Red Hat sells commercial offerings under the umbrella name of Red Hat Enterprise Linux (RHEL). This is the most popular commercial Linux version ever and is widely used in businesses and universities. Technically, the software itself is free. When you buy a license, you are actually purchasing a support contract, which entitles you to installation and configuration support as well as security fixes and program updates.

The true value add of RHEL is the Red Hat Network. This collection of services makes it easier to deploy large numbers of systems, install new software, maintain your system, and even roll back to earlier program versions if something goes wrong. This is one of the enterprise-class features that make Red Hat so popular in the business world. You can read more about Red Hat and its offerings at *http://www.redhat.com.*

SUSE/Novell

SUSE Linux was originally produced by SUSE, LLC, a company based out of Germany. In early 2004, SUSE was purchased by the well-known American software company Novell, which in 2003 had also purchased the highly respected Linux developer business called Ximian. With these recent acquisitions, Novell is showing that it believes in the future of the Linux operating system. In fact, it is betting its business on Linux becoming a dominant force in computing.

SUSE has long been a favorite of European users. The company has been a strong backer of the KDE project, and SUSE features one of the nicest implementations of KDE. Now that it has been teamed up with Ximian, a major developer of the GNOME desktop environment, you can expect releases going forward to include well-featured versions of both desktop environments.

SUSE is known for its powerful but confusing YAST configuration utility. With this program you can configure your Linux system, add and remove software, create users, and perform other administrative tasks. After Novell acquired SUSE it open-sourced YAST, but don't expect it to show up in other distributions anytime soon.

The current version of SUSE is the Professional 9.3 boxed set, sold at stores like Best Buy, Comp USA, and Fry's, as well as from various online vendors. It comes with over 1000 pages of documentation in two books, one focused on using the OS, the other on administering it.

SUSE 9.3 has the ability to resize hard drive partitions, including NTFS ones, so you can easily install it alongside existing Windows installs to create a dual-boot system. SUSE provides a downloadable ISO image of the Personal edition, but only the Professional edition is available via an FTP install; see the instructions on the SUSE web site. SUSE also offers a live CD that functions as a demo, and is a great way to try out SUSE and see if it recognizes your hardware. SUSE should definitely be on your short list of distributions to try out.

More information is available from these resources:

http://www.suse.com
http://forums.suselinuxsupport.de/
#suse channel on IRC freenode
The newsgroup alt.os.suse

Slackware

Though Slackware isn't the oldest distribution, it's the oldest one that has been continuously developed. It was created by Patrick Volkerding in 1993 and is currently maintained by him. Slackware is free software, so you can install it on as many computers as you like. A supported version can be purchased from *http://www.slackware.com.*

Slackware is a no-frills distribution that does little to customize the desktop environments or other software packages. That's bad news for someone who wants a Windows-like experience, but fantastic news for someone who wants a very clean, uncomplicated, and stable system.

The simplicity of a basic install of Slackware combined with its very Unix-like approach to Linux makes it popular as a server distribution, but usually only experienced Linux users use it as a desktop. Though it requires a knowledgeable user to configure it properly, the reward is a secure and stable operating system. As with Gentoo, I wouldn't recommend using this distribution until you have tried a few others. As users gain experience, they often find that they actually prefer working with hands-on distributions such as Slackware, Debian, and Gentoo.

Slackware favors KDE over GNOME, but maintains packages of both. For the best GNOME experience on Slackware, use Dropline GNOME available at *http://www.dropline.net/gnome*.

To test-drive Slackware, check out the live CD distribution called Slax. It is available at *http://slax.linux-live.org*.

Getting More Information

Learning about Linux is an ongoing process, and the more resources you have available the better. Linux users are a technically savvy group, so they make use of a variety of information channels.

Books

For initial forays into Linux, it's best to have a comprehensive guide. Hopefully, this book has provided you with the information you need to move beyond introductory Linux books, but obviously it can't be all things to all people. If you want another take on the subject, check out *Linux for Non-Geeks* (No Starch Press). This book focuses on the GNOME desktop environment, which makes it a nice complement to this book and a good introduction to the Fedora distribution.

If you're ready to tackle more than the pretty desktop environment in Linux, try *Running Linux* (O'Reilly). This is the best-selling Linux book of all time, and it provides everything you need to know to become a power Linux user. This includes not just understanding how to use a desktop environment, but how to administer a Linux machine and set up network services like web, file sharing, and email servers.

Sometimes you just need a quick reference to turn to. Once again, O'Reilly provides the two best-selling reference titles with *Linux in a Nutshell*, a detailed 1000-page reference book, and *Linux Pocket Guide*, a mini command reference that fits in your coat pocket. (Don't let the Fedora banner on the pocket guide fool you; the commands covered apply to all Linux distributions.)

And finally, if you're intrigued by the power of live CDs, you might want to look at *Knoppix Hacks* (O'Reilly), which provides 100 cool things you can do with the most popular live CD variant, Knoppix.

Magazines

There are several Linux-oriented magazines that you can find at most bookstores:

Linux Journal

This was the first magazine on Linux in the United States, and the editors still seem to relish their role of keeping readers current with every aspect of Linux. The journal's focus is administration, but its articles range from end-user tools to journalistic reportage on the most cutting-edge projects. Insightful overviews of political, legal, and market issues get tucked in around the edges.

Linux Magazine

Another magazine with practical information for Linux administrators, similar to *Linux Journal* but with generally shorter and more basic articles. There is less interest in highly advanced topics and more articles on everyday components such as MySQL and Perl.

Linux Format

This is a British magazine that is often available in the U.S. at bookstores such Barnes & Noble and Borders. It is flashy and hip, and contains a lot of useful tips and tricks for desktop-focused users, but it has far less coverage of Linux as a server system than the previous two magazines do. *Linux Format* is often bundled with a CD, which raises the price substantially. The software on the CD is usually downloadable for free, so if you have plenty of bandwidth it is seldom worth the cost.

Tux

Tux magazine, named after the lovable Linux mascot, is a new digital magazine that is available for free at its web site, *http://www. tuxmagazine.com.* It is focused on the particular needs of the growing number of Linux desktop users.

Web Sites

A large number of web sites provide information about Linux. Some cover specific problems people have solved with Linux; others give exact instructions about how one person installed and configured Linux; and many others are general Linux and open source software news sites.

If you're interested in freely available Linux documentation, your first stop should be the Linux Documentation Project at *http://www.tldp.org.* This web site is a collection of HowTos and Guides for all aspects of Linux. It is particularly good at providing information about specific problems, such as making fonts look better (anti-aliasing) or getting wireless network cards to work.

For an invaluable resource to installing Linux on a laptop, there is no better place than the Linux on Laptops web site at *http://www.linux-laptop.net.* This is another example of how the Linux community provides for itself, not just with software but with documentation. The site is really just a bunch of links to individual pages written by Linux users that provide detailed instructions about how they installed Linux on their laptops. Laptops contain a lot of proprietary hardware that may not be fully supported under Linux, so it is often very helpful to learn from other users' experiences. If you haven't yet purchased the laptop you intend to run Linux on, visit this site first.

The Google search engine has a nifty feature that makes it just a little bit easier to find Linux-related information. Simply go to *http://www.google. com/linux* to get a specialized search page that will only return information from Linux sites. If you go to this page and perform a search on "wireless", for example, Google will only return results that relate to Linux.

There are dozens of web sites out there that provide helpful information to Linux users. One of the best for new users is found at *http://www. linuxquestions.org.* You can learn a lot just from browsing the forums or wiki and reading entries on topics that interest you.

There are several news sites that Linux users frequently visit. The most popular of these is *http://www.slashdot.org,* the self-proclaimed news site for nerds. This large community of technology enthusiasts has a very open source slant, but it is not exclusive to Linux. The news articles it links to run the gamut from Linux-related issues to how current patent law has the potential to ruin the software industry.

Another great site is the Linux news aggregator *http://www.linuxtoday. com.* This web site has links to all of the most popular or relevant Linux and open source articles posted on the Web that day.

When you purchase a new sound card, scanner, printer, or other peripheral, it will almost always come with a CD that contains drivers and program installers for Windows. It is very rare to find a vendor that provides Linux drivers in the box. Sometimes you will find drivers on the vendor's web site, but these will usually be listed as beta and unsupported. However, none of this means that the hardware will or won't work with Linux. If you want to know if your particular hardware works with Linux, check a hardware compatibility list. There are several such lists; here are just a few:

> *http://www.linuxcompatible.org/compatibility.html*
> *http://hardware.redhat.com/hcl/*
> *http://cdb.suse.de/?LANG=en_UK*

Other sites of general interest include:

> *http://www.newsforge.net*
> *http://www.osnews.com*
> *http://www.desktoplinux.com*
> *http://www.lwn.net*

Linux User Groups

In cities around the world, Linux users gather on a regular basis to talk about things that interest them. As you can imagine, much of this talk revolves around Linux itself, but it also extends to discussions of open source software and technology in general. Recent meetings of the Boston Linux User Group had presentations on making your computer into a TiVo-like video recorder using the MythTV software, converting PCs into useful thin client desktops with the Linux Terminal Server Project, and an InstallFest to help new users get Linux installed and configured on their machines (a great way to get someone else to help you with any difficulties).

To find out if your city has a Linux User group, visit *http://www.linux.org/ groups/index.html* or *http://glue.linuxgazette.com* where you can perform a search for your city.

Summary

Henry Ford is reputed to have said, "Any customer can have a car painted any color that he wants, so long as it is black." One reason he may have said this was because black paint dried the fastest on the assembly line. That means the choice of paint color was expedient for the manufacturer, not for the customer. Thankfully, the automobile industry has changed since his time, and it is now possible to buy cars from dozens of manufacturers, in hundreds of styles, painted in practically every color under the sun.

Unfortunately, the same has not yet been true of the computer world. You can buy a PC computer from dozens of vendors but they all come with just one operating system: Microsoft Windows. Though it is expedient for Microsoft to continue to sell an overpriced, buggy, and insecure operating system, the situation really isn't that good for you, the customer.

Don't let this test drive of Linux be the end of your Linux experience. Pick a distribution to try out; in fact, pick several. Most are free or can be obtained at little expense. (If you can't decide, I recommend trying both Mandrake and the open circulation version of Xandros.) Though it does take a little bit of time to try each distribution, your gain is a stable, secure, and low-cost operating system that will enrich your computer experience.

SOLUTIONS TO
COMMON
PROBLEMS

The folks over at Mandrakesoft have put together a list of the most common support issues for *Move* and the usual solutions. If you're having trouble getting the *Move* CD to work, if your hardware isn't getting recognized, or if you have problems with the USB key, this handy resource should save you a lot of time and frustration. Keep in mind, however, that the version of *Move* included with this book is unsupported, so please don't call Mandrakesoft with problems.

Your Computer Won't Boot from the CD

Most modern computers are configured to attempt to boot from the CD before booting from the hard drive. The reason for this is to make it easier for you to use the Windows Restore CD when your computer gets messed up with viruses and spyware. But sometimes the settings get changed, and when you need to boot from a CD like *Move*, you find that it doesn't work.

The problem is almost always that a setting in your computer's startup code has changed the boot order to make your computer boot from the hard drive first. To fix this problem, boot up your computer and read the text that appears on the screen when your monitor first comes to life—you should see something like "Press F2 to Enter Setup" in the lower left or right corner. Press the specified key to enter your computer's setup configuration screen. Look for the setting that specifies boot order; the exact location will vary depending on your computer's manufacturer. When you find this setting, simply change it to boot from the CD-ROM before the hard drive, save the setting changes, reboot your machine, and you should be all set.

Alternately, some computers display the available boot devices during bootup, so booting from your CD-ROM may be as simple as choosing it from this list. Pay attention at boot time, as often these lists appear for only a few seconds before accepting a default like the hard drive and continuing to load Windows.

Move Won't Boot Completely

When *Move* always hangs during the boot process, it may be having a hard time configuring itself for some of the features of your hardware. One workaround is to disable some of the hardware checks *Move* performs during boot. To do this, press F1 when the *Move* boot splash first comes up, then enter one of the following commands and press Enter:

```
linux noapic acpi=off nolapic pnpbios=off
linux noapic acpi=off nolapic
```

Oddly enough, the *Move* CD sometimes starts booting and then gets hung up at a later point, because its boot program suddenly thinks the CD-ROM drive itself has disappeared from the system. If *Move* reports that your CD-ROM drive cannot be found, try entering the following command after pressing F1 at the *Move* boot prompt:

```
linux noprobe acpi=off noapic
```

If this command doesn't do the trick, one of these two commands might work:

```
linux noapic acpi=off nolapic pnpbios=off
linux noapic nolapic
```

You may experience problems booting *Move* with a PCMCIA card in your laptop. If so, try booting the laptop without the card, and once KDE is fully loaded, put the card back into your laptop and it should be automatically recognized.

Problems with the USB Memory Key

One great thing about the *Move* live CD is its ability to save your settings and data to a USB key. If this feature isn't working for you, there are a few things you can try:

- Plug the USB key into a different USB port and try again.
- Some USB keys are not supported. Visit *http://www.mandrakesoft.com* to see if your USB key is in the supported hardware database.
- If you have a powered USB hub, plug the USB key into it and try again.
- Check your BIOS setup for a USB setting and toggle the setting between USB 1.1 and USB 2.0.

If you get the USB key error "Bad Size Recognized" or if *Move* refuses to boot when you are using a key, your USB key's format is probably corrupted. To fix this problem, simply reformat it as a FAT filesystem. Your USB key probably came with a utility to do this; if you can't find this utility, you can format your key from inside the Windows My Computer window by right-clicking on the USB key icon and selecting Format. Another option is to format the key during the *Move* boot process. To do this, press F1 during bootup to bring up the Advanced screen. At the command prompt, type the following command and press Enter:

```
linux formatkey
```

During the boot process, after you accept the license, you are told that formatting the USB key will cause all data on the key to be lost, and you are asked if you really want to do this. Click Yes and continue as you normally would.

Setting Up Your Monitor

I've tried out *Move* on about a dozen different desktop and laptop computers, and although it almost always configured the video card correctly, it only got the monitor's configuration right about half the time. You'll know that *Move* failed to figure out your monitor correctly if the text is much larger than you expect it to be, if the fonts are blocky, or if your screen "scrolls" when you drag your mouse to the edges.

The solution to this problem is usually quite simple. First, launch the hardware configuration tool by clicking K Menu → Administer your system → Configure your computer. (If you can't see the K Menu, drag your mouse to the bottom left corner and the screen will scroll so you can see it.) This brings up the MandrakeLinux Control Center, a centralized place for several different configuration tools common to all distributions of Linux made by Mandrakesoft. The control center is used to configure your video card, monitor, network connections, printer, mice, and so on.

Click once on the Hardware icon and then on the Monitor icon to bring up a list of hundreds of different monitors. You need to find and select your monitor model from the Vendor list (click the triangle to expand the list), choose a generic setting that is similar to your monitor, or enter some custom settings. Generic settings work particularly well for laptops and LCD displays; you usually just need to select the maximum resolution for your monitor from the flat-panel options. When you click OK, you will be told that you need to log out and back in again for the change to take effect. Click OK again to close this screen, but don't log out yet.

Back at the Hardware screen, click the Screen Resolution icon. This brings up a simple screen with just two options: the resolution drop-down list and the choice of how many colors to display. LCD and laptop screens have a preferred resolution, which is usually 1024×768 for 15" screens and smaller, and 1280×1024 for 17" screens and larger. Pick the resolution and color depth that is appropriate for your monitor and click OK. You'll again be told that you have to log out and back in for the changes to work.

Back at the main screen, click File → Quit to exit the control center, and log out of KDE by clicking K Menu → Logout and selecting "End session only." KDE will shut down and restart, and your monitor should now be configured correctly.

Setting Up the Network

Move usually does a good job of configuring your network card, particularly if you have a typical Ethernet card built into your desktop or laptop. *Move* doesn't do so well, however, when you use a wireless card. And if you use a modem to make your network connection, you need to know how to configure *Move* to dial out. This section helps you to set up your network in the event that *Move* fails to do so automatically.

Ethernet and Wireless Cards

As with your monitor configuration, most of your network configuration will be done from the MandrakeLinux Control Center. Go to K Menu → Administer your system → Configure your computer, click the Network & Internet icon, and then click New Connection. This launches a wizard that will help you set up your network connection. Choose the connection type appropriate to your network and click Next. If the next screen contains only the choice to configure a network device manually, it means that *Move* did not detect your network device. This is somewhat common with wireless network adapters, but it should be rare with Ethernet cards. You can try to manually configure your network card, but don't be surprised if it doesn't work. My suggestion at this point is to add a separate Ethernet card to your computer and try that, or, if you're using a laptop, insert a different PCMCIA wireless card or use your laptop's built-in Ethernet jack instead of wireless.

Wireless does work well in Linux

Although *Move* has limited wireless network card support, a hard drive install of Linux usually does much better. Even if an installed Linux version doesn't detect your network card right away, you'll have a much better chance of successfully troubleshooting the problem.

Modems

When setting up a modem, I find I have to use a two-step process. The first part involves getting *Move* to recognize the modem, and the second part involves configuring a dial-up program to connect to your ISP. (If you have an external modem, make sure it is plugged in and powered on before continuing.)

To set up your modem, go to the MandrakeLinux Control Center, click Network & Internet, and then click New Connection. In the New Connection window, select Modem connection and click Next. *Move* will pause for a few seconds, and then it should tell you it has detected a modem. Now just keep clicking Next to move through all the remaining screens; don't bother entering any information. When you are finished, you will get an error message in the top left corner telling you that *kppprc* has failed because of a read-only filesystem. Just click OK to close the error window, and then close the Control Center.

Now go to K Menu → Surf the Internet → Connect to the Internet. This launches the KDE KPPP dialer program. Before you can use this program, though, you need to configure an account. Click Configure to bring up the configuration window.

The configuration program opens with the focus on the Accounts tab, so just click New to create a new account. You'll then be asked if you want to use a Wizard or to configure your connection manually. Choose Manual Setup, because the Wizard tries to force you to select a European

ISP, which isn't much use for people living in the U.S. In the next screen, simply fill out a connection name, click Add, type in your ISP's dial-up number, and click OK. Click OK once more to get back to the Accounts tab and OK again to get to the main screen, where you should now have an entry in the "Connect to" drop-down list. Type in your username and password and click Connect. KPPP will dial your ISP, and you will be on the Internet.

Unsupported modems

Not all modems are created equal. Some modems, known as Win-modems, require Windows-only software to be installed on the computer. These modems are not supported by *Move*, and generally have very poor support in Linux.

Configuring Your Printer

If your printer is plugged in and powered on when you boot *Move*, it should be recognized and set up during the boot process. You know your printer has been detected if you are presented with a window asking you if you want CUPS to be configured to start each time you boot *Move*. You should answer Yes to this screen and finish booting *Move*. Once you are in KDE, you should be able to use the printer from any application.

Printing system

CUPS is the Common Unix Printing System, and is the default print system in most distributions of Linux and Mac OS X.

But if you didn't set up your printer during bootup, you can still do so after you are in KDE. To do this, first make sure the printer is connected and powered on. Go to the MandrakeLinux Control Center (K Menu → Administer your system → Configure your computer), click the Hardware icon, and then click the Printers icon. This launches a printer detection program that should open up a window telling you which printers it has detected. If it didn't detect your printer, try clicking the Quit button, double-checking your printer connections, and powering the printer off and back on. If it's a USB printer, unplug the USB cable from the computer and reinsert it. Once you've completed this little ritual, click the Printers icon again.

Your printer should now be detected, so click the Yes button. After the computer thinks some more about your printer setup, you'll be presented with a window asking you if the CUPS printing system should be started automatically next time you boot. Go ahead and click Yes for this too. After some more thinking, you'll be presented with a window for the Mandrakelinux Printer Management Tool. At this point your printer is fully set up, so you can just close this window by selecting File → Quit.

You should now be able to print from any application by clicking the print icon on the toolbar, choosing File (Location in Konqueror) → Print, or using the keyboard shortcut Ctrl-P.

Index

We'd like to hear your suggestions for improving our indexes. Send email to *index@oreilly.com.*

X

Y

Z

About the Author

David Brickner is an editor of Linux and open source books at O'Reilly Media, Inc. Prior to that, he worked as a Windows system administrator for eight years. He has used Linux servers since 1998, and has run Linux as his full-time desktop for the past four years. David lives near Boston with his wife, Claire, and two well-behaved cats. He enjoys reading fantasy and science fiction books, eating his own pumpkin bread, and going to the movies with Claire. David wishes his hobbies were woodworking and camping, but he hasn't done enough of either for this to be true.

Colophon

Our look is the result of reader comments, our own experimentation, and feedback from distribution channels. Distinctive covers complement our distinctive approach to technical topics, breathing personality and life into potentially dry subjects.

Emily Quill was the production editor and copyeditor for *Test Driving Linux*. Sada Preisch was the proofreader. Mary Brady and Claire Cloutier provided quality control. John Bickelhaupt wrote the index.

Mike Kohnke designed the CD label and the cover of this book. Karen Montgomery produced the cover layout with Adobe Photoshop CS and InDesign CS using Bitstream Futura font.

Marcia Friedman designed the interior layout. This book was converted by Andrew Savikas, Keith Fahlgren, and Emily Quill to FrameMaker 5.5.6 with a format conversion tool created by Erik Ray, Jason McIntosh, Neil Walls, and Mike Sierra that uses Perl and XML technologies. The text font is Berthold Baskerville; the heading font is Helvetica Neue; and the code font is LucasFont's TheSans Mono Condensed. The illustrations that appear in the book were produced by Robert Romano, Jessamyn Read, and Lesley Borash using Macromedia FreeHand MX and Adobe Photoshop CS.

Related Titles Available from O'Reilly

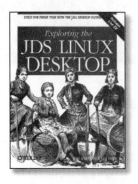

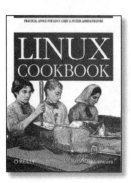

Linux

Building Embedded Linux Systems

Building Secure Servers with Linux

The Complete FreeBSD, *4th Edition*

Even Grues Get Full

Exploring the JDS Linux Desktop

Extreme Programming Pocket Guide

Knoppix Hacks

Learning Red Hat Enterprise Linux and Fedora, *4th Edition*

Linux Cookbook

Linux Desktop Hacks

Linux Device Drivers, *3rd Edition*

Linux in a Nutshell, *4th Edition*

Linux iptables Pocket Reference

Linux Network Administrator's Guide, *3rd Edition*

Linux Pocket Guide

Linux Security Cookbook

Linux Server Hacks

Linux Unwired

Linux Web Server CD Bookshelf, *Version 2.0*

LPI Linux Certification in a Nutshell, *2nd Edition*

Managing RAID on Linux

OpenOffice.org Writer

Programming with Qt, *2nd Edition*

Root of all Evil

Running Linux, *4th Edition*

Samba Pocket Reference, *2nd Edition*

Understanding the Linux Kernel, *2nd Edition*

Understanding Open Source & Free Software Licensing

User Friendly

Using Samba, *3rd Edition*

Keep in touch with O'Reilly

1. Download examples from our books

To find example files for a book, go to:

www.oreilly.com/catalog

select the book, and follow the "Examples" link.

2. Register your O'Reilly books

Register your book at *register.oreilly.com*

Why register your books? Once you've registered your O'Reilly books you can:

- Win O'Reilly books, T-shirts or discount coupons in our monthly drawing.
- Get special offers available only to registered O'Reilly customers.
- Get catalogs announcing new books (US and UK only).
- Get email notification of new editions of the O'Reilly books you own.

3. Join our email lists

Sign up to get topic-specific email announcements of new books and conferences, special offers, and O'Reilly Network technology newsletters at:

elists.oreilly.com

It's easy to customize your free elists subscription so you'll get exactly the O'Reilly news you want.

4. Get the latest news, tips, and tools

http://www.oreilly.com

- "Top 100 Sites on the Web"—PC Magazine
- CIO Magazine's Web Business 50 Awards

Our web site contains a library of comprehensive product information (including book excerpts and tables of contents), downloadable software, background articles, interviews with technology leaders, links to relevant sites, book cover art, and more.

5. Work for O'Reilly

Check out our web site for current employment opportunities:

jobs.oreilly.com

6. Contact us

O'Reilly & Associates
1005 Gravenstein Hwy North
Sebastopol, CA 95472 USA
TEL: 707-827-7000 or 800-998-9938
        (6am to 5pm PST)
FAX: 707-829-0104

order@oreilly.com
For answers to problems regarding your order or our products.
To place a book order online, visit:
www.oreilly.com/order_new

catalog@oreilly.com
To request a copy of our latest catalog.

booktech@oreilly.com
For book content technical questions or corrections.

corporate@oreilly.com
For educational, library, government, and corporate sales.

proposals@oreilly.com
To submit new book proposals to our editors and product managers.

international@oreilly.com
For information about our international distributors or translation queries. For a list of our distributors outside of North America check out:
international.oreilly.com/distributors.html

adoption@oreilly.com
For information about academic use of O'Reilly books, visit:
academic.oreilly.com

O'REILLY®

Our books are available at most retail and online bookstores.
To order direct: 1-800-998-9938 • *order@oreilly.com* • *www.oreilly.com*
Online editions of most O'Reilly titles are available by subscription at *safari.oreilly.com*